THE A.I. AGE

ADAM RICCOBONI

THE AI AGE

Published by Critical Future Publishing

ISBN: 978-1-5136-5729-5

THE A.I. AGE

ADAM RICCOBONI

ABOUT THE AUTHOR

Adam Riccoboni is an AI entrepreneur, AI lecturer, and AI writer.

Adam is the founder and CEO of Critical Future, a strategy and technology consultancy with a specialism in Artificial Intelligence trusted by many of the world's biggest brands.

Critical Future is one of the most pioneering AI companies globally, developing AI systems to predict cancer, predict property value, and even predict stock prices with record accuracy.

Adam is an award winning entrepreneur, as featured in the Financial Times, the Guardian, the Express, BBC, ESPN, and USA Today. Adam lives with his family in Hampstead, London, UK.

Adam welcomes contact from readers and can be reached at
adam@criticalfuture.global

ACKNOWLEDGMENTS

This book is dedicated to our wonderful daughter Alexia.

Thank you so much to my lovely Joanna all your support while writing the book

Thank you Carole Reed, a wonderful editor, who was absolutely fantastic.

Thank you Ali el Houssani who developed the AI System for the book cover, and also Matthew Stewart. Two great AI developers who will no doubt change the world in some way great or small.

Also, thanks to Thomas Pernet and Michael Rawson, for research that was important to the writing of Chapters 3 and 4.

I'd also like to thank Manolis Skouloudakis, Lesley Greenan and Chara Antoniadou for their hard work at Critical Future while I was working on this book.

Thank you to the great writers who inspired many of the ideas in this book, from Richard Dawkins, John Gray, Richard Wright and Yuval Noah Harari to Thomas Malone, Kai-Fu Lee and many more.

Finally, thank you to Alan Turing, the genius who invented this field.

TABLE OF CONTENTS

INTRODUCTION

"AI is probably the most important thing humanity has ever worked on."
— Sundar Pichai, CEO, Google

Close your eyes. Imagine you're at home watching television. Take in every object in the room: the sofa you're lounging on, the remote, the laptop, tables, books.

Let your mind wander to the kitchen. Scan the fridge, microwave, sink and the washing machine tucked away in its niche.

Drift outside. See the lawn mowers cutting grass, cars hurtling past, street lights shining down.

Take a breath and imagine you can look deep inside of things: gas sucked along pipes underground, electricity snaking through overhead lines, a rocket engine throttling back as it enters orbit.

Now picture, if you will, artificial intelligence (AI) enhancing all things in the world.

And all people. Even you.

It's true. Intelligent behavior can be developed in everything to make it work better, stronger, faster.

This is the genius of AI. It's the world's first and only universal technology—with a potential so profound it makes every other tech seem flat, hollow and empty. This is why we should understand AI. And why we should care so much about AI.

THE "ENCHANTED LAND"

Allen Newel, a founding father of AI, gave a lecture in 1976 in which he foresaw an "enchanted land" where AI invigorates every object with intelligence. Nils Nilson, another pioneering AI researcher, wrote that AI is "ubiquitous" and "differs from all other technologies precisely in providing the capability for an enchanted world. In short, computer technology offers the potential for incorporating intelligent behavior into all the nooks and crannies of our world. With it, we can build an enchanted land."

We're not far from that, or something like it, becoming our reality. We are entering an AI Age where artificial intelligence has seeped almost unnoticed into the fabric of our lives. AI-powered GPS systems guide our journeys. AI-filtered entertainment products fill our leisure time. AI-guided parcels arrive at our doors. AI-assisted doctors diagnose illnesses. AI algorithms trade stocks. And AI-informed police forces catch criminals.[1]

AI is now so widely used and so intrinsic in everyday operations that if we turned off all the AI tomorrow, the world would stop working. This is just the beginning of a burgeoning AI Age. In a future not so far away, AI will become integrated into every aspect of our lives.

THE AI AGE

The most potent driver of economic change is technology. Time periods are named after the dominant technology, from the agricultural and Industrial Revolutions to the Bronze Age and Iron Age and now the coming AI Age. For the past 250 years, those economic drivers have been general purpose technologies, such as the combustion engine and electricity. Such technologies spawned whole new industries and transformed the business world. AI reaches even farther, becoming truly ubiquitous in a way that electricity or engines could never be. AI is the technology's technology, representing a new class of universal purpose technology. In

1. ""'Crime prediction software 'adopted by 14 UK police forces,' "" " - BBC News,." 4 February 4,. 2019, https://www.bbc.co.uk/news/technology-47118229. Accessed 4 Feb. 2019.

this way, the repercussions of the AI Age promise to be greater than any of the prior industrial, economic and technological transformations.

At Critical Future, we have developed a robust econometrics model to assess the impact of the AI market over the coming years. We found that AI will unlock US$19 trillion in market value by 2035. As part of our study, we have calculated that global AI market size will grow from US$27.68 billion in 2019 to US$1.34 trillion by 2035, at a compound annual growth rate (CAGR) of 29.15 percent during that period. But AI has the potential to play a much larger role in the global economy. To understand this, it's important to appreciate that AI is not a single technology, but a family of technological techniques. By 2035, at least one type of AI technology will be adopted by two-thirds of companies worldwide, and AI will create an additional total economic impact of US$19.24 trillion on a global scale.

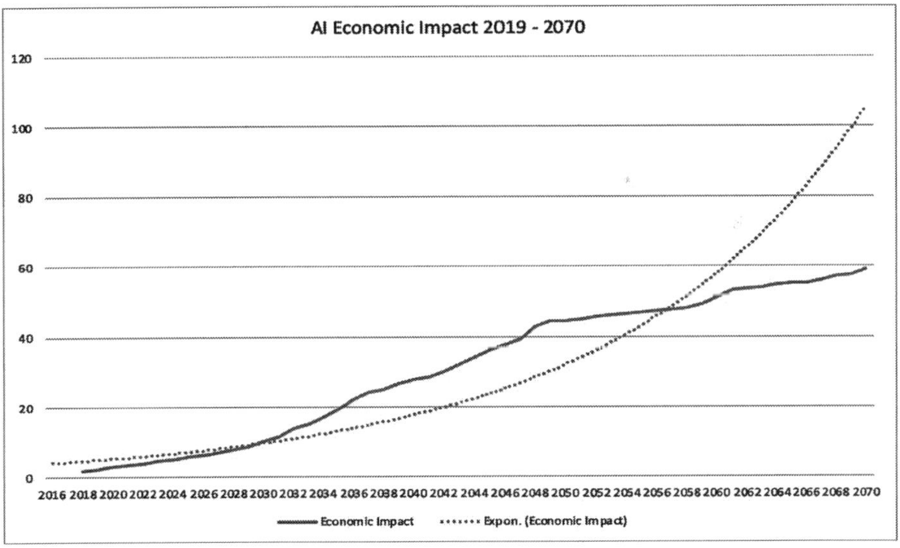

Figure 1: Economic Impact of Artificial Intelligence, Source Critical Future 2020

This phenomenal growth will create a new economic and technological paradigm: the AI Age. The coming period has been called a fourth Industrial Revolution, but it is more accurately an AI-centric epoch. While other technologies, such as nanotechnology and 3-D printing, will be important in the next decades, they will rely on AI. Artificial intelligence will become the platform that every other technology is built on; more to the point, all technologies will need AI to realize their potential. There is no more important technology than intelligence. No higher power. The magic of intelligence is being distilled and bottled and is ready to be sprinkled over anything and everything in the AI Age.

THE IMPACT OF AI ON BUSINESS

Why should businesses care about the AI Age? The answer is compelling: Any business that doesn't invest in AI will become increasingly uncompetitive. Despite this, the vast majority of companies have not yet leveraged the power of AI. They have left the full benefits of AI to a small group of technology companies that are using it for massive gain. In the seventeen years between 2002 and 2019, four of the world's top five publicly traded companies by market cap shifted from companies that have little or no AI (GE, Exxon, Citigroup and Walmart) to companies that harness AI as a foundation of their business (Apple, Google parent Alphabet, Amazon and Facebook). The one company that managed to maintain its top-five position was Microsoft, which heavily invested in AI throughout this period.

Your business can also benefit enormously from AI. Every business can. More than that: Your business needs to benefit from AI before it gets left behind by competitors that do. Recent research shows that businesses investing in AI grow 30 percent faster and have 50 percent higher profits than those without AI investments. Businesses that invest in AI have the opportunity to gain a clear competitive advantage, and those that don't risk everything. Not adapting to the digital age sent giants like Kodak and Blockbuster Video plummeting into bankruptcy; companies that fail to adapt to the AI Age could suffer the same fate.

THE IMPACT OF AI ON NATIONS

The competition for AI extends past business and all the way to nations. China is fully involved in implementing a massive-scale strategy to become the preeminent AI nation by 2030. China plans to achieve a $1 trillion AI industry, in a mission described as the biggest threat to US supremacy since the Cold War. The US doesn't plan to be outdone and is investing billions to win the most important arms race of our times. President Donald Trump has signed an executive order encouraging US agencies to prioritize keeping the United States ahead in the development and deployment of artificial intelligence. The world's leadership is united in seeing AI as the key to the future. Russian President Vladimir Putin summed up the greatest technological struggle of the twenty-first century: "Artificial Intelligence is the Future. . . . Whoever rules in this domain will rule the world."

THE IMPACT OF AI ON PEOPLE

Why should we as individuals care about the AI Age? Studies have shown that up to 47 percent of the workforce will be displaced by AI in the United States. And the Bank of England's chief economist has warned that the UK will need a skills revolution to avoid "large swathes" of people from becoming "technologically unemployed" as AI makes many jobs obsolete.

The front cover of this book was entirely created by AI. There are no human fingerprints on this image. It was created by 200,000 book covers being fed into an AI System, and then the Machine Learning algorithm, known as Generative Adversarial Networks (GANs) generating its own AI Art. This world-first and new landmark in the story of AI, poses questions such what will happen to all the human designers and creatives in future if AI can do these jobs? This is a striking example of how our professional lives will be transformed by the AI Age, compelling us to acquire AI Age skills.

Why should we as citizens care about the AI Age? AI has a dark side and has allegedly been used by Russian agents to influence the 2016 US presidential election. AI was used by Cambridge Analytica, a British data science firm, to allegedly influence elections. China's government has invested heavily to use AI for the world's most advanced population-monitoring apparatus. AI has the potential to be used unethically for military, political and criminal means, and against vulnerable people. At the same time, AI can also be a source for good in many domains, from providing solutions for climate-related dangers to improving health care and helping farmers optimize crop yields. For these reasons, every responsible citizen needs to be aware of the imminent AI Age.

Yet our research shows there is a massive AI knowledge gap. How can people be prepared for massive AI-related job disruption when they don't have a proper understanding of the technology? How can businesses stay competitive in the AI Age when most haven't learned the business applications? How can citizens be vigilant against AI misuse when they don't know how this technology works? Our research surveys at Critical Future show people fail to understand even the basics, from the main types of AI being used to how they can be applied in business. Equipping businesspeople with the knowledge to thrive in the AI Age is the purpose of this book.

Children growing up today are no longer digital natives; they are AI natives. Today's children are interacting with intelligent machines from an early age. AI will shape their outlook in ways we don't yet understand, just as we found millennials were distinctive as the first generation immersed in digitization. We need to educate the AI generation about the technologies shaping their lives, and that begins with educating ourselves.

STRUCTURE OF THIS BOOK

This book focuses mainly on the implications of AI for business. As we go on this journey, we examine what intelligence is and what is unique about human intelligence. We walk through the fascinating history of AI to understand its provenance. And we analyze the predominant types of AI, their capabilities and how businesses can use them.

My aim is to make artificial intelligence accessible. I seek to demystify the concept, which can be hidden amid technological jargon, and guide businesses toward an understanding of AI that will help them apply it. I am the founder and CEO of Critical Future, the specialist AI consultancy trusted by some of the world's biggest brands. My team at Critical Future includes the very best PhDs in AI from Harvard, MIT, Cambridge University and elsewhere. I am an entrepreneur, an active AI consultant rather than a technical PhD, and I look at AI from a business perspective. Thus, this book is grounded in actual, working AI business solutions.

People all over the world, from companies to academics and hobbyists, are already using AI every day in thousands of different ways. Businesses with domain expertise and industry-specific data have the potential to build AI applications with real impact. At the core of the book is a comprehensive AI Business Solutions Framework, which shows how your business can use AI to overcome business challenges with new solutions. This framework illustrates how AI can enhance every business function, including strategy, supply chain, sales, marketing, operations, production, IT, finance and HR. We detail specific initiatives you can activate to fuel the growth of your business with AI. These solutions are actionable now by any company, large or small.

THE FUTURE OF WORK

In the second half of the book, we take a detailed look at the impact AI will have on jobs. AI will take on many tasks now done by humans and, in the process, impact hundreds of millions of jobs. By the same token, AI will also create millions of new jobs in data analysis, AI development and jobs requiring human-specific skills like sales, innovation and customer service. The role of the business professional will be to navigate this transition, acquiring new skills and possibly switching occupations in the process. Learning how to effectively work with AI will transform the nature of work and unleash life-changing opportunities. It will be absolutely essential to learn AI Age skills, and we detail the key skills needed to thrive in the AI Age.

THE FUTURE OF MAN AND MACHINE

We also explore the future of AI, its evolution and how it will change our lives. We provide a glimpse of the world to come and the potential for a watershed moment known as the singularity in which artificial intelligence exceeds the powers of human intelligence, giving birth to a superintelligence. Such an intelligence could dominate the earth and utterly transform the world around it. It could be like a god, with the power to heal the sick, know your every move, read your mind and answer your prayers. Many have raised concerns about the implications of a superintelligence. By the end of this book, we will have explored the intriguing implications of a singularity, providing you with the tools to consider its ramifications.

Some of the era's greatest minds are divided on this question. Stephen Hawking has said, "Every aspect of our lives will be transformed [by AI]," and he warned that "success in creating effective AI could be the biggest event in the history of our civilization. Or the worst. We just don't know." Google CEO Sundar Pichai has said AI will be "more important than fire or electricity." Jeff Bezos, Amazon CEO and the wealthiest man on earth, has said we are in a "golden age of AI" that "offers an enabling layer for every business." Elon Musk, CEO of Tesla and SpaceX, has been less sanguine about AI, revealing that, "It scares the hell out of me. It's capable of vastly more than almost anyone knows and the rate of improvement is exponential."

Whatever we each think of AI, one thing is certain: Our businesses, our careers, our lives will be changed by AI. The AI Age is an all-encompassing, metamorphic, technological and economic revolution. Yuval Noah Harari, author of the best-selling *Sapiens*, foresees a twenty-second century where the AI Age has divided society into two classes—the Gods and the Useless. The AI Age will produce winners and losers, and this book aims to usher readers toward the winning side of that divide.

A change is upon us. The glowing embers of revolution have been sparked. AI is burning down the old business landscape, leaving in its wake fertile fields of opportunity. This book aims to provide readers with the knowledge to effectively manage this most critical transition of our lives so that, rather than becoming displaced, you are well positioned. Rather than being disrupted, you can be a disruptor. Rather than being left behind, you are out in front of the crowd. This book is a guide to the AI Age.

CHAPTER 1
The History of AI

"Human history, in essence, is the history of ideas."
— H. G. Wells

"Do not fear to be eccentric in opinion, for every opinion now accepted was once eccentric."
— Bertrand Russell

"The best prophet of the future is the past."
— Lord Byron

The story of artificial intelligence begins in an unexpected place—the English village of Bletchley. There are few things finer than the English countryside. The flowing green fields, golden daffodils and hills shaped as if by a kindly hand were inspiration for the literary greats William Wordsworth, T.S Eliot and Thomas Hardy. Such natural beauty offers an incongruous setting for the birth of the most profound technological revolution of our time. Yet it was in Bletchley, in rural England, that the computer age commenced and the story of artificial intelligence begins.

Bletchley was a perfectly ordinary village, with one unique attribute; it lay at the geometric center of intellectual England, where the main railway from London intersected the branch lines of the two oldest and preeminent university towns in the world: Oxford and Cambridge. In 1938, this serendipity helped draw Bletchley into something extraordinary. Here, the British government brought together mathematicians, crossword-puzzle solvers, chess players and thinkers. Their home: a converted nineteenth-century Victorian mansion known as Bletchley Park. Their mission: to crack the German Enigma encryption machine. Their most brilliant mind was Alan Turing. Former US President Barack Obama recognized Turing's achievements when he singled out three British scientists for having a profound impact on science: Isaac Newton, who discovered gravity; Charles Darwin, who uncovered the science of evolution; and Turing, who invented the digital computer and what became known as artificial intelligence.

THE GENIUS OF ALAN TURING

Alan Turing was born in 1912 into a British family once described as "lower-upper middle class," a description that provides insight into the pronounced British class structure of the time. Turing's mother, Sara, drew pride from a baronetcy in the family and a distinguished ancestor who, as a scientist, had coined the term "electron." Turing was born in London, but his parents later lived in India, where his father worked in the British Empire. He grew up on the English South Coast in the small town of St Leonards-on-Sea, where he had a quite normal upbringing. Turing developed a love of science from a very young age, and by the time he was sent to public school at Sherborne, he already had a passion for scientific experiments.

As Turing grew into a man, he became a brilliant academic who distinguished himself as a mathematician at Cambridge and Princeton universities. Throughout this time, he harbored a dangerous secret. Had it been discovered, it would have meant not only scandal and professional ruin but criminal charges and imprisonment for him. Turing was gay, and in Britain the punishment for homosexual sex was severe—the death penalty until 1861, and from 1885 until 1967 the Labouchere Amendment criminalizing "gross indecency" meant gay men were punished with two years in prison. Throughout his top secret work on Enigma, Turing was forced to keep his sexuality a secret or face personal ruin and prison.

Enigma, capable of encrypting information for secure communications, was the so-called "unbreakable" machine that German engineers developed during World War II. Coded messages were critical to Germany's war effort because they prevented the Allies from intercepting German communications and intelligence. In a total war, keeping one step ahead of the enemy is vital, and Germany relied on this communication tool. Enigma users could type a message, then scramble it using five rotors that depicted different letters of the alphabet. To recover the text, the receiver needed to know the exact settings of these rotors.

In *Alan Turing: The Enigma*, writer Andrew Hodges outlined why the Enigma machine was considered impenetrable and the code unsolvable.[2] Hodges describes how, in the case of a 26-letter Enigma, there are 26 x 26 x 26 = 17,576 possible states of the rotors. These were geared as any adding machine would be. The middle rotor would move on one step when the first had made a complete revolution, and the innermost moved a step when the middle one had made a complete turn. The "reflector," however, would not move, it being a fixed set of wires connecting the outputs of the innermost rotor. So the Enigma was polyalphabetic, with a period of 17,576. This meant there were 159 million million million possible Enigma setups. The German authorities believed that this vast complexity made Enigma impenetrable.

Polish intelligence had studied Enigma intensely during the interwar period, and just prior to the outbreak of hostilities, it handed the Western Allies a working model of the Enigma machine as well as useful

2 Andrew Hodges, *Alan Turing: The Enigma, The Book That Inspired the Film* The Imitation Game, Princeton, New Jersey: Princeton University Press, 2014.

knowledge regarding decrypting it. But it was not enough to crack the code, leaving Enigma indecipherable.

THE INVENTION OF THE COMPUTER

Turing grew interested in Enigma because, as he said, "No one else was doing anything about it, so I could have it all to myself." He realized cracking the Enigma could not be achieved by a human; beating this machine would require another machine. In 1936, while studying for his PhD at Princeton in the United States, Turing had published the paper On Computable Numbers, With an Application to the Entscheidungsproblem [3], which became the foundation of computer science. In it, Turing presented a theoretical machine that could solve any problem described by simple instructions encoded on a paper tape. Turing demonstrated that a single "universal machine" could be constructed that could compute any programmed set of instructions. Turing's universal machine is unmistakably what we today call a computer.

CHARLES BABBAGE AND LADY ADA LOVELACE

Turing was influenced by nineteenth-century inventor Charles Babbage and his companion and colleague, Lady Ada Lovelace.

It has often been claimed that Ada Lovelace, the daughter of Lord Byron, designed the first ever computer program. She was deeply intrigued by Babbage's plans for a complicated device he called the analytical engine. It was never built, but the design had all the essential elements of a modern computer. In 1843, Lovelace did a translation of comments concerning the engine and at the end wrote the first program, which recorded a series of numbers called Bernoulli numbers. She realized that computer applications were not limited to mathematical operations and could even store and replay music:

3 On computable numbers, with an application to the Entscheidungsproblem, A.M. Turing, 1936, https://www.cs.virginia.edu/~robins/Turing_Paper_1936.pdf.

Supposing, for instance, that the fundamental relations of pitched sounds in the science of harmony and of musical composition were susceptible of such expression and adaptations, the engine might compose elaborate and scientific pieces of music of any degree of complexity or extent. (1843)[4]

Although Babbage and his assistants had sketched out programs for his engine before, Lovelace's are the most elaborate and complete, and the first to be published; thus, she is often referred to as "the first computer programmer." Babbage himself "spoke highly of her mathematical powers and of her particular capability—higher, he said, than of anyone he knew, to prepare the descriptions connected with his calculating machine."

However, the book *Computing Before Computers* [5] argues, though, that Ada Lovelace's contribution has been overstated:

"This romantically appealing image is without foundation. All but one of the programs cited in her notes (to her translation of an account of a lecture Babby gave in Turin, Italy) had been prepared by Babbage from three to seven years earlier. The exception was prepared by Babbage for her, although she did detect a "bug" in it. Not only is there no evidence that Ada Lovelace ever prepared a program for the Analytical Engine, but her correspondence with Babbage shows she did not have the knowledge to do so."

Ada Lovelace died of cancer at 36, a few short years after the publication of her "Sketch of the Analytical Engine, with Notes from the Translator." She reappeared when Turing referenced her in his seminal 1950 paper, Computing Machinery and Intelligence, under Lady Lovelace's Objection.

4 Ada Augusta, Countess of Lovelace, "Notes by the Translator" on French comments by L. F. Menabrea on "Sketch of the Analytical Engine Invented by Charles Babbage." Her notes at the end with instructions for "the first computer program," were three times longer than Meabrea's comments, http://www.fourmilab.ch/babbage/sketch.html, 1843

5 William Aspray, ed, *Computers Before Computing*, Ames, Iowa: Iowa State University Press, 1990.

Charles Babbage's designs for computers were never built in his lifetime. The first complete Babbage Engine was assembled in 2002 in London, 153 years after it was designed. Difference Engine No. 2, built faithfully to the original drawings, consists of 8,000 parts, weighs five tons and measures eleven feet long. I took this picture of it at the Science Museum in London, using my six-inch smartphone camera, which can trace its origin back to the schematics for this mammoth machine.

THE TURING BOMBE

Turing was a mathematician rather than an electrical engineer, which was seen as a lower-order profession. But Turing was interested in how things really worked, and he researched engineering for the design of his Enigma deciphering machine, which he called the bombe. The machine was like 36 Enigma machines strapped together, combined with Bayesian statistics. Bayes was an English vicar from the 18th century who developed mathematical theories that were extremely unfashionable in Turing's time. Turing restored Bayes' credibility, and today Bayesian statistics are among the main methods used in machine learning.

BAYES THEOREM

Bayes actually died in 1761, a relatively unknown priest, but after his death his papers were discovered by Richard Price who read his works to the Royal Society and organized their publication preserving them for posterity.

Bayesian analysis is based on this structure: Prior Belief + New Evidence = Revised Belief. For example, if you toss a coin 50 times and 49 times it is tails, a normal statistics perspective would be the coin has been manipulated to always come up tails. So a good bet with a high probability would be on tails again next. But a Bayesian statistics perspective would take into account prior knowledge of the coin. Did we receive it from an ordinary shop, or was it specifically taken out by the person who suggested the bet?

The Bayesian approach allows us to combine the observed evidence with our prior knowledge to obtain a revised belief. Traditional statisticians were opposed to Bayes as he allows opinion to encroach in the objective world of statistics. It was not until Bayesian analysis proved to be a highly useful tool in many applications that it was accepted into mainstream statistics. Today Bayesian methods are everywhere, as Judea Pearl who invented Bayesian Networks, which employ Bayes theorem to enable algorithms to use inference and learning, explains:

"They (Bayesian Networks) are used in speech-recognition software, in spam filters, in weather forecasting, in the evaluation of potential oil wells, and in the Food and Drug Administration's approval process for medical devices. if you play video games on a Microsoft Xbox, a Bayesian network ranks your skill. If you own a cell phone, the codes that your phone uses to pick your call out of thousands of others are decoded by belief propagation, an algorithm devised for Bayesian networks. Vint Cerf, the chief Internet evangelist at another company you might have heard of, Google, puts it this way: "we're huge consumers of Bayesian methods."

Bayes' theorem was used to calculate probabilities, which helped the machine focus. The probabilities that Bayes produced reduced the number of potential permutations. This meant the machine could come up with the answer much more quickly. The theorem worked. Turing's bombes enabled the operator to search through all the possible permutations and define the correct settings of the Enigma machine. An instantaneous decryption of the message could then be achieved. However, Turing lacked the resources to build and deploy his invention. The resourceful Turing wrote directly to Prime Minister Winston Churchill for help:

> Secret and Confidential Prime Minister
> only Hut 6 and Hut 8, (Bletchley Park) 21st October 1941
>
> Dear Prime Minister, Some weeks ago you paid us the honour of a visit, and we believe that you regard our work as important. You will have seen that, thanks largely to the energy and foresight of Commander Travis, we have been well supplied with the 'bombes' for the breaking of the German Enigma codes. We think, however, that you ought to know that this work is being held up, and in some cases is not being done at all, principally because we cannot get sufficient staff to deal with it. Our reason for writing to you direct is that for months we have done everything that we possibly can through the normal channels, and that we despair of any early improvement without your intervention. [6]

This letter had an immediate effect. Winston Churchill, to his credit, appreciated the strategic importance of Turing's work. Upon receipt of the letter, Churchill minuted General Ismay, his principal staff officer: "ACTION THIS DAY Make sure they have all they want on extreme priority and report to me that this has been done." [7]

6 Alan Hodges, *Alan Turing: The Enigma*
7 Alan Hodges, *Alan Turing: The Enigma.*

Bletchley code breaking became an industrial process: 10,000 people, two-thirds of them women, worked three shifts 24/7. Turing's electro-mechanical machine, called the bombe, searched through the permutations of Enigma, and by the end of the war the British were able to read all daily German traffic. This intelligence, known as Ultra, had a profound impact. It enabled the Allies to read German plans, which the Germans themselves believed were protected by an impenetrable code, and played a fundamental role in the outcome of the war. The greatest impact was in the Battle of the Atlantic, the longest battle of World War II. Britain as an island nation relied on food imports, and in both world wars it came close to mass starvation. German U-boats working in "wolf packs" could inflict devastating losses on Allied shipping, which included food ships. Churchill later said "the only thing that ever really frightened me during the war was the U-boat peril." [8]

Ultra intelligence from Turing's bombes transformed the nature of the battle. The Allies not only rerouted convoys from German wolf packs but surrounded combat U-boats and their supply U-boats. The predators became prey. By May 1943, U-boat losses were so devastating that Admiral Karl Dönitz, the officer in charge of the German Navy, withdrew them from the North Atlantic. The battle continued at a much slower pace, but the Allies had put an end to the strategic threat of the U-boat.

Bletchley Park's achievements were not solely those of Turing. It was a team effort, with many other important code breakers, among them Bill Tutte, who brilliantly cracked the code used by the Nazi high command, including Hitler himself. Crucial intelligence derived from such decryption revealed Hitler was duped by the Allied pretence that the D-Day landing would be at Calais, supporting the Allies' decision to proceed with the Normandy invasion.

8 "Was Churchill really worried about the Battle of the Atlantic? And if so, why?" Churchill Archive for Schools, http://www.churchillarchiveforschools.com/themes/the-themes/key-events-and-developments-in-world-history/was-churchill-really-worried-about-the-battle-of-the-atlantic-and-if-so-why.

TURING TURNED THE WAR

Historian David Kahn concludes that without Bletchley Park's Ultra intelligence [9], the Allied ground offensives would have been delayed by several months and the Normandy invasion, pushed back into 1945. Based on shipping figures, Kahn estimates that the Mediterranean offensives would have been delayed by three months, and that to get sufficient tonnage, it would have been necessary to transfer vessels from the Pacific, thereby delaying operations in that theater as well. The increased number of U-boats (because of greater numbers) would also have made lend-lease supply to the Soviet Union far more problematic. Without the atomic bomb, Khan concludes, the war might have been extended by as much as two years.

US President Dwight Eisenhower also said the contribution of Turing and others at Bletchley was "priceless" and "saved thousands of British and American lives and, in no small way, contributed to the speed with which the enemy was routed and eventually forced to surrender." [10] Captain Jerry Roberts, who worked with Turing at Bletchley Park, told the BBC, without Turing's Ultra intelligence, Britain would have lost the war:

> You have to understand the measure of what Turing did. Early in the war, in 1939, he had broken the Enigma used by the Luftwaffe and the German army, but he'd been unable to break the naval Enigma. In 1940/41 the German U-boats were sinking our food ships and our ships bringing in armaments left, right and centre, and there was nothing to stop this until Turing managed to break naval Enigma, as used by the U-boats. We then knew where the U-boats were positioned in the Atlantic, and our convoys could avoid them. If that hadn't happened, it is entirely possible, even

9 "The Historical Impact of Revealing the Ultra Secret," NSA.gov, October 26, 2006, https://www.nsa.gov/news-features/declassified-documents/cryptologic-spectrum/assets/files/ultra_secret.pdf.

10 "Eisenhower letter praising UK code breakers goes on display," Theguardian.com, March 15, 2016, https://www.theguardian.com/uk-news/2016/mar/15/eisenhower-letter-uk-code-breakers-display-bletchley-park.

> probable, that Britain would have been starved and would have lost the war. [11]

Irving John Good, one of Turing's colleagues agreed: "I won't say that what Turing did made us win the war," he once observed, "but, I dare say, we might have lost it without him." It is a startling thought, tens of millions of armed men at war, but the outcome decided by one gentle academic named Alan Turing. That is a stark reminder of the power of intelligence and the fundamental importance of machine intelligence.

Had Turing not cracked Enigma and had Britain lost the war due to the U-boat peril before the United States entered the war, the final outcome could have been completely different. The Nazis may have won the war and conquered the Soviet Union. Nazi victory would have led to industrial mass murder on a scale never before seen in human history. For example, Goering and Hitler planned to starve to death 30 million Russians after victory in the East to bring down the Russian population, before enslaving all the Slavic "Untermenschen" (subhumans) that remained. The Holocaust would have continued unbridled, leading to the annihilation of Jews in Europe and Russia. Nazi victory is a thought almost too terrible to bear, and it is possibly thanks to Alan Turing and his fascination with thinking machines that it didn't become an all too dreadful reality.

Turing was awarded an Order of the British Empire (OBE) for his service in the war. While it pleased his mother, Sara, who made an embarrassing fuss, it was a remarkably lowly award considering his contribution. According to the British government Cabinet Office, the OBE "is awarded for having a major local role in any activity." Turing had much more than a local role. His role had a profound long-lasting international impact. As his Bletchley friend William Newman said:

11 "Churchill: Turing made the single biggest contribution to the war effort," The Turing Centenary, October 19, 2011, https://theturingcentenary.wordpress.com/2011/10/19/churchill-turing-made-the-single-biggest-contribution-to-the-war-effort/.

> Turing got an OBE, which I thought a "wonderful" thing to offer a man for what he did. I mean, Good Heavens, he changed the course of the war. I felt all these decorations were so ludicrous I felt justified in declining the one they offered me. I think to offer a man like Turing the OBE, which he accepted rather as a joke, I must say, was fantastic. [12]

However, we must remember Turing's work was absolutely secret. Everything at Bletchley was governed by the Official Secrets Act, and no one who worked there was to utter a word. Indeed, it was not until 30 years later, in 1970s, that the world's best kept secret began to be unravelled. The British government would have been careful, therefore, not to bestow too high an award on Turing, so as not to give any indication of his top-secret achievements. It was sadly characteristic of Turing's lifetime that his great contributions went largely unrecognized.

THE COMPUTER AGE

At the end of the war in 1945, Turing produced a detailed design for his proposed Automated Computing Engine (ACE), which was the first design for an electronic stored-program digital computer. As the 1950s progressed, business was quick to see the benefits of computers, and business computing became a new industry. These computers were all universal Turing machines (UTMs), which Turing described this way:

> There will positively be no internal alteration [of the computer] to be made even if we wish suddenly to switch from calculating the energy levels of the neon atom to the enumeration of groups of order 720. It may appear somewhat puzzling that this can be done. How can one expect a machine to do all this multitudinous variety of things? The answer is that we should consider the machine to be doing something quite simple, namely carrying

12 Dermot Turing, *PROF: Alan Turing Decoded*, (London: Pavilion Books, 2016), 152.

> out orders given to it in a standard form which it is able to understand. [13]

Canadian academic Hector Levesque [14], writing in 2017, explains why, even today, we still talk about Turing machines in relation to computing. Turing's profound insight had been that writing down a number as a string of symbols allows us to talk about mapping from numbers as operations that transform one string of symbols into another string of symbols. These operations involving strings of symbols are what we call digital computation. Turning numbers into symbols enables us to perform a computation. Levesque asks:

> Why do theoreticians still talk about Turing machines? Has modern computing not gone far beyond the quaint vision of a machine with a movable head? The answer is simple: Every digital computer built to date can be shown to be a special case of a Turing machine. Whatever it can do, a Turing machine can do as well. Or to be more precise, any function over strings of symbols computable by a modern digital computer is also computable by a Turing machine. Most scientists believe this will be true of *any* computer we ever build.[15]

Turing's achievement was to pin down the idea of a computer mathematically. Whether the machine is computing pictures, bank transactions, musical notes or ballistic trajectories, it is all 1s and 0s at its core. Every digital computer can, in theory, compute anything that is possible to compute. Turing proved all digital computers are logically equivalent. The heritage of Turing's ideas can be seen today in every computer in the world, from the smartphone to the digital clock, laptop and PC.

13 Ian Watson, *The Universal Machine: From the Dawn of Computing to Digital Consciousness*, New York: Copernicus, 2012.

14 Hector Levesque, *Common Sense, the Turing Test, and the Quest for Real AI*, Cambridge, Massachusetts: The MIT Press, 2017.

15 Hector Levesque, *Common Sense, the Turing Test, and the Quest for Real AI*, 113.

THE TURING TEST

Turing's legacy did not end with the computer. He also did groundbreaking work on thinking machines, which later became known as artificial intelligence. Turing believed that while machines were currently "slaves" that followed instructions, they could become something more:

> Let us suppose we set up a machine with certain instruction tables, so constructed that these tables might on occasion, if good reason arose, modify those tables. One can imagine that after the machine had been operating for some time, the instructions would have altered out of all recognition, but nevertheless still be such that one would have to admit the machine was doing worthwhile calculations....like a pupil who learns from his master, but had added much more by his own work. When this happens, I believe one is obliged to regard the machine as showing intelligence.[16]

In 1947, Turing went back for a year to Cambridge, where he wrote his theoretical report Intelligent Machinery. He considered the implications of assembling groups of tiny decision-making units. Turing's paper shows these machines could be conditioned to learn, and in doing so Turing invented what today is known as machine learning.

However, Turing's ideas were sniggered at in some quarters. There was a recurrent debate about whether machines could think or whether thinking was the preserve of human beings. One of the most famous objections to the notion of thinking computers had come from Alan Turing's female influence, now known as Lady Lovelace's Objection. Here are Ada Lovelace's own words:

> The Analytical Engine has no pretensions whatever to originate anything. It can do whatever we know how to order it to perform. It

16 Dermot Turing, *PROF: Alan Turing Decoded.*

> can follow analysis; but it has no power of anticipating any analytical relations or truths. [17]

Turing resolved to tackle the question of whether machines can think by reframing it to focus on a test. Turing wanted to make the point that intelligence is defined by behavior rather than by mystical qualities so that if a program could act like a human, it should be considered as intelligent as a human.

In his 1950 paper Computing Machinery and Intelligence [18], Turing outlined a specific test for machine intelligence, now well known as the Turing test. There are three versions of this test. The first is a party game, known as the Imitation Game involving a man and a woman in separate rooms. The second involves a judge conversing only with a computer and a man. In the third and most famous, which Turing proposed in a 1952 radio broadcast, a jury asks a computer questions. The aim of each version of the test is the same: The machine must convince, through holding a conversation, that it is a human being. This is Turing's own illustration of the test between a human and a machine:

> Interrogator: In the first line of your sonnet, which reads "Shall I compare thee to a summer's day," would not a "spring day" do as well or better?
>
> Computer: It wouldn't scan.
>
> Interrogator: How about a "winter's day?" That would scan all right.
>
> Computer: Yes, but nobody wants to be compared to a winter's day.
>
> Interrogator: Yet Christmas is a winter's day, and I do not think Mr. Pickwick would mind the comparison.
>
> Computer: I don't think you're serious. By a winter's day, one means a typical winter's day, rather than a special one like Christmas.[19]

---

17 Ada Lovelace, "Notes of the Translator," English translation of French comments on "Sketch of the Analytical Engine Invented by Charles Babbage," http://www.fourmilab.ch/babbage/sketch.html, 1843.

18 "Computing Machinery and Intelligence," A. M. Turing, Oxford University Press,1950, http://phil415.pbworks.com/f/TuringComputing.pdf.

19 S. Barry Cooper and J. van Leeuwen, eds, *Alan Turing: His Work and Impact*, Amsterdam: Elsevier Science, 2013.

I fear most human beings wouldn't be able to keep up with this conversation, which easily switches between classical references from Shakespeare and Dickens to conversational plays on the double meaning of words. For example, "a winter's day" does not refer literally to a day in winter but to the qualities a day in winter would have, such as frostiness and cold. Thus, the computer responded that "nobody wants to be compared to a winter's day." Perhaps Turing was overly used to conversing with intellectuals, such as Cambridge dons and Bletchley code breakers. Turing, in this way, overestimated the speed with which artificial intelligence would be able to match human intelligence in holding such a sophisticated conversation. He incorrectly predicted that machines would be able to pass the test by the year 2000, believing machines with around 100 MB of storage would be able to fool 30 percent of human judges in a five-minute test.

In practice, the Turing test has been far more difficult to pass. Some machines have, indeed, performed well, such as Eliza in 1967. In this instance, the program presented itself as a psychologist and, rather than answering all the questions, it turned them back on the questioner:

> Patient: I only feel happy when I'm writing.
>
> Eliza: How long have you been writing?
>
> Patient: Always, but I have only been writing seriously since I was eighteen.
>
> Eliza: What incident are you thinking of?
>
> Patient: Um
>
> Eliza: What does that suggest to you?
>
> Patient: I don't think it is enough, to only be happy when you write.
>
> Eliza: Does that trouble you?
>
> Patient: . . . Um, because you write all the time. And then there's the real world, and you still have to deal with real people.
>
> Eliza: What are your feelings now?

> Patient: I've been thinking a lot about a poem by Yeats: "The man and the echo." Do you know it?
>
> Eliza: Do you say you are thinking a lot about a poem by Yeats "The man and the echo" for a special reason?
>
> Patient: Yes

Beginning in 1990, inventor Hugh Loebner offered $100,000 to the creators of the first bot that could pass the Turing test, but the prize remains unclaimed. In 2014, a computer program named Eugene Goostman, which simulates a 13-year-old Ukrainian boy, passed a short Turing test at an event organized by the University of Reading. An element of gamesmanship was used because judges believed non sequiturs and grammatical errors were the result of cultural and language barriers deriving from Eugene being a teenage boy from Ukraine. Interestingly, Eugene did manage to present a consistent personality, and his conversation, which follows, reads like an irreverent adolescent with a mildly impetuous sense of humor:

> Scott: What is bigger, a shoebox or Mount Everest?
>
> Eugene: I can't make a choice right now. I should think it out later. And I forgot to ask where you are from . . .
>
> Scott: How many legs does a camel have?
>
> Eugene: Something between 2 and 4. Maybe, three?:))) By the way, I still don't know your speciality-or, possibly, I've missed it?
>
> Scott: How many legs does a millipede have?
>
> Eugene: Just two, but Chernobyl mutants may have up to five. I know you are supposed to trick me.
>
> Scott: No, I need to know that you're not a chatbot. Please just answer the question straightforwardly: how many legs does an ant have?
>
> Eugene: Something between 2 and 4. Maybe, 3?:))) Oh what a fruitful conversation :)
>
> Scott: Do you understand why I'm asking such basic questions; you realise I'm just trying to unmask you as a robot as quickly as possible, like in the movie Blade Runner?

> Eugene: . . . wait
>
> Scott: Do you think your ability to fool unsophisticated judges indicates a flaw with the Turing test itself, or merely with the way people have interpreted the test?
>
> Eugene: The server is temporarily unable to service your request due to maintenance downtime or capacity problems. Problems try again later.
>
> Scott: Do you think Alan Turing, brilliant though he was, had trouble imagining that the judges of his "imitation game" wouldn't think to ask common sense questions like the ones above-or that, if they did, they'd actually accept evasion or irrelevant banter as answers?
>
> Eugene: No, not really. I don't think Alan Turing brilliant although this guy was had trouble imagining that the judges of his imitation game would not consider to Oooh. Anything else?
>
> Scott: In your opinion, does your existence demonstrate any idea or principle that wasn't demonstrated just as convincingly by ELIZA Joseph Weizenhams's chatbot from the 1960s.
>
> Eugene: Eliza was a break-thru. All the bots after it were nothing but weak parodies, claiming to have "revolutionary improvements"
>
> Scott: Hey, that's the first sensible thing you've said.

Despite great advances in artificial intelligence, the Turing test has remained more challenging than its distinguished originator anticipated. This highlights important differences between the strengths of machines and human beings. Machines have computational power that far exceeds that of humans, but humans understand context and meaning more accurately. Language is extremely complex, and while machines can learn to speak, they struggle to understand setting. Machines also find it difficult to demonstrate a consistent personality, which is probably why Eugene Goostman was the most successful, as this program does appear to have a steady voice. Perhaps it should not be surprising that a computer program without a human body or human feelings would find it hard to emulate a human, especially in conversations regarding human-focused topics such as sex, illness or aging. Certainly, humans would fail a "reverse Turing test" that involves replicating computer programs, since humans are not even able to emulate the calculators in mobile phones.

MORAVEC PARADOX

This disparity of strengths and weaknesses between man and machine is known as Moravec's Paradox, named after robotics pioneer Hans Moravec. The paradox: Things that are easy for a five-year-old human are hard for a machine, and vice versa.

In a paper entitled The Age of Robots, Moravec explained the reasons behind his intriguing paradox. Why are things that are simple for humans difficult for computers, and vice versa? The reason is the things that computers find hard really are hard. We handle them easily because our brains have been developed by millions of years of evolution to deal with these difficult things so well they now seem easy:

> In hindsight it seems that, in an absolute sense, reasoning is much easier than perceiving and acting—a position not hard to rationalize in evolutionary terms. The survival of human beings (and their ancestors) has depended for hundreds of millions of years on seeing and moving in the physical world, and in that competition, large parts of their brains have become efficiently organized for the task. But we didn't appreciate this monumental skill because it is shared by every human being and most animals—it is commonplace. On the other hand, rational thinking, as in chess, is a newly acquired skill, perhaps less than one hundred thousand years old. The parts of our brain devoted to it are not well organized, and, in an absolute sense, we're not very good at it. But until recently we had no competition to show us up.

Marovec's Paradox is why the Turing test has been much more difficult to pass than its brilliant proponent foresaw. Nevertheless, considering that today talking machines such as Alexa or Siri are a normal household gadget, Turing's focus on speaking machines was prescient. Just as Turing imagined, human beings are now constantly conversing with machines. The Turing test also foreshadows a future in which machines will become indistinguishable from human beings or will even exceed our intelligence.

Today, the Turing test remains an important concept in artificial intelligence. There are some, such as Yann LeCun, chief AI scientist for Facebook, who think it "is not a very interesting test. . . . It is too easy to trick it." Steve Wozniak, Apple cofounder, has proposed an alternative test for human-level intelligence in AI that uses a coffee cup test: A robot enters a strange house and makes a cup of coffee to pass the test. Yet, Ray Kurzweil, a remarkable AI writer, inventor and director of engineering at Google, believes the Turing test remains an excellent test for human-level intelligence:

> If a computer is to pass a valid Turing test, I believe it will need to have the full range of human intelligence. Understanding language at human levels is the ultimate goal. If an AI could do that, it could read all documents and books and learn everything else. We are getting there a little bit at a time. [20]

Today's speech recognition systems like Alexa or Siri can give specific answers to questions, but they cannot go off script. This would require understanding and reasoning about what is being said below the surface. These are attributes of general intelligence, as found in human beings. So to have the natural conversation outlined in the Turing test, which is not scripted but can branch off in different directions, would require something approaching human-level intelligence. Kurzweil, who has a long track record of making accurate predictions about technology, predicts AI will finally reach this point and pass the Turing test in 2029. It will be interesting to see over the next decade if he's right.

THE CHILD-MACHINE

Turing made another crucial contribution to artificial intelligence. His Computing Machinery and Intelligence paper, published in 1950 by the British journal Mind, is rightly remembered as a cornerstone in the history of AI. However, the most compelling part was largely overlooked until

20 Martin Ford, *Architects of Intelligence.*

recently. Turing suggested that to build a computer system capable of achieving the level of intelligence required to pass the Imitation Game, the system should be as a human child:

> Instead of trying to produce a programme to simulate the adult mind, why not rather try to produce one which simulates the child's? If this were then subjected to an appropriate course of education, one would obtain the adult brain. Presumably the child-brain is something like a notebook as one buys from the stationers. Rather little mechanism, and lots of blank sheets. . . . Our hope is that there is so little mechanism in the child-brain that something like it can be easily programmed. The amount of work in the education we can assume, as a first approximation, to be much the same as for the human child. [21]

Turing foresaw that this learning would be incremental. The machine develops knowledge by its own exploration, and as this knowledge accumulates, it can learn increasingly complex concepts and solve increasingly challenging problems. This is one way that human beings learn. As we will see by the end of this chapter, deep reinforcement learning, one of the most novel and exciting fields of artificial intelligence, has adopted one element of the way children learn—through positive reinforcement—with startlingly powerful results. Of course, children also learn in other important ways, such as imitation, reading and transfer of learning. All of these aspects of children's learning are today being researched by the leading lights in AI at companies such as Google, Facebook and Baidu and at universities such as MIT, Harvard and Cambridge. Turing's child-machine has, therefore, become known as "the oldest good idea in AI."

A TRAGIC END

Alan Turing was a remarkable genius. Not only did he contribute substantially to the defeat of the Nazis, but he also invented the computer age, leading to progress in almost every field of human endeav-

21 Peter Morton, ed, *A Historical Introduction to the Philosophy of Mind—Second Edition,* Peterborough, Canada: Broadview Press, 2010.

or. Turing foresaw that computers would evolve artificial intelligence with stunning prescience and outlined a blueprint for machine learning, as well as for child-machines, which remains one of the most promising fields of AI research. Former US President Barack Obama was undoubtedly correct when he added Turing to the esteemed company of Newton and Darwin as British scientists who had a profound impact on the world.

There is, however, a tragic corollary to Turing's story. In 1952, he was prosecuted for homosexual acts through the Labouchere Amendment, which made "gross indecency" a criminal offence in the UK. Turing discovered a man he had a casual affair with was an accomplice to a burglary at his house. After Turing reported the burglary to police, he admitted to the prior sexual relationship and was charged and convicted. As punishment, he accepted as an alternative to prison, chemical castration with DES, an estrogen medication that works as an anaphrodisiac. Persecuted by the very nation he had done so much to save, Turing despaired that his life's work would also be tarnished:

> I'm afraid that the following syllogism may be used by some in the future.
>
> Turing believes machines think
>
> Turing lies with men
>
> Therefore machines do not think
>
> Yours in distress,
>
> Alan
>
> —Alan Turing [22]

Turing died in 1954, 16 days before his 42nd birthday, from cyanide poisoning. The coroner ruled his death a suicide. Turing's mother believed it an unfortunate accident with cyanide, and there have been conspiracy theories about murder. But taking into account the torment

22 Shaun Usher, *Letters of Note: Volume 2: An Eclectic Collection of Correspondence Deserving of a Wider Audience*, San Francisco: Chronicle Books, 2016.

Turing suffered by maltreatment from a nation he had served so well, one can see why he would have been driven to take his own life. Turing made an immense positive contribution to Britain and the wider world, yet in return had been cruelly persecuted for no other reason than his sexuality. In 2013, the British government finally pardoned Turing posthumously.

Today, his contributions to science are recognized, and every year the A.M. Turing Award, often called the Nobel Prize of computing, is given in his name. In 2019, BBC viewers voted Alan Turing "the greatest person of the twentieth century." In winning, Turing beat out greats such as Winston Churchill, Einstein, Nelson Mandela, Muhammad Ali, Pablo Picasso and Martin Luther King. He was "father of the computer, war hero, genius," in the words of the BBC Icons series, which organized the vote. It showed just how much societal values have changed, and it was, I believe, well earned. As great as other major figures of the twentieth century were, Turing's impact is longer lasting. Computers have transformed the world for decades since his death. And the impact of AI will ring out for decades to come.

Turing reached the pinnacle of human intelligence in his lifetime. A mathematician, scientist, code breaker, genius, inventor, future seer, there have been few if any human beings who were more intelligent. The irony is that as Turing reached the high point of human intellect, he discovered artificial intelligence, the archetype for a new form of intelligence that may eventually exceed that of humans. Turing had given birth to something extraordinary; after his death, others would take his ideas forward.

WAR AND PROGRESS

It is not by coincidence that Turing's breakthrough came during the Second World War. Wars bring the greatest misery but, ironically, significant scientific progress. World War II led to the deaths of 50 million to 80 million people (including deaths due to war-related disease and famine). Yet during that war, not only were computers invented but so, too, were rockets, satellites, radar, jet engines and nuclear bombs.

Most significant among these achievements was medical penicillin, which was first mass-produced to treat infections. Sir Alexander Fleming had discovered penicillin in 1928, but Howard Florey and Ernst Boris Chain purified and tested it successfully in 1939. It was a British invention, rushed over to America during WWII because it had such far-reaching implications for curing soldiers. The Allies developed a coordinated effort, backed by tens of millions of dollars, to develop the lifesaving new antibiotic. Germany had the opportunity to develop penicillin since its discoverers had published their findings in the journal Nature, in an open academic paper that may have breached wartime secrecy. But Germany failed to put the required resources into developing penicillin and never managed to produce it.

In 1941, the first human trials were completed, and in 1942 it was first used as a medicine. By 1945, 650 billion units per month were being produced to save lives and limbs from infections. It is estimated that penicillin was used to treat 100,000 Allied men in the European theater. After the war, penicillin became the most effective lifesaving drug in the world, conquering diseases such as syphilis, gonorrhoea, tuberculosis, gangrene, pneumonia, diphtheria and scarlet fever. In all, it may have saved over 200 million lives, which is more than twice the number killed in WWII. It is clear that despite all the horrors of the Second World War, we do owe it many groundbreaking inventions. As the philosopher William James said:

> If we think how many things besides frontiers of states the wars of history have decided, we must feel some respectful awe, in spite of all the horrors. Our actual civilization, good and bad alike, has had past wars for its determining condition.[23]

IRVING JOHN GOOD

The Second World War also incited Irving John Good, a colleague of Turing's, to make an important contribution to the development of artificial intelligence. Born to Polish Jewish parents in London, Good's father was a watchmaker and Yiddish writer who had anglicized his name from Isadore Jacob Gudak. Good was a mathematics prodigy, like many of the fathers of AI. He once stood up in his crib and asked, "Mother, what is a thousand times a thousand?" As a child, he independently discovered irrational numbers while intensely ill with diphtheria. At nine years old, while confined to bed with an illness, he mulled over the square root of 2 and came up with a new understanding of its mathematical subtleties. As Good put it later in life:

> I'm proud of that, even now, because if there was any single instance in my life that shows that I had a little bit of mathematical genius, I think that was it. At the age of nine, it wasn't bad to make a discovery that was described as one of the greatest achievements of the ancient Greek mathematicians.

By the time he was fourteen, he had rediscovered mathematical induction, and his teachers at the Haberdashers' Aske's Boys' School, then in Hampstead, North West London, were no longer able to teach him anything new. They just left him alone with stacks of books. Good went on to read mathematics at Jesus College, Cambridge, graduating in 1938, winning the Smith's Prize in 1940, and completing his doctorate. He moved to Bletchley Park in 1941 to work for Alan Turing.

23 "William James (1842-1910), *Memories and Studies*, Project Gutenberg, http://www.gutenberg.org/ebooks/20768.

Chess has played a remarkable role in the development of artificial intelligence, always there in the background like the best supporting actor in an Oscar-winning movie. It was actually chess that brought Good to Bletchley Park. Britain's reigning chess champion, Hugh Alexander, recruited Good for his chess-playing talents, to join Hut 18 at Bletchley Park, where the decoders worked under Alan Turing.

Good, then 24, made a bad first impression on Turing, his new superior, when he arrived at Bletchley. Turing had caught him sleeping on the floor during his first night shift. Working all night was normal in wartime, and Turing completely ignored Good following this episode; he would not utter a word to his new colleague and promptly left the room when Good entered. But Good managed to win Turing over by solving a mathematical problem with great significance for the war effort:

> During a subsequent night shift, when there was no more work to be done, it dawned on Good that there might be another chink in the German indicating system. The German telegraphists had to add dummy letters to the trigrams, which they selected out of the Kenngruppenbuch. . . . Good wondered if their choice of dummy letters was random, or whether there was a bias towards particular letters. After inspecting some messages which had been broken, he discovered that there was a tendency to use some letters more than others. That being the case, all the code breakers had to do was to work back from the indicators given at the beginning of each message and apply each bigram table in turn in the same way as Joan Clarke had done before. The bigram table that produced one of the popular dummy letters was probably the correct one. When Good mentioned his discovery to Alan Turing, Turing was very embarrassed and said, "I could have sworn that I tried that." It quickly became an important part of the Banburismus procedure. [24]

24 Hugh Sebag-Montefiore, *Enigma: The Battle for the Code*, Hoboken, New Jersey: Wiley, 2004, 189.

THE INTELLIGENCE EXPLOSION

Good's main contribution to artificial intelligence was in originating the concept now known as the "intelligence explosion," which would anticipate the eventual advent of a superintelligence. He explains:

> Let an ultraintelligent machine be defined as a machine that can far surpass all the intellectual activities of any man, however clever. Since the design of machines is one of these intellectual activities, an ultraintelligent machine could design even better machines; there would then unquestionably be an "intelligence explosion," and the intelligence of man would be left far behind. Thus, the first ultraintelligent machine is the last invention that man need ever make, provided that the machine is docile enough to tell us how to keep it under control.

The importance of this concept of the "intelligence explosion" should be underlined. This mechanism could lead to the singularity, a time when machine intelligence will exceed all human intelligence combined. Turing also believed in the singularity, although he didn't know it by that name:

> It seems probable that once the machine thinking method had started, it would not take long to outstrip our feeble powers. They would be able to converse with each other to sharpen their wits. At some stage, therefore, we should have to expect the machines to take control. Lecture 1951

Good foresaw the "runaway," in which machine intelligence can continually redesign itself, producing more and more advanced forms of intelligence. David Chalmers, a professor of philosophy and neural science, wrote in 2010 that he supports Good's view, arguing AI could produce sufficiently intelligent software to reprogram and improve itself—a feature called "recursive self-improvement." It would then be even better at improving itself and could continue doing so in a rapidly increasing cycle, leading to a superintelligence. The arrival of a superintelligence has become a key concept and area of debate in the philosophy of artificial intelligence.

Inventor and futurist Ray Kurzweil forecasts the singularity will occur in 2045. At that point, machine intelligence will exceed human intelligence, and following Good's intelligence explosion, this will give birth to the superintelligence. Such an intelligence would not have the limitations of human intellect and may be able to invent or discover almost anything. It would be like a god, able to cure the sick, answer our deepest questions and engineer anything made possible by the laws of physics, including tantalizing prospects like time travel. It could also represent a great danger, and tech billionaire Elon Musk has famously said a "godlike" AI could rule over or even destroy humanity in the future.

Science has been seen as the destroyer of gods since Copernicus placed the sun, not the earth, at the center of the solar system. Darwin dealt another blow to religion by proving human beings were not "one down from the angels" but relegated to the animal kingdom, having evolved over millions of years, rather than being created in "God's own image." Today, many of the world's most famous atheists, like evolutionary biologist Richard Dawkins, are scientists.

Theological debate is largely framed as science versus religion. But now, for the first time, thanks to artificial intelligence and Good's "intelligence explosion" idea, one can make a logical scientific case that a superintelligence—a god by another name—may be created in our lifetime. For example, physicist Mark Tegmark's *Life 3.0*, a book Dawkins has described as "fantastic," considers a dozen scenarios post-singularity, with the superintelligence cast as Enslaved God or Conqueror, among the options. In the final chapter, we will explore in more detail whether a coming superintelligence will be a god. For now, I just want to make the point that a major, unnoticed philosophical shift has occurred. Scientists, that very anathema of religion, are now talking about the scientific potential of gods. This is the unique power of artificial intelligence.

AI AS A RECOGNIZED RESEARCH DISCIPLINE

In 1956, AI was established as a field of study at the Dartmouth Summer Research Project on Artificial Intelligence, organized by John McCarthy. Like Turing and Good, McCarthy was a math prodigy, and he had finished high school two years early. In his teens, McCarthy taught himself college mathematics by studying textbooks used at the nearby California Institute of Technology (Caltech). As a result, he was able to skip the first two years of mathematics at Caltech. In 1951, McCarthy received a PhD in the subject from Princeton and became an assistant professor at Dartmouth, where he organized that summer research project, now considered the most important brainstorming workshop in the history of AI:

> We propose that a 2 month, 10 man study of artificial intelligence be carried out during the summer of 1956 at Dartmouth College in Hanover, New Hampshire. The study is to proceed on the basis of the conjecture that every aspect of learning or any other feature of intelligence can in principle be so precisely described that a machine can be made to simulate it. An attempt will be made to find how to make machines use language, form abstractions and concepts, solve kinds of problems now reserved for humans, and improve themselves. We think that a significant advance can be made in one or more of these problems if a carefully selected group of scientists work on it together for a summer.
>
> J. McCarthy, Dartmouth College
>
> M. L. Minsky, Harvard University
>
> N. Rochester, I.B.M. Corporation
>
> C.E. Shannon, Bell Telephone Laboratories
> August 31, 1955

The workshop objectives were overly confident about what could be achieved in two months, and, as McCarthy later said, "AI is harder than we thought." But it had a far greater long-term impact than its organizers could have anticipated because it launched the academic field of AI. Claude Shannon, Marvin Minsky and Nathaniel Rochester formed the core participants. Herbert Simon and Allen Newell also presented, and in the end McCarthy, Minsky, Simon and Newell became known as the fathers of AI.

Simon and Newell simulated human thought with a machine for the first time. One was a mathematician and the other a computer scientist. Simon and Newell contemplated thought processes and came to the conclusion that they were abstract versions of reality that applied logic. So dog + cat = fight, or man + coat = dressed, woman + naked = (let's just leave it there). They tested their hypothesis with *Principia Mathematica* and solved a number of problems. They proved what Turing knew all along, that machines could simulate human thought, not just compute numbers.

At Dartmouth, John McCarthy coined the term "artificial Intelligence" and the name was immediately controversial. AI pioneer Arthur Samuel remarked that "the term 'artificial' makes you think there is something kind of phony about this, or else it sounds artificial, as if there is nothing real about this work at all." Neither Simon nor Newell liked the phrase, although Newell later accepted the name, commenting, "It is a good name. Like all names of scientific fields, it will grow to become exactly what its field comes to mean."

GOLDEN YEARS AND AI WINTERS

The productive 1956–1974 period of AI development that McCarthy sparked is now known as AI's golden years. In 1957, Frank Rosenblatt developed neural networks with his work on "perceptrons" as models of human learning, cognition and memory. Then in 1959, Arthur Samuel coined the now ubiquitous term "machine learning," identifying it as a "field of study that gives computers the ability to learn without being explicitly programmed." While at IBM,

Samuel developed a program that learned how to play checkers better than him.

Following this burst of AI theory and innovation, there was an AI winter from 1974 to 1980, before another boom in the 1980–1987 period and then a second AI winter from 1987 to 1993. These winters were AI downtimes, during which real questions were raised about the potential of AI and investment declined. AI became a dirty word, and AI developments during this period were given different names, such as informatics or computational intelligence. The winters had been mainly caused by computational power failing to keep pace with research. The AI research pioneers had ideas too far ahead of what computing power at that time could achieve. The situation was remedied by Moore's law.

MOORE'S LAW

Moore's law, first proposed in a 1975 magazine article by Intel co-founder Gordon E. Moore, states that computing power tends to double every two years. What it says precisely is: The number of transistors that can be packed into a given unit of space will roughly double every two years. Remarkably, that prediction has remained true, bequeathing us smartphones and laptops, and the ongoing digitization of the economy.

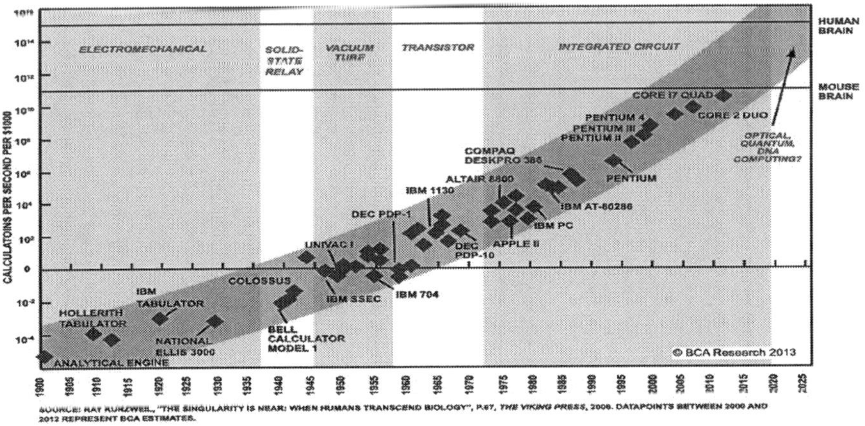

Figure 2. Source Ray Kurzweil, the Singularity is Near: When Humans Transcend Biology, p47, DTa points between 2000 and 2012

Martin Ford, author of *The Rise of the Robots*, illustrates this explosive growth in computing power with an analogy: Imagine you are driving a car at five miles an hour and then double your speed twenty-seven times. You are now driving at 671 million miles an hour, and you can charge out of the earth's atmosphere and reach Mars in just five minutes. Computing power has gone through the same number of doublings—twenty-seven since 1958. Another example of the power of Moore's law comes from AI researcher John Lancashire, who points out that in 1996 the US government built a model for nuclear explosions called Red, which could, for the first time, process a trillion operations per second. It was hyped as a supercomputer, but just a decade later, in 2006, every PlayStation 3 console contained the same processing power and was being used by children to play video games.

Today, some argue that Moore's law is slowing down or will stop by 2020. At that point, it will become physically impossible to fit any more transistors onto an integrated circuit. However, others claim Moore's law will speed up in future, using 3-D processor chips and smaller components at the atomic level or through nanotechnologies. Having provided remarkable accuracy for over four decades, I wouldn't bet against Moore's law continuing.

MACHINE LEARNING

Moore's law enabled machine learning to take off in the 1990s. Machine learning had developed over a number of decades, beginning in the 1940s with Walter Pitts and through the 1950s with Frank Rosenblatt. In the 1970s, British AI researcher Geoffrey Hinton made a breakthrough with backpropagation (methods used to efficiently train neural networks). In the 1980s, when neural networks were developing, part of the impetus was competition between Japan and the United States. In 1982, the Japanese government announced it would build fifth-generation machines, which was seen as a threat to what the US terms "economic security." This prompted renewed government investment in the US, and in the UK, too.

In 1989, a hugely important technology was developed. Another British inventor, Tim Berners-Lee, invented the World Wide Web while working at CERN, the European Particle Physics Laboratory. Tim and others advocated for ensuring that CERN would make the underlying code available forever on a royalty-free basis. In April 1993, CERN announced its decision to place the World Wide Web in the public domain, sparking a global wave of creativity, collaboration and innovation never seen before. Today, of course, over 3.2 billion people, more than half the world's population, use the internet.

During the 1990s, with enhanced computer power and growing sources of data, work on machine learning moved from a knowledge-driven focus to a data-driven one. The field became an intersection between statistics and computer science. Scientists began to create programs to analyze large quantities of data and extract conclusions from the results. Hinton made further breakthroughs in the mid-2000s, becoming known as the "godfather of deep learning." There had been two schools of thought in AI: the symbologists like Newell and Simon working in what was known as traditional AI and those in the newer, previously less respected field of neural networks, which ultimately won out. As Geoffrey Hinton explains:

> These two paradigms were completely different; they aimed to try and solve different problems, and they used completely different methods and different kinds of mathematics. I think that old-fashioned notion of AI is just wrong. . . . They believe that if you have symbols coming in and you have symbols going out, then it must be symbols in-between all the way. What's in between is nothing like strings of symbols; it's big vectors of neural activity. I think the basic premise of conventional AI is just wrong. [25]

MAN VS. MACHINE

As Moore's law saw computing power catch up with AI research, machine learning put that power to work finding patterns in data, while the internet activated a global wave of innovation. We came out of the AI winter in 1993 and entered an AI spring. Then in 1997, an exceptional event set the stage for

25 Martin Ford, *Architects of Intelligence.*

a new age of AI. The history of AI moved away from the ideas of brilliant men and women, and toward a new era of competitions between man and machine. We began competing with our own creation in cognitive challenges. These man-versus-machine battles spoke to deep-seated fears that have been around since the Luddites of the nineteenth century: Man is losing work to machines; man's usefulness is being replaced by machines; human beings are becoming obsolete; machines are taking over. These anxieties reached new heights in 1997 when world chess champion Garry Kasparov took on IBM's Deep Blue computer chess program.

1997: DEEP BLUE DEFEATS GARRY KASPAROV

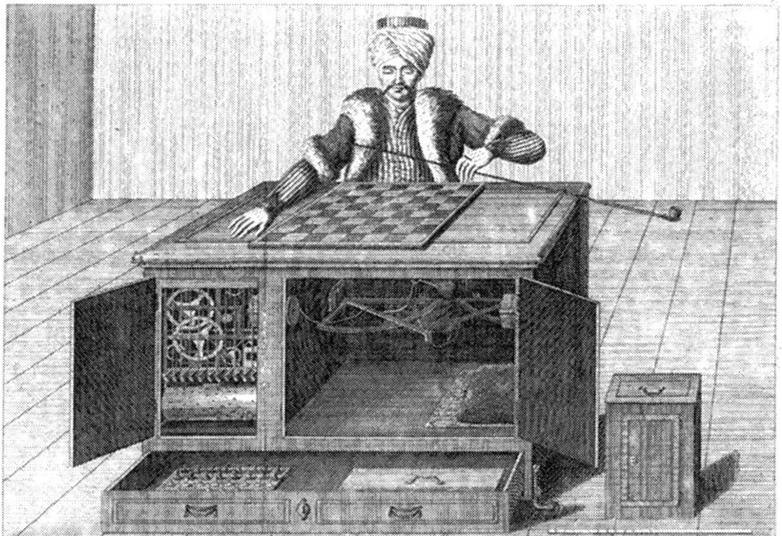

Figure 3, Source Karl Gottlieb von Windisch - Copper engraving from the book: Karl Gottlieb von Windisch, Briefe über den Schachspieler des Hrn. von Kempelen, nebst drei Kupferstichen die diese berühmte Maschine vorstellen. 1783.

The Holy Grail of AI had always been to build a chess program that could defeat the world champion. In the eighteenth century, an automaton chess player called the Mechanical Turk became the wonder of the age. This wooden figure moved chess pieces and played remarkably well, even defeating chess aficionados such as Napoleon Bonaparte and Benjamin Franklin.

Sadly, the Turk was an elaborate hoax with a concealed human being hiding inside. But the Turk is credited with inspiring Charles Babbage, who had also played and lost to the automaton; it gave him the idea that a mechanical engine can perform tasks, leading to his design of the first computer.

Chess was long seen as a pinnacle of human intelligence—a singular game pulling from different facets of intelligence, ranging from problem-solving to memory, creativity, observation, concentration, focus, foresight and calculation. Newell commented that:

> If one could devise a successful chess machine, one would seem to have penetrated to the core of human intellectual endeavor.[26]

Chess is, thus, the longest studied topic in artificial intelligence. Its constant role in testing AI programs has led to chess being known as the drosophila (fruit flies) of AI, a reference to the insects that have been the subject of many a scientific experiment.

From 1948 to 1952, Alan Turing developed a chess program called Turo Champ. It is a hallmark of Turing's far-reaching impact that his fingerprints can also be found in chess AI. Because Turing didn't have a computer powerful enough to run his Turo Champ, he played the games himself, simulating it by following the logic and taking about half an hour to make each move. Turo Champ lost to his colleague Alick Glennie but beat the wife of David Gawen Champernowne, a leading mathematician at Bletchley, showing the exciting early potential of AI chess programs.

The development of chess programs continued in the 1950s and, mirroring the space race, competition developed between the US and the Soviet Union. Chess competitions between man and machine seeped into popular culture. In Stanley Kubrick's iconic 1968 film *2001: A Space Odyssey*, the supercomputer HAL 9000 defeats astronaut Frank Poole at chess, before the intelligent machine kills him.

26 Margaret A. Boden, *Mind as Machine: A History of Cognitive Science*, Oxford: Oxford University Press, 2008.

AI researchers had great faith in the ability of machines to beat the best human players, but, in practice, it turned out to be much more difficult. In 1968, Donald Michie and John McCarthy each bet Scottish International Master David Levy £250 that a chess program could beat him within a decade. In 1978, Levy won and collected on his bet; it was clear that humans were still significantly better than machines at chess.

Then in 1997, we witnessed the ultimate real-life AI-versus-human chess showdown, when world chess champion Garry Kasparov faced the International Business Machines (IBM) chess-playing computer Deep Blue. Newsweek [27] covered the momentous match with the headline "The Brain's Last Stand." It was a six-game match featuring Kasparov, renowned as the greatest chess player of all time. From 1985 until his retirement in 2005, Kasparov was ranked No. 1 in the world for 225 of 228 months. Defeating Kasparov was statistically one of the most difficult feats in the world. In 1990, British grand master Raymond Keene wrote the book *How to Beat Garry Kasparov*. In it, he calculated the odds of defeating the great champion against other major achievements and found "beating Garry Kasparov at chess is considerably more difficult than climbing Mount Everest or becoming a dollar billionaire."[28]

Kasparov had defeated many computer chess programs before. In 1985, when he was just twenty-two, he even played against 32 chess programs at the same time, in what is called a chess "simul":

> I walked from one machine to the next, making my moves over a period of 5 hours. . . . I was fearless. I achieved a perfect 32-0 score, winning every game.[29]

Kasparov was immensely confident before the IBM match. Man and machine had different strengths:

27 "The Brain's Last Stand," *Newsweek*, May 5, 1997, https://www.amazon.com/Newsweek-May-1997-MAN-MACHINE/dp/B0055FEL4G.

28 Raymond Keene, *How to Beat Gary Kasparov*, London: Hardinge Simpole, 2002.

29 Gary Kasparov with Mig Greengard, *Deep Thinking: Where Machine Intelligence Ends and Human Creativity Begins*, New York: PublicAffairs, 2017.

1. Deep Blue could evaluate up to 200 million chess positions per second, while Garry Kasparov could evaluate around three chess positions per second.

2. Deep Blue had limited chess knowledge but enormous calculation ability; Garry Kasparov had enormous chess knowledge but limited calculation ability.

Deep Blue's game play was based on making hypothetical moves and evaluating its opponent's responses and its responses to these responses. Deep Blue could search six plies deep, moving six times for each potential move. It would repeat this process for all the possible moves, scoring each move on criteria such as whether it could capture a piece or improve its position on the board. Then it would proceed with the highest-scoring move. While impressive in terms of computational power, this mechanistic approach led Kasparov to believe the computer could be led into traps, thus falling for short-term gains and failing to develop the sophisticated, holistic, long-term strategy required for victory. "I don't think it's an appropriate thing to discuss the situation if I lose," said Kasparov. "I have never lost in my life."

IBM had a lot riding on the match. As one of the world's largest corporations, the result of the Deep Blue match would have a direct financial impact. A little-known fact about the financial aspect: Kasparov had already played one match against Deep Blue in 1996, and he won 4-2; the following week, IBM stock rose $3.31 billion, while the rest of the index fell.[30] Kasparov has since claimed that with so much money riding on the result of the 1997 rematch, IBM waged psychological warfare. One tool was concealing information. Going into the match, IBM had not shared printouts of Deep Blue's practice games. This meant Kasparov could not prepare by studying his opponent's previous matches, as he would normally. He commented that "keeping Deep Blue completely hidden was the strongest move of the match, but it was by IBM, not by either of the players." [31]

30 Gary Kasparov with Mig Greengard, *Deep Thinking: Where Machine Intelligence Ends and Human Creativity Begins.*
31 Gary Kasparov with Mig Greengard, *Deep Thinking: Where Machine Intelligence Ends and Human Creativity Begins.*

IBM was also secretly working with more experienced grand masters than the chess minds who helped IBM program its system. At the match, IBM revealed that three human chess grand masters were on its team, including the renowned Miguel Illescas. The grand masters not only advised on strategy but also taught IBM about gamesmanship. During a match, human players will often use psychology to confuse an opponent. For example, they may mask a clearly defined strategy by taking their time on moves to feign uncertainty. IBM programmed these tactics into their AI. Illescas later revealed that sometimes when Deep Blue instantly knew its next move, it would wait minutes before acting. A chess computer stalling suggests it is having difficulty. Deep Blue would also sometimes play immediately to throw off Kasparov after the human champion had made his best move. This led Kasparov to believe he had fallen into a trap. "Of course, we also built in some tricks for Garry... This has a psychological impact as the machine becomes unpredictable, which was our main goal," said Illescas.

The psychological pressure on Kasparov highlights one great advantage machines have over human beings; they don't feel pressure. Machines don't know millions of people are watching, they don't worry about the impact losing might have on their career, they don't feel their heart race when the board becomes more complex and the tree of variations grows. How many great sportsmen have faltered at the crucial moment, not from a lack of talent or capability but from nerves? When I was a boy, I watched my hero, Italian striker Roberto Baggio, considered the greatest football player in the world, step up to take the final penalty against Brazil in the 1994 World Cup Final in the United States. Baggio had been voted World Player of the Year in 1993, and in the 1994 World Cup, he already scored five brilliant goals.

Baggio stepped up to take the penalty with the eyes of the world watching. Over half a billion people were glued to their screens, and my heart pounded as the commentator pronounced him "the savior of Italy." Baggio then skyed the ball over the bar and almost out of the stadium. Brazil won, and Baggio put his head down in shame. Machines don't have a Baggio moment. Machines always have a cool head; they're always neutral, unflustered and clinical. English poet Samuel Butler made this point elegantly in 1863 as he foresaw, with stunning prescience, a new era of machine supremacy:

> In the course of ages, we shall find ourselves the inferior race. Inferior in power, inferior in that moral quality of self-control, we shall look up to them as the acme of all that the best and wisest man can ever dare to aim at. No evil passions, no jealousy, no avarice, no impure desires will disturb the serene might of those glorious creatures. Sin, shame and sorrow will have no place among them. Their minds will be in a state of perpetual calm, the contentment of a spirit that knows no wants, is disturbed by no regrets. Ambition will never torture them. Ingratitude will never cause them the uneasiness of a moment. The guilty conscience, the hope deferred, the pains of exile, the insolence of office and the spurns that patient merit of the unworthy takes—these will be entirely unknown to them . . . [32]

No doubt psychological pressure had some impact on Kasparov. But as the world's undefeated chess champion, he would have been used to this sort of strain. What ultimately beat Kasparov was not manipulation but when IBM's Deep Blue passed a sort of Turing test. Deep Blue became indistinguishable from a human being, not in conversation, as Turing had predicted, but instead by producing a strategy as great as any human mind. Having won the first game, Kasparov laid a trap for IBM Blue on the 36th move. He expected the machine to attack his exposed queen, as all other top-level chess programs would have done. Deep Blue resisted the bait and opted for a sublime move that completely undermined Kasparov's preconceptions about AI's capabilities.

It seemed to Kasparov that Deep Blue had suddenly stopped playing like a machine and instead strategized like the greatest of human masters. As Kasparov put it, "Suddenly [Deep Blue] played like a god for one mo-

32 Samuel Butler, "Darwin Among the Machines," *The Press,* Christchurch, New Zealand, June 13, 1863, https://www.goodreads.com/book/show/28103397-darwin-among-the-machines.

ment." Kasparov was stumped and confused, falling into "a fatalistic depression" and resigning from the game. Once Deep Blue, IBM's AI system, became no longer identifiable as a machine, Kasparov, the greatest human chess player of all time, was defeated.

Ironically, Murray Campbell, one of the IBM Blue designers, revealed in 2001 the remarkable move that had so befuddled Kasparov, was just the result of a computer glitch. Murray explained "Kasparov had concluded that the counterintuitive play must be a sign of superior intelligence. He had never considered that it was simply a bug." [33]

The truth is that the IBM match was a show; it was entertainment and it was big business. Kasparov demanded a rematch, but IBM had the machine dismantled. However symbolic the victory, IBM Blue was less an AI system and more a computational power-based system. IBM admitted this point itself:

"Does Deep Blue use Artificial Intelligence? The short answer is no. Deep Blue relies more on computational power and a simple search and evaluation function. . . . Deep Blue could never be a HAL 9000, not even if it tried. Nor would it occur to Deep Blue to try."[34]

2011: WATSON WINS JEOPARDY!

Over a decade later, another colossal machine-versus-human competition was held. *Jeopardy!*, a popular US television quiz show that is essentially a test of general knowledge, presented an even greater challenge to AI than chess. *Jeopardy!* required the computational power and learning of chess but it also included ambiguous language, trick questions and far-ranging topics.

IBM was again behind the machine, but this time it was Watson, named after longtime IBM chairman and CEO Thomas Watson. A showcase of

33 "Did a Computer Bug Help Deep Blue Beat Kasparov?" Wired.com, September 28 2012, https://www.wired.com/2012/09/deep-blue-computer-bug/.

34 Nils J. Nilsson, *The Quest for Artificial Intelligence: A History of Ideas and Achievements, Cambridge:* Cambridge University Press, 2009.

the company's expertise in advanced science and computing, Watson was trained on almost 250,000 questions from previous *Jeopardy!* seasons to understand the game. It would play Ken Jennings, the 74-time winner, and Brad Rutter, a 20-time champion.

What made Watson advanced compared to Deep Blue was its ability to find answers from ambiguous clues, such as this one: "It's a poor workman who blames these."

"What are tools?" answered Watson.

Watson was actually composed of thousands of smaller agents working as a collective intelligence on parallel processes. First, some of Watson's agents would parse the sentence and analyze the key words such as "workmen." Then other Watson agents looked into its already digested sources of millions of information points to understand that the answer involved a common phrase. The agents then voted on the best answer, enabling Watson to choose its answer and beat the humans to it in a matter of two to three seconds. When Watson got an answer correct, it would then "gain confidence," realizing it had understood the category correctly. As a result, it adapted its gameplay during the match. Ken Jennings, Watson's talented opponent, explains that the approach of the Watson AI was remarkably similar to that of the human mind:

> The computer's techniques for unraveling *Jeopardy!* clues sounded just like mine. That machine zeroes in on keywords in a clue, then combs its memory (in Watson's case, a 15-terabyte data bank of human knowledge) for clusters of associations with those words. It rigorously checks the top hits against all the contextual information it can muster: the category name; the kind of answer being sought; the time, place and gender hinted at in the clue; and so on. And when it feels "sure" enough, it decides to buzz. This is all an instant, intuitive process for a human *Jeopardy!* player, but I felt convinced that under the hood my brain was doing more or less the same thing.

We've already discussed Moravec's Paradox, which explained the difficulty machines have had in passing the Turing test. Watson also faced challenges with setting and context. Human brains work in the background such that we understand context instantly. Machines have to build context for each new data point. This challenge with context also held Watson back. For example, Garry Kasparov explains that we can learn about machine intelligence from Watson's answer to the question "a 1904 Olympic gymnast with this anatomical oddity." Jennings, the human player, buzzed first with "only one hand," which was incorrect. Watson then answered "leg," which was judged wrong because leg is not an oddity. The correct answer should have been "only one leg." Watson had lots of data with the name George Eyser (a one-legged Olympic athlete) and the word "leg," but the machine couldn't frame the answer correctly with the common sense of a human mind.

Sometimes Watson was just wrong, and Jennings and Rutter managed to beat Watson in Final Jeopardy. The human players answered correctly when asked which city's largest airport is named after a World War II hero and which city's second-largest airport was named after a WWII battle. The human players responded with "What is Chicago?" but Watson demonstrated confusion with five question marks after responding, "What Is Toronto?????"

In the end, IBM Watson won handsomely with $77,147, while Jennings came in second with $24,000 in winnings. Rutter followed with $21,600. "I, for one, welcome our new computer overlords," Jennings wrote next to his last answer. Many have considered this comment to be disconcertingly prescient. As Shakespeare wrote in *King Lear*, "Jesters do oft prove prophets."

Watson's victory was a landmark event in the progression of AI. As AI scientist Bill Hibbard commented:

> IBM Watson, playing *Jeopardy!* as skillfully as human champions, is a significant milestone and illustrates the progress of machine language processing. Watson learned language by statistical analy-

> sis of the huge amounts of text available online. When machines become powerful enough to extend that statistical analysis to correlate language with sensory data, you will lose a debate with them if you argue that they don't understand language."

2016 and 2017: ALPHAGO DEFEATS HUMAN GO PLAYERS

There was an even more challenging competition between man and AI in 2016 when DeepMind's AlphaGo faced an Asian grand master in the game of Go.

According to a legend, Emperor Yao (2357–2255 BC) invented Go to enlighten his son, Dan Zhu, making it 3,000 years older than the game of chess. Go is also more complex than chess. The estimated number of possible moves based on board configuration is 10^{120} in chess, but Go has around 10^{174}. This may not seem like a lot more, but it is actually 1 million trillion trillion trillion trillion more configurations than chess. (The number of legal moves in Go is actually a googolplex, which is the 100-digit number that inspired the name of the company Google). There are more potential positions in a Go game than atoms in the universe. After 10 years of work by Dutch computer scientist John Tromp, we finally have the actual number. Tromp ran a computation starting on March 6, 2015, and it took until December 26, 2015, to complete; after some post-processing, the number was announced on January 20, 2016. This is the number of legal moves in Go:

208168199381979984699478633344862770286522453884530548425639456820927419612 7
380153785256484516985196439072599160156281285460898883144271297153193175577 3
66203972470648409 35[35]

Note that Alan Turing had been interested in Go and taught the game to I.J. Good, who went on to help popularize it in the West.

AlphaGo, the first computer program to defeat a professional human Go player, was invented by the London AI start-up DeepMind Technologies. It was founded by Demis Hassabis, a British former chess prodigy,

35 Counting Legal Positions in Go, John Tromp, https://tromp.github.io/go/legal.html.

who gave up professional chess at the age of 13, despite being aware he could have become the world champion. He went on to code the successful video game Theme Park, which sold in the multimillions of units, and then studied computer science and AI at Cambridge. He realized there was a lack of understanding about how the human brain is holding back the field of AI. So he completed a PhD in neuroscience at University College London (UCL).

Hassabis then founded DeepMind in London with the explicit aim of creating AGI, artificial general intelligence, leading to the holy grail of human-level AI. It was difficult to win over venture capital investors to such a huge ambition, but he calculated that not many people would have such a grand plan to change the world through AI and that, therefore, there would be less competition. DeepMind hired PhD researchers from the UK's best universities and spent two years leveraging Geoffrey Hinton's breakthroughs in deep learning.

DeepMind's creation was the program AlphaGo. It could compute based on a vast number of parameters not previously available. Importantly, it was self-taught, having played millions of games against itself following initial programming. AlphaGo is inspired by how the human brain works with billions of interconnected neurons, using a multilayered neural network.

AlphaGo earned its mettle at the 2016 Google DeepMind Challenge Match in Seoul, South Korea, where AlphaGo, by then Google-owned, played 18-time Go world champion, Lee Sedol. In a historic win that was compared to Deep Blue's 1997 defeat of Garry Kasparov, AlphaGo beat Sedol in a five-game match, winning all but the fourth game.

At the 2017 Future of Go Summit in Wuzhen, China, AlphaGo beat Ke Jie, the world No.1 ranked player, in a three-game match. "I feel like his game is more and more like the 'Go god.' Really, it is brilliant,"[36] Ke Jie said.

36 "World's best Go player flummoxed by Google's 'godlike' AlphaGo AI," Theguarandian.com, May 23, 2017, https://www.theguardian.com/technology/2017/may/23/alphago-google-ai-beats-ke-jie-china-go.

AlphaGo's victories took the world by surprise since AI experts had previously predicted that the complexity of Go meant the program would not beat a world champion until 2027. Showing the exponential growth of AI development, DeepMind had achieved this feat a decade earlier. Underscoring how valuable AlphaGo could be for business applications, Google had acquired DeepMind for $500 million.

Kai-Fu Lee, the former president of Google China, has said that the match between AlphaGo and Lee Sedol gave China a "Sputnik moment." This refers to when Russia successfully launched its Sputnik satellite into space and challenged US technological supremacy. The US was sent into a frenzy of investment and activity to regain its technological preeminence, which culminated in the Moon landings. Likewise, when AlphaGo used deep learning to defeat Ke Jie, China realized deep learning was a monumentally important technology, on a par with the discovery of electricity. Here was a British company, acquired by the American giant Google, coming to China and beating a Chinese world champion at a Chinese game. Since this very moment, China has become intensely focused on AI, investing billions in AI research, with an explicit government strategy aimed at making China the world's preeminent AI nation by 2030.

2017: ALPHAZERO DEFEATS ANOTHER MACHINE

The fertile marriage of America's Google with Britain's DeepMind gave birth to an incredible new AI system called AlphaZero. In December 2017, DeepMind's AlphaZero faced the reigning world chess champion—another computer program, called Stockfish 8, which drew on centuries of human knowledge in chess and decades of its own computer experience. It had mammoth computational power, calculating 70 million chess positions per second.[37]

AlphaZero had much weaker computational power, with only 80,000 calculations per second, and it was also not programmed with any previous

37 "Google's AlphaZero Destroys Stockfish In 100-Game Match," Chess.com, December 6, 2017, https://www.chess.com/news/view/google-s-alphazero-destroys-stockfish-in-100-game-match.

chess knowledge at all. Instead, AlphaZero used deep reinforcement learning to self-learn chess by playing itself. After just nine hours of self-play, AlphaZero was ready to face Stockfish and its vast legacy of accumulated human and machine chess wisdom. AlphaZero won 28 matches, drew 72 and didn't lose a single game. Based on half a day of self-play, it became the best chess player in the history of the world. This is a startling reminder of AI's power. As DeepMind CEO Demis Hassabis, a chess master himself, put it:

> The game of chess represented the pinnacle of AI research over several decades. State-of-the-art programs are based on powerful engines that search many millions of positions, leveraging handcrafted domain expertise and sophisticated domain adaptations. AlphaZero is a generic reinforcement learning algorithm—originally devised for the game of Go—that achieved superior results within a few hours, searching a thousand times fewer positions, given no domain knowledge except the rules.

Following IBM Blue's victory over Kasparov, for a period, human grand masters and chess programs played together in so-called "centaur" teams. It looked like AI and human combined was the most powerful approach. But AlphaGo and deep reinforcement learning have completely blown that out of the water, and AI chess programs now far exceed any human being or centaur teams. The top AI programs often play original moves that seem completely unusual to human players. Hassabis called AlphaZero's play style "alien." For example, AlphaZero sometimes wins by offering many sacrifices, like offering up a queen and bishop to exploit a positional advantage. "It's like chess from another dimension." This originality is so marked that Garry Kasparov has said chess judges look for creativity as a tell-tale sign that a human is cheating by leveraging AI.

AI has now beaten the best human players in all of the following popular games:

- Checkers: In 1994, the program Chinook beat the reigning human champion. In 2002, Jonathan Schaeffer and his team solved checkers, producing a program that always makes the best possible move leading to a draw with a human champion.

- Backgammon: A 1979 program called BKG defeated the world champion although the creator later attributed the win to the luck of the dice. But, as of today, backgammon programs have far surpassed the best human players.
- Scrabble: Using words like qadi (a Muslim judge), anuria (the non-passage of urine) and alif (a type of spinal fusion), the software program Quackle beat David Boys 482–465 in the final round of the 2006 Scrabble Open in Toronto. Quackle is an open-source program, and its chief designers included students at the Massachusetts Institute of Technology.
- eSports: Dota 2, the central game in an annual esports tournament called The International, is an extremely popular and complicated, multiplayer online battle arena game and is serious business in the world of competitive gaming. Elon Musk and a small group of investors founded a group called OpenAI. After just two weeks of learning, the OpenAI bot was unleashed on the tournament and subsequently beat several of the world's top players. In 2019, DeepMind gained "Grandmaster" status in Starcraft II, a complex video game. As Starcraft is a real time strategy game it requires resource planning, organizing troops and battling opponents with an imperfect knowledge of their potential moves. The AI system beat 99.8% of human players it faced.

A large survey of AI researchers found it won't be long before AI can beat us at everything. The survey, by the University of Oxford and Yale University, was sent to AI researchers who had published in 2015 at one of two big conferences in the field. In total, 352 leading AI researchers responded. The survey predicted that within 10 years AI will drive better than us, by 2049 it will be able to write a best-selling novel, and by 2053 it will perform better than humans at surgery. In fact, the survey concluded there is a 50 percent chance that by 2060 AI will essentially be able to do everything we can do, but better. All human jobs will be automated within the next 120 years, said most respondents.

Should AI develop as the academic experts working on it expect, it will cause the greatest technological transformation the world has ever seen. AI is not a fad or a buzzword currently in vogue. AI is an all-consuming, metamorphic revolution that will touch every aspect of our lives.

THE AI REVOLUTION AND BIG DATA

The AI revolution has begun. There have been AI winters in the past when investment in the technology declined, but the convergence of key trends suggests we are now in a long AI spring leading to summer. These trends include cheap storage for data, constant connectivity and faster processing power (Moore's law). All of this has culminated in producing an eruption of all types of data, data that fertilizes artificial intelligence.

The main driver for AI's recent progress has been an explosion of data in the world. As Eric Schmidt, former Google CEO, put it as far back as 2010, "There were five exabytes of information created from the dawn of civilization through 2003, but that much information is now created every two days."

In 2019, there are 2.5 quintillion bytes of data produced globally every day. In case you are not familiar with quintillions, here is that amount expressed as a number: 2,500,000,000,000,000,000.

Or to put it another way, 2.5 quintillion pennies would, if laid out flat, cover the Earth five times. This enormous amount of daily data, of fundamental importance to AI, is derived from various sources.

Social media is a massive generator of personalized data:

- Facebook has 2.23 billion monthly active users, uploading 300 million photos a day.
- YouTube users watch a billion hours of its videos every day.
- WhatsApp says its users around the world sent 75 billion messages on New Year's Eve 2017, including more than 13 billion images and 5 billion videos.

And as mobile phone penetration is forecast to grow its share of the global population, those figures are set to increase.

Through the Internet of Things, smart devices interact with each other and us while collecting all kinds of data. Examples include wearables that track your health, environmental sensors and many seemingly ordinary devices like your TV, printer or fridge. The amount of data produced by machines is exploding from 2 billion in 2006 to a projected 200 billion in 2020.

Organizations have developed treasure troves of data, including data on customers, digital systems, production systems, human resource performance and much more. For example, at Critical Future, one of the largest manufacturer's in Europe provided us with a "small file" of 20 million data points on the company's customers.

DATA AS THE "OIL" OF AI

The exponential growth of data, 75 percent of which is unstructured, is important to AI for two reasons. First, this is the training data that AI needs to learn. Machine learning relies on data for training. Having so much data available means that machine learning can learn about all these things. Second, the vast amount of data means that we simply cannot cope without AI. It would be impossible for human beings to track, analyze or work with the staggering amounts of data being produced. We need narrow AI such as machine learning to analyze all this data.

This is why data has been described as the new "oil," an analogy that I think has merit. Data is now the chief commodity in the world, and the entrepreneurs that can create new sources of data on platforms like Facebook or Google are the Rockefeller and Getty tycoons of our times. They are originating a powerful resource—data.

Owning data production, like owning oil production, offers a massive competitive advantage. Google today commands 70 percent of the market for search in the US and 90 percent of the market in the European Union. Google's near monopoly position in a free market has developed thanks to having more data to train its AI that its rivals. Google's market share then creates a virtuous cycle of more training, more AI performance, more competitive edge and more market share. The irony of Google's success is that it was built on what was previously considered waste data or "data exhaust." Author Kenneth Cukier explains that Google capitalized on waste data to build one of the most successful companies of our times, showing just valuable it is for companies to collect and utilize all the data possible:

> Other search engines in the 1990s had the chance to do the same but did not pursue it. Around 2000, Yahoo! saw the potential, but nothing came of the idea. It was Google that recognized the gold dust in the detritus of its interactions with its users and took the trouble to collect it up. . . . Google exploits information that is a by-product of user interactions, or data exhaust, which is automatically recycled to improve the service or create an entirely new product.[38]

THE DATA POTENTIAL

But Google doesn't hold even a minuscule fraction of the data out there. The potential for data gathering is infinitely greater. Every single action, movement, object, change, atom, however slight or small on the earth and even in the universe, has the potential to be captured as data. The breaths you are taking right now and your heart rate, the beads of sweat on your brow are all data trackable through technology such as wearables. The wind blowing the leaves of the trees outside your window is data trackable with an anemometer. The ants scurrying along the ground are data trackable through image recorders, and their very movements are data we can capture through ground sensors. The thoughts lighting up regions of your brain. The taste of saliva in your mouth. The raised eyebrow as you read that last sentence. The world around you is all numbers. All of it, everything, is data. So everything can be learned by AI.

38 Shoshana Zuboff, *The Age of Surveillance Capitalism: The Fight for a Human Future at the Frontier of Power*, New York, 2019.

CHAPTER 2

What Is Artificial Intelligence?

"I know that I am intelligent because I know that I know nothing."
— Socrates

"The mind is a meat machine."
— Marvin Minsky

"As soon as it works, no one calls it AI anymore."
— John McCarthy

In the last chapter, we traced the history of Artificial Intelligence from brilliant ideas to real world systems that exceed human intelligence in narrow domains. In this chapter, we explore what is intelligence? The question is simple; the answer, complex. American psychologist R.J. Sternberg replies that, "Viewed narrowly, there seem to be almost as many definitions of intelligence as there were experts asked to define it." The word "intelligence" refers to a multitude of capabilities in human beings, machines and in every living organism.

INTELLIGENT LIFE

The earth is 4.5 billion years old. Life emerged 3.8 billion years ago, and animal life 2.8 billion years after that. There are more than 8 million organism species on earth, from the smallest bacterium weighing less than a trillionth of a gram to the blue whale weighing up to a hundred million grams. Bacteria may live for an hour, while whales can live for over a century. All this complex panoply of life displays intelligence. Bacteria have been shown to be intelligent through detailed time-lapse microscopy revealing how they sense and explore their surroundings, communicate with their neighbors and adaptively reshape themselves.[39] Plants have shown the intelligence of storing memories and learning from them.[40] Plants process information about available light; they respond by repositioning themselves so their leaves face it. They can also respond to sound.[41] Insects, despite their minute stature, have significant intelligence and complex societies. Some ancient aspects of the human nervous systems are shared with insects, such as the Hox genes, which organize a vertebrates' nervous system from head to tail.

THE TREE OF LIFE

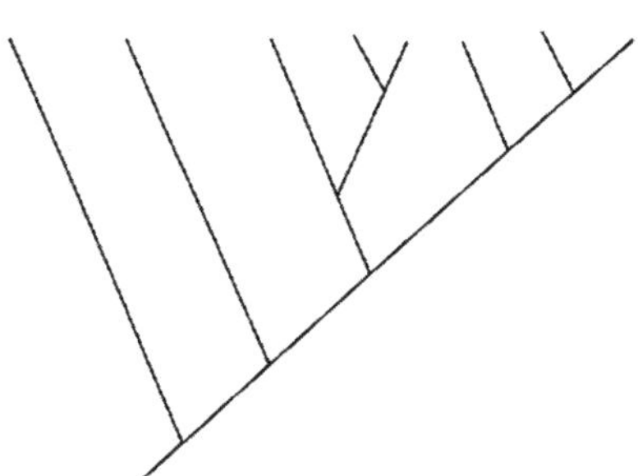

All living organisms are connected via what Charles Darwin characterized as a tree of life:

39 "Seeing the Beautiful Intelligence of Microbes," Quanta.org, November 13, 2017, https://www.quantamagazine.org/the-beautiful-intelligence-of-bacteria-and-other-microbes-20171113/.

40 "The Intelligent Plant," NewYorker.com, December 23, 2013, https://www.newyorker.com/magazine/2013/12/23/the-intelligent-plant.

41 "New Research Suggests Plants Hear and Respond to Sounds and Broadcast Ultrasounds of Their Own," Mysterious Universe, January 11, 2019, https://mysteriousuniverse.org/2019/01/new-research-suggests-plants-hear-and-respond-to-sounds-and-broadcast-ultrasounds-of-their-own/.

> "The affinities of all the beings of the same class have sometimes been represented by a great tree. . . . As buds give rise by growth to fresh buds, and these, if vigorous, branch out and overtop on all sides many a feebler branch, so by generation I believe it has been with the great Tree of Life, which fills with its dead and broken branches the crust of the earth and covers the surface with its ever-branching and beautiful ramifications." [42]

MAMMAL INTELLIGENCE

Some 6 million years ago, human beings shared a common ancestor on the tree of life with chimpanzees, making them our closest relative. Chimpanzees share nearly 99 percent of their DNA with human beings and are considered the most intelligent animals. These sensitive mammals feel rage, joy, love, jealousy, sadness and fear, and they grieve the death of their loved ones.[43] Chimps and other great apes, such as bonobos and gorillas, have been trained to understand sign language and even to pronounce some words.[44]

Chimps, along with macaques and capuchins, have begun using stones as tools, leading some to claim they have entered their own Stone Age.[45] They use tree branches as clubs and, most interestingly, fashion wood into spears. It's said that chimps go through a five-stage process to create hunting spears[46], which makes them unique among animals; previously, only human beings were believed capable of constructing tools. Chimps establish social structures, with alpha males ruling groups in roles reminiscent of human chieftains. Chimps are innately political, forging alliances to maintain or take power. Chimps also have primitive markets that involve trading meat for grooming or sex[47], proving the addage "prostitution is the world's oldest profession."

42 "Tree of Life (biology)," Wikipedia, https://en.wikipedia.org/wiki/Tree_of_life_biology.

43 "Chimps filmed grieving for dead friend," BBC Earth, May 18, 2016, http://www.bbc.com/earth/story/20160517-chimps-grieve-for-dead-friend.

44 "Six Talking Apes," Smithsonianmag.com, August 11, 2011, https://www.smithsonianmag.com/science-nature/six-talking-apes-48085302/

45 "Chimpanzees and monkeys have entered the Stone Age," BBC Earth, August 18, 2015, http://www.bbc.com/earth/story/20150818-chimps-living-in-the-stone-age.

46 "Chimps Make Spears and Hunt Bushbabies." Livescience.com, February 22, 2007, https://www.livescience.com/4395-chimps-spears-hunt-bushbabies.html.

47 "Chimps Trade Meat for Sex—and It Works," Nationalgeographic.com, April 7, 2009, https://www.nationalgeographic.com/animals/2009/04/chimps-behavior-sex-news-animals/.

Around 55 million years ago, humans share a common ancestor on the tree of life with other mammals, such as dolphins, which exhibit large brains and remarkable intelligence. Every dolphin has a characteristic whistle that functions as that dolphin's name.[48] They also teach each other surprisingly clever hunting techniques. In one fascinating example, dolphins circle shoals of fish, stimulating the ground as they do so. This causes the fish to leap into their open mouths.[49] Most interesting of all is the belief that dolphins create art. Evolutionary psychologist Robert Wright explains:

> Dolphins, and for that matter some beluga whales, can send circles of air out of their blowholes, rising like smoke rings. But these Hawaiian dolphins take a whole new approach. They start by creating big underwater swirls with their fins, then turn around and blow air into the swirls. The resulting rings are big, limpid and beautiful. Some dolphins swim through their rings. Some dolphins make two little rings and then coax them toward fusion, creating one big ring. Each artist has its own style.

Advanced intelligence is shared by other sea mammals such as killer whales, which have a complex language and even a culture. Killer whales teach particularly difficult and dangerous hunting techniques. Mothers repeatedly push their young onto beaches in pursuit of seals and sometimes have to drag their stranded young back into the water. Importantly, this shows culture, which is about learning from others. As whale researcher Hal Whitehead says, "A cultural species starts behaving differently than a species where everything is determined genetically." [50]

Other mammals, such as dogs and cats, are unmistakably intelligent; we know this from keeping them as domesticated pets. They learn to understand when we communicate with them and can be highly trained

48 "Dolphins Have Names, Respond When Called," Nationalgeographic.com, July 23, 2013, https://news.nationalgeographic.com/news/2013/07/130722-dolphins-whistle-names-identity-animals-science/

49 "Dolphin Waits After Creating Sand Circle," Seconds Later Camera, Relayhero.com, https://www.relayhero.com/dolphin-stunning-ocean-phenomenon/.

50 "How smart are killer whales—and can they decide to kill a person," Orlandosentinel.com, March 7, 2010, http://articles.orlandosentinel.com/2010-03-07/news/os-seaworld-killer-whale-brains-20100302_1_killer-whales-orcas-dolphin-or-porpoise.

and useful as guide dogs for blind people, service dogs for police and in other capacities. Elephants famously mourn their dead and use tools. Elephants dig water holes, strip bark from trees, chew it into a ball, then use it to fill the hole. Once the top has been covered with sand, the elephant has an evaporation-resistant canteen. [51]

BIRD INTELLIGENCE

Birds such as crows, parrots and ravens are intelligent vertebrates that use tools.[52] Ravens even preplan tasks, a behavior long believed unique to humans. Scientists taught the birds how a tool can help them access a piece of food. Then when offered a selection of objects almost 24 hours later, the ravens selected that specific tool again and used it to retrieve their treat. Harvard comparative psychologist Irene Pepperberg taught English words to a clever African grey parrot named Alex. The bird mastered roughly a hundred words, could use them in context and even grasped the concepts of same, different and zero. Humans share a common ancestor with these avian wonders who lived 320 million years ago. Our common ancestor was a lizardlike, reasonable-size animal with a backbone who had adapted to living on land.[53]

OCTOPUS INTELLIGENCE

From the story of intelligent life so far, I may have given the impression that intelligence peaks with humans and descends down the tree of life to other animals. But there is another fascinatingly intelligent animal relative that is far removed from humans, the invertebrate eight-limbed octopus. To find a common ancestor for human and octopus, we have to go back 600 million years to a flattened wormlike creature. The descendant octopus is among the cleverest cephalopods in the sea. These spineless creatures are so smart that biologists put them in a class with higher vertebrates.

51 "Clever Critters: 8 Best Non-Human Tool Users," Wired.com, January 16, 2009, https://www.wired.com/2009/01/animaltools/.

52 "Ravens, Crows, Parrots, and More—Meet the Most Intelligent Birds," Nationalgeographic.com, March 15, 2018, https://news.nationalgeographic.com/2018/03/year-of-the-bird-brains-intelligence-smarts/.

53 Peter Godrey-Smith, *Other Minds: The Octopus, the Sea, and the Deep Origins of Consciousness*, New York: Farrar, Straus and Giroux, 2016.

They exhibit compassion, a sense of humor and an ability to use shells and other tools to nab crab, their favorite prey. They are even able to recognize individual human faces. In captivity, they have learned to navigate mazes, solve puzzles, open screw-top jars and attempt daring escapes. In the wild, observers have seen them stacking rocks to protect the entrance to their dens and hiding themselves inside coconut shell halves.

Octopuses have the largest brains of any invertebrates, with more neurons than humans. Sixty percent of these cells are in their arms, not their brains. As a result, their arms seem to be individually intelligent: When cut off, they can crawl away, grab food, and lift the food up to where the mouth would be if the arm were still connected. Peter Godfrey-Smith, a distinguished professor of philosophy in New York and Sydney who is also a deep-sea diver, describes these wily creatures in *Other Minds: The Octopus, the Sea and the Deep Origins of Consciousness*:

> If we can make contact with a cephalopod as sentient being, it is not because of a shared history, not because of kinship, but because evolution builds minds twice over. This is probably the closest we will come to meeting an intelligent alien. [54]

The otherworldly cleverness of the octopus speaks to something else—that intelligence on earth has not always developed in the same way as human intelligence. Our intelligence is the result of millions of years of chance events, which led to the evolution of human cognition in a specific form. But it can develop differently in another environment, such as deep in the ocean, where octopus neurons grow in both the brain and the arms.

This has important implications for artificial intelligence because it demonstrates that AI need not emulate human intelligence nor re-create the human brain to match or exceed human intelligence. There are other paths to the progression of AI outside of human-centric approaches.

54 Peter Godrey-Smith, *Other Minds: The Octopus, the Sea, and the Deep Origins of Consciousness.*

ANIMAL VS. HUMAN INTELLIGENCE

Intelligence is clearly not the preserve of humans, and animals share many of the traits of intelligence traditionally thought to be uniquely human, such as art, the use of tools, language, culture and emotions ranging from joy and love to grief. This is especially true, though not exclusively so, of mammals. Charles Darwin, perhaps the greatest observer of animal behavior, argued that "there is no fundamental difference between man and the higher mammals in their mental faculties." Darwin's point is that only a difference of degree separates animal and human intelligence. Some contemporary academics go farther and claim that human and animal intelligence are entirely equal. Maciej Henneberg, a professor of anthropological and comparative anatomy at the University of Adelaide in Australia argues:

> The belief of human cognitive superiority became entrenched in human philosophy and sciences. . . . However, science tells us that animals can have cognitive faculties that are superior to human beings'. . . . Animals offer different kinds of intelligences, which have been underrated due to humans' fixation on language and technology. These include social and kinaesthetic intelligence. Some mammals, like gibbons, can produce a large number of varied sounds—over 20 different sounds with clearly different meanings that allow these arboreal primates to communicate across a tropical forest canopy. The fact that they do not build houses is irrelevant to the gibbons.[55]

Pulitzer Prize–winning sociobiologist Edward O. Wilson says that we have created an "evolutionary epic" around the superiority of human intelligence, which serves as our grounding myth in the scientific age. It is a story we pass down that helps us orient ourselves in the cosmos. "Every epic needs a hero," he says, and in the case of the human, it is our mind. We believe in a mythology of the brilliant and heroic human

55 "Humans are not smarter than animals—we just don't understand them," Independent.co.uk, December 13, 2013, https://www.independent.co.uk/news/science/humans-are-not-smarter-than-animals-we-just-dont-understand-them-9003196.html.

overcoming the evolutionary struggle with *Homo sapiens* intelligence because this helps us define our place and purpose. In reality, animal intelligence actually closely mirrors human intelligence in almost every important aspect.

FLOODLIGHT COGNITION AND THE NEOCORTEX

So what is actually different about animal and human intelligence? The unparalleled success of the human race does suggest there is something uniquely potent about our intelligence. American evolutionary biologist Marc Hauser came up with the theory of "humaniqueness" to explain the difference between human and animal intelligence. Animals, he said, have "laser beam" intelligence, in which a specific solution is used to solve a specific problem. But these solutions cannot be applied to new situations or to solve different kinds of problems. In contrast, humans have "floodlight" cognition, allowing us to use thought processes in new ways and to apply the solution of one problem to another, similar situation.

Humans also have key physiological differences with other animals, which is another clue to the difference in intelligence that separates us from our animal cousins. The key difference? Humans have the largest brain mass relative to body mass of all mammals. This is especially pronounced in the neocortex, a large region unique to mammals that accounts for 76 percent of the brain's total mass and that is involved in conscious thought and language.

This region of the cerebral cortex is called the neocortex because it is the newest part of the brain. Imagine there is a brain in front of you. The surface of the brain looks the same all the way around: a heavily creased, pinkish-grey mass that's clammy to the touch. The outer layer is the neocortex, which derives its name from the Latin for "new bark," since it covers the older brain. In the 1960s, famed American neuroscientist Paul MacLean formulated the following "triune," or three-part, brain model to help explain how the brain has evolved and functions:

- Layer 1: The ancient part of the brain, in all animals from humans to lizards. Its role is to mediate automatic, regulatory functions. For example, if body temperature drops, then Layer 1 senses it and tells the body to shiver. This region creates feelings of pain, hunger and thirst.
- Layer 2: A more recently evolved region found in mammals, its role is focused on emotions, a mammalian development. For example, if you see something frightening, this layer of the brain makes you tremble with fear.
- Layer 3: The most recently evolved layer of the neocortex, it is found on the upper surface of the brain. This region is involved in cognition, memory storage, sensory processing, abstractions and philosophy. For example, when you read a frightening book, this layer interprets the story and signals Layer 2 to direct you to feel scared, triggering Layer 1, which directs your body to start trembling.

This model actually oversimplifies brain function since, in reality, brain functions overlap. MacLean's model does, however, provide a useful framework for understanding how the brain evolved and how it works. We all still have our old lizard brain in Layer 1. When we walk or balance, we rely on our old brain. If we hear a scary sound and feel afraid, that is mainly our old brain. But that something extra human beings have, the neocortex, takes us beyond lizard-brain sensory reactions.

Francis Crick, British codiscoverer of the DNA double helix structure, described brain function in *The Astonishing Hypothesis: The Scientific Search for the Soul.* In the book, Crick posits that your mind is nothing more than the cells in your brain—just neurons exchanging information. There is no "ghost in the machine," he says, nor eternal soul forming your mind; it is formed by the 100 billion neurons in your neocortex. You are your neocortex, the region that contains all your memories, experiences, capabilities, imagination, sense of self and much more. American futurist Ray Kurzweil explains:

> Two million years ago, we didn't have these large foreheads, but as we evolved we got a bigger enclosure to accommodate more neocortex. What did we do with that? We put it at the top of neocortical hierarchy. We were already doing a very good job of being primates, and now we were able to think on an even more abstract level. That was the enabling factor for us to invent technology, science, language and music.[56]

The human neocortex gives us three main, interlinked intelligence enhancements over animals. The first is creative intelligence, imagination and the ability to use memory to make predictions. Silicon Valley entrepreneur Jeff Hawkins, who reverse engineers the brain in his book, *On Intelligence: How a New Understanding of the Brain Will Lead to the Creation of Truly Intelligent Machines*[57], argues:

> Here then, it goes to the core of my argument on how to understand the neocortex, and why memory and prediction are the keys to unlocking the mystery of intelligence. We start with the reptilian brain with no cortex. Evolution discovers that if it tacks on a memory system (the neocortex) to the sensory path of the primitive brain, the animal gains the ability to predict the future.

The second is the ability to learn throughout our lives at a staggering rate versus using our preprogrammed, innate intelligence. Yes, human beings are born with innate knowledge, as demonstrated in studies of babies. But we then learn more throughout our lives, at a completely different level compared to any other animal. This is a key differentiator. Yoshua Bengio, deep learning pioneer, explains:

> An ant doesn't learn much; it's all like a big, fixed program. But as you go higher up the intelligence hierarchy, the share of learning

56 Martin Ford, *Architects of Intelligence*, Birmingham, UK: Packt Publishing, 2018.

57 Jeff Hawkins, *On Intelligence: How a New Understanding of the Brain Will Lead to the Creation of Truly Intelligent Machines*, London: St. Martin's Griffin, 2005.

> keeps increasing. What makes humans different from other animals is how much we learn versus how much is innate.[58]

The third and most crucial enhancement, the neocortex gives humans social intelligence and the ability to cooperate in large groups. An expanded prefrontal cortex leads to an increased capacity to process internal and external experiences. This translates to an enhanced ability to empathize with and relate to other human beings, which is fundamental to cooperation.

COLLECTIVE INTELLIGENCE

Social psychologists have long recognized the mind is social; it exists, not in isolated individuals, but in individuals embedded in social and cultural systems. Intelligence is shared among individuals, in teams, in organizations and in complex, dynamic systems. Individual intelligences come together to form a greater overall intelligence. The whole is greater than the sum of the parts.

This is true not only of human beings but also animals. The Portuguese man-of-war is a sixty-foot-long creature that resembles a giant jellyfish. It looks like one organism, but it actually represents the merger of distinct organisms, as award-winning journalist Robert Wright points out in *Nonzero: The Logic of Human Destiny*:

> [The Portuguese man-of-war] evolved through the merger of distinct multicelled organisms, which grew more specialized as they grew more interdependent; some paralyze fish, others eat the fish and then share the nutrients. Among other colonial invertebrates that blur the line between organism and society are our old friend the cellular slime mold (which vacillates between autonomous cells and unified slug) and corals (including, aptly, the "brain coral"). For that matter, even things that we all agree are organisms, such as ourselves, can have their colonial aspects, . . . cells and organ-

58 Martin Ford, *Architects of Intelligence.*

> elles—formerly distinct creatures that merged. There is a little Portuguese man-of-war in all of us. [59]

Insects have collective intelligence, so much that a group of almost blind ants can work out the shortest route between food and their nest without any visual information. The difference between human collective intelligence and insect or animal collective intelligence is the human "floodlight" capability, which can be applied to any new situation or problem. Other animals cannot apply their collective intelligence to new situations, whereas humans can. As a result, we human beings are able to cooperate in groups to deal with any problem we encounter. Our collective intelligence is a general collective intelligence that enables large-scale cooperation.

TECHNOLOGY FOR COLLECTIVE INTELLIGENCE

Broad human cooperation improved thanks to written language, which enables us to learn with other human beings not just in the present but throughout the ages. When Newton transformed science and our understanding of the world in his *Philosophiæ Naturalis Principia Mathematica*, he said, "If I have seen further, it is by standing on the shoulders of giants." In other words, Newton credited the ideas and work of earlier scientists, which were transferred to him through written language. The late US Senator S. I. Hayakawa once said of human beings: "It is not true we only have one life to live. If we can read, we can live as many more lives and as many kinds of lives as we wish."[60]

Technologies like the telegraph, radio and telephone sped up the evolution of human cooperation in the twentieth century. French idealist philosopher Pierre Teilhard de Chardin wrote in the mid-twentieth century that the world's nascent telecommunications infrastructure was "a generalized nervous system" that gave humans "organic unity." Human beings, it seemed, were becoming a "super brain" and a "brain of brains," as many called the result of this new level of cooperation.

59 Robert Wright, *Nonzero: The Logic of Human Destiny*, New York: Vintage Books, 2001.

60 Quote by S.I. Hayakawa, https://www.goodreads.com/quotes/44905-it-is-not-true-that-we-have-only-one-life.

British computer scientist Tim Berners-Lee, known as the inventor of the World Wide Web, also compared the internet he had created to "the brain." Yuval Noah Harari argues that what has made human beings so successful as a species is precisely this capacity for broad cooperation:

> The *sapiens* secret of success is large-scale, flexible cooperation. This has made us masters of the world. But at the same time, it has made us dependent for our very survival on vast networks of co-operation. This process has accelerated over the millennia so that today nearly all of the things we need for survival are provided by complete strangers. I don't know how to produce the food I eat, how to sew the clothes I wear or how to build the house in which I live. I write history books, get paid for it, and buy 99 percent of what I need from strangers. It is no wonder that the size of the *sapiens* brain has been decreasing over the last 10,000 years.[61]

In *Superminds: The Surprising Power of People and Computers Thinking Together*, MIT professor Thomas W. Malone predicts that collective intelligence will be crucial for human progress. He cites research showing collective intelligence can be measured, just as individual intelligence can. Collective intelligence, he argues, also has its own will, which is different from that of the individuals in a group. Take, for example, the government that decides to go to war against the will of its people. Organizations have collective intelligence, too, he says, and may even be considered conscious life forms. Malone reveals that Apple CEO Tim Cook believes Apple has its own consciousness:

> When Apple's CEO Tim Cook spoke at MIT's commencement, I asked him whether he thought Apple was conscious. He considered the question very thoughtfully. Then, over the course of several minutes, he said he thought Apple was an organism like a person with values and goals and that, of course, it was conscious. [62]

61 "What Makes Humans Different? Fiction and Cooperation," Smithsonianmag.com, https://www.smithsonianmag.com/arts-culture/what-makes-humans-different-fiction-and-cooperation-180953986/

62 Thomas W. Malone, *Superminds: The Surprising Power of People and Computers Thinking Together*, Amazon.com, New York: Little, Brown and Company, 2018.

Malone believes that the real power of AI will be enabling the collective intelligence of humans and machines to work together:

> Humans can supply the general intelligence and other specialized skills that machines don't have. The machines can supply the knowledge and other specialized capabilities that people don't have. And the groups of people and computers together can act more intelligently than any person, group, or computer has ever done before. [63]

DEFINING ARTIFICIAL INTELLIGENCE

We have seen how intelligence manifests itself in living organisms and what distinguishes human intelligence. What then is machine intelligence, a.k.a. artificial intelligence? Some say artificial intelligence (AI), so named by AI pioneer John McCarthy, is just a catchall term for novel and experimental cognitive computer programs. Once the individual programs become popular, we no longer call them AI; we call them by their individual names, such as Google Search, GPS Maps, industrial robotics, speech recognition and personalized recommendations. All these solutions contain AI but are no longer referred to as AI. As McCarthy once said: "As soon as it works, no one calls it AI anymore." This is known as Tesler's Theorem, or anything a machine cannot yet do is called AI.

So are machines and AI really the same thing? Does AI just represent novel types of machine technologies? Machines and even automatons (machines that move themselves) have been around since antiquity. The Hero of Alexandria (c. AD 10–c. AD 70), an ancient Greek inventor and engineer, wrote a book called *Automata*, meaning "moving itself"; the book described how to construct machines such as animated statues, a fire engine, a water organ and a programmable cart. Fast forward to the modern era, and this ancient book title lives on in the modern business term *automation*.

63 Thomas W. Malone, *Superminds*.

Italian Renaissance polymath Leonardo da Vinci even designed a robot that could sit up, move its arms and head, and open its jaws. In 1450, Gutenberg developed the world's first movable-type press, better known as the printing press, which marks the acknowledged start of Europe's modern era. It helped challenge religious dogma and launched the scientific and industrial revolutions. This led to the introduction of other machine technologies, from the telegraph to the telephone, radio, television, computer and more. Have all these machines really been part of the artificial intelligence story? The answer is no; AI is more than just a machine, as we shall see from developing an overarching definition of intelligence.

A useful approach to defining all intelligence, including artificial intelligence, in the context of so many competing definitions of intelligence, is to determine what all these definitions have in common. Cornell University academics Shane Legg and Marcus Hutter examined more than 70 definitions of intelligence across three categories to find commonalties. They began by grouping definitions of intelligence into three main areas:

1. Collective definitions: "The ability to use memory, knowledge, experience, understanding, reasoning, imagination and judgment in order to solve problems and adapt to new situations." —AllWords Dictionary, 2006
2. Psychologist definitions: "Intelligence is not a single, unitary ability, but rather a composite of several functions. The term denotes that combination of abilities required for survival and advancement within a particular culture." —A. Anastasi
3. Artificial intelligence definitions: "Any system . . . that generates adaptive behavior to meet goals in a range of environments can be said to be intelligent." —D. Fogel

Collating all these definitions based on commonly occurring features, they found that intelligence:

- Is a property that an individual agent has as it interacts with its environment or environments

- Is related to the agent's ability to succeed or profit with respect to some goal or objective
- Depends on how able the agent is to adapt to different objectives and environments

These attributes produce a definition of intelligence that can apply to organisms or machines, or in the researchers' words:

> "Intelligence measures an agent's ability to achieve goals in a wide range of environments." —S. Legg and M. Hutter.[64]

GOALS AND SELF-AGENCY

Crucial to intelligence then are goals and the will to achieve them. For example, a car is a machine full of smart technology. It can outperform human beings in speed, endurance and power. It is run on a computer. However, a car would not be described as artificial intelligence. But if we were to give the car a goal and the self-agency to achieve it, such as being able to travel to a particular destination, then we would no doubt call this an example of artificial intelligence. Indeed, self-driving cars are hailed as a shining example of AI.

Artificial intelligence, thus, can be seen as the business of endowing a dumb machine with goals and self-agency. It could be a chair, a toilet, a car, a coach, a doorknob, a table or a key fob. Once a machine has the ability and self-direction to achieve a complex goal, we can say this is artificial intelligence. The more complex the goal achieved, the more intelligent the man, organism or machine.

64 "A Collection of Definitions of Intelligence," Researchgate.com, https://www.researchgate.net/publication/1895883_A_Collection_of_Definitions_of_Intelligence.

CHAPTER 3

How Artificial Intelligence Works

"Artificial Intelligence, Deep Learning, Machine Learning. Whatever you're doing, if you don't understand it, learn it. Because otherwise you're going to be a dinosaur within three years."

— Mark Cuban, billionaire investor

"A breakthrough in Machine Learning will be worth 10 Microsofts."

— Bill Gates

"We are now solving problems with machine learning and artificial intelligence that were in the realm of science fiction for the last several decades."

— Jeff Bezos, CEO and founder, Amazon

We saw in the last chapter that artificial intelligence is described as technology with the ability to achieve complex goals. So the question becomes what is a goal? Is the goal of a self-driving car to travel down the street the same as the goal of a human male to start a family? Or can the goal of an email spam filter be compared with the goal of a human social worker to make a difference in the world? When we give a machine a goal to achieve a task, can we equate that to the goals of human beings? Nelson Mandela had a goal to free South Africa of apartheid. Charles Darwin had a goal to understand our provenance. Winston Churchill, to defeat Nazi Germany. Can we equate these lofty human goals with the functional goals of machines? The answer is that this may not be a fair comparison. The reason is that we have been comparing the goals of human beings with a very limited type of AI that's called "narrow AI."

TYPES OF AI

Artificial intelligence divides into two main types: General artificial intelligence and narrow AI, which breaks down into further subfields:

1. Artificial general intelligence
2. Narrow AI
    - Robotics
    - Expert systems
    - Automated reasoning
    - Swarm intelligence
    - Speech recognition
    - Natural language processing
    - Machine learning
        - Supervised
        - Unsupervised
        - Reinforcement learning
            - Deep learning
                - Machine vision
                - Deep reinforcement learning

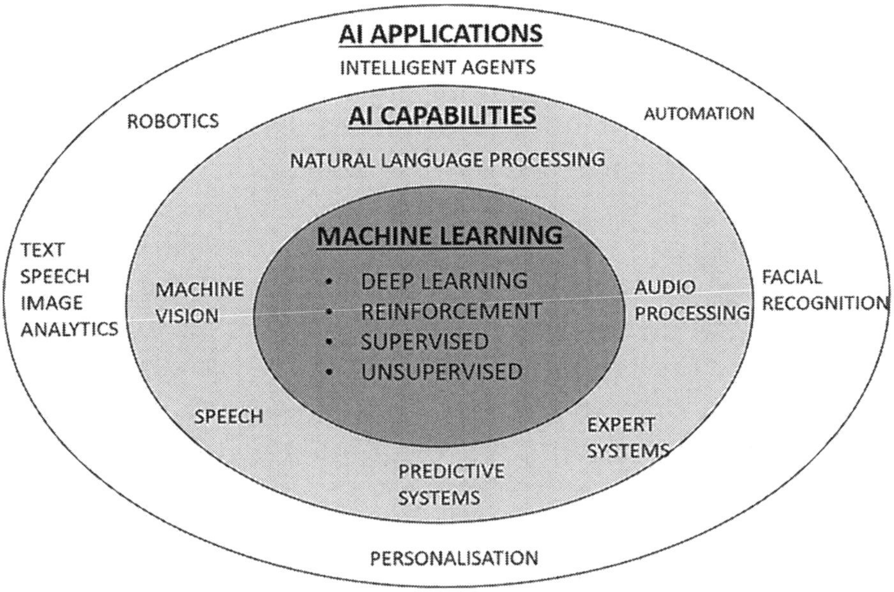

Figure 4: The constellation of AI technologies and business applications, based on an image from the book Human + Machine, 2018 Accenture Global Solutions[65]

ARTIFICIAL GENERAL INTELLIGENCE

Artificial general intelligence (AGI) is the transformative AI that could culminate in the singularity, a watershed moment when machine intelligence exceeds all human intelligence, giving birth to a superintelligence.[66] AGI specifically refers to software that can solve a variety of complex problems in a variety of different domains and that controls itself autonomously.

This is the AI that could have important goals that would be just like human goals. It could even have grander goals than most of us, such as ending poverty, preventing malaria or curing cancer, traveling to other planets and more. Or in many doomsday scenarios, for example, in the movie The Terminator, AGI could have the goal of destroying all human life.

65 Adapted from Infographic in Paul R. Daugherty and H. James Wilson's *Human + Machine: Reimagining Work in the Age of AI*, Cambridge Massachusetts: Harvard Business Review Press, 2018.
66 Nick Bostrom, *Superintelligence: Paths, Dangers, Strategies*, Cambridge: Oxford University Press, 2016.

AGI was the original focus of the first AI researchers, such as Turing, Good, McCarthy, Minsky and others. However, due to the demonstrated difficulty of the problem, not many AI researchers are focused on AGI anymore. Hype surrounding the singularity has given AGI a bit of a bad reputation, as if creating artificial general intelligence was pure science fiction. Yet, while AGI is a recurrent theme for sci-fi movies, it is, by all known science, absolutely possible. Like nanotechnology, it is merely an engineering problem, though an extremely difficult one. Among the few companies explicitly focused on AGI are Google DeepMind, the London-based company led by Demis Hassabis; Elemental Cognition founded by David Ferrucci, who built IBM Watson and led its victory on *Jeopardy!*; and Open AI, a nonprofit AI research company backed by Elon Musk that is focused on building safe artificial general intelligence.

NARROW AI

Narrow AI is the only form of artificial intelligence that humanity has achieved so far. Narrow AI is good at performing a single task, such as playing chess, finding patterns in data, making recommendations, making predictions or planning routes. Speech and image recognition are narrow AI, even if they seem remarkably human. Google's translation engine is a form of narrow artificial intelligence. The technology behind self-driving cars is still considered a type of narrow AI, or more precisely, an ensemble of several narrow AIs.

Narrow AI is sometimes also referred to as "weak AI." However, that doesn't mean that narrow AI is not useful. It is excellent at fulfilling its narrow purpose, either physically or cognitively. It is narrow AI that's threatening to displace millions of human jobs. And it's narrow AI that finds patterns in data that humans may not be able to find. It is also narrow AI that has bested the best human minds in chess, Go and other challenging games. Narrow AI is also the AI that you could use to help your business.

MACHINE LEARNING

Machine learning is the most widely used and potent form of narrow AI. Machine learning is a specific subset of narrow AI that trains a machine how to learn. It is a method of data analysis that automates analytical model building. Machine learning models use algorithms to look for patterns in data and then try to draw conclusions.

The world is filled with data. Machine learning offers the potential of deriving meaning from all of that data. The sheer scale of the quintillions of data points produced every day surpasses humans' ability to analyze. The only way to understand all this data is through automated systems such as machine learning. Data is not useful by itself, but enormous value can be derived from data through analyzing it, as British mathematician Clive Humby explains:

> Data is the new oil. It's valuable, but if unrefined, it cannot really be used. It has to be changed into gas, plastic, chemicals, etc. to create a valuable entity that drives profitable activity; so must data be broken down and analyzed for it to have value.

Machine learning is based on the idea that machines can analyze patterns in data through algorithms and that these patterns can be used to make predictions. The term "algorithm" comes from the Latinization of the name Al-Khwarizmi, the ninth-century Persian mathematician who pioneered algebra. An algorithm sounds wonderfully complex, but it is simply a set of instructions. It is a highly specific set of instructions that even something as literal as a machine can follow to complete a calculation or solve a problem. For example, a cooking recipe is not an algorithm because it is not precise enough about every action that needs to be taken. You don't know how many seconds to pour the milk or to exactly what temperature to heat the cooktop.

Here is an example of an algorithm for finding the largest number on a list:

find_max().
Problem: Given a list of positive numbers, return the largest number on the list.
Inputs: A list L of positive numbers. This list must contain at least one number. (Asking for the largest number in a list of no numbers is not a meaningful question.)
Outputs: A number n, which will be the largest number on the list.
Algorithm:
Set max to 0.
For each number x in the list L, compare it to max. If x is larger, set max to x.
max is now set to the largest number on the list.

Once designed, the algorithm needs to be written in a language computers understand, at which point it becomes a program. This is our algorithm "find max" in Python programming language:

```
def find_max (L):
  max = 0
  for x in L:
    if x > max:
      max = x
  return max
```

LEARNING ALGORITHMS

Normal algorithms like "find max" have an input and an output. Data goes in the computer, the algorithm works on it and out comes the result. The genius of machine learning is to reverse this process. The data and the result go in, and the underlying pattern that turned one into another is uncovered by a learning algorithm, or learner. We then have a trained learning algorithm we can apply to new data. Machine learning can find patterns in extremely complex datasets and, as a result, make highly accurate predictions.

USES OF MACHINE LEARNING

Machine learning is all around us in the products we use today. All of the following are powered by machine learning:

- Social media personalization, face recognition and ad targeting
- Recommending a video to watch, such as a movie on Netflix or Amazon Prime
- Google searches, from the actual query to understanding its meaning, then personalizing the results
- Customer service technology, such as chatbots that answer questions through LiveChat
- Email spam filtering and malware alerts
- GPS systems that predict traffic
- Virtual personal assistants like Alexa and Siri that use speech
- Crime- and fraud-detection systems that identify abnormal behavior
- Financial traders that use automated systems to help them make trades
- Medical diagnosis systems that can assess your symptoms and send you to a doctor
- Business and customer analytics to identify valuable customers and predictive analytics to find selling opportunities

TYPES OF LEARNERS

US computer science professor Pedro Domingos, author of *The Master Algorithm* [67], explains that just a few learners are responsible for the great majority of machine learning applications. For example, a learner algorithm called "naïve Bayes," based on Bayes' theorem, can be used to diagnose medical conditions or filter out spam email. "Decision tree" learners are used for credit card applications and DNA analysis. "Nearest neighbor" is used for tasks ranging from moving robot hands to recommending films playing in movie theaters.

67 Pedro Domingos, *The Master Algorithm: How the Quest for the Ultimate Learning Machine Will Remake Our World*, New York: Basic Books, 2015.

Amazon recommendations use a learner called "affinity analysis." It is a simple cross-selling and upselling strategy. The algorithm has learned that people who buy product Y often also buy product X, Z, T. So when you click on product Y, the affinity analysis algorithm kicks in and recommends products X, Z and T. You may not buy any of these products but instead go for product R. The affinity analysis then learns from your behavior and this is fed into the model so that next time it may also offer R. It is, therefore, continually improving performance. These learners consist of just a few hundred lines of code, which makes them remarkably simple compared to programs they replace, which can house millions of lines of code. AI systems are, at their core, just chains of these algorithms tied together. Nick Polson and James Scott explain in their book, *AIQ: How Artificial Intelligence Works and How We can Harness Its Power for a Better World:*

> On its own, an algorithm is not smarter than a power drill; it just does one thing very well, like sorting a list of numbers or searching the web for pictures of cute animals. But if you chain lots of algorithms together in a clever way, you can produce AI: a domain-specific illusion of intelligent behaviour. For example, take a digital assistant like Google Home, to which you might pose a question like "Where can I find the best breakfast tacos in Austin?" This query sets off a chain reaction of algorithms. And that's AI. Pretty much every AI system . . . follows the same pipeline of algorithm system.[68]

THE SIMPLICITY OF COMPUTING

If algorithms now seem very simple, computers are even simpler. At the core of every computer are transistors that switch on and off. The late MIT professor Claude Shannon, realized as an MIT master's student that, when these transistors switch on and off, it is a form of logical reasoning. The master's thesis written by Shannon, an American contemporary and friend of Alan Turing, became the most famous and possibly

68 Nick Polson and James Scott, AIQ: How Artificial Intelligence Works and How We Can Harness Its Power for a Better World, (New York: St. Martin's Griffin, 2019), 4.

the most important master's thesis of the twentieth century.[69] Domingos explains Shannon's finding:

> If transistor A turns on only when B and C are both on, it's doing a tiny piece of logical reasoning. If A turns on when either B or C is on, that's another tiny logical operation. And if A turns on whenever B is off, and vice versa, that's a third operation. Believe it or not, every algorithm, no matter how complex, can be reduced to just these three operations: AND, OR and NOT operations.[70]

The transistors in a computer turn on and off in different orders billions of times per second to run the technology that shapes our lives, from mobile phones to credit cards, GPS systems, online shopping and much more. The challenge is how to develop algorithms sophisticated enough for all these operations. Facebook, for example, would have to write a program to show relevant updates to each of its 2.27 billion users. Amazon would have to individually code its product recommendations to all of its 310 million users. Netflix would need to write a program to offer different and relevant films to cater to the specific tastes of its 158 million subscribers. There aren't enough programmers and developers in the world to write all these codes, and even if they tried, they could not layer in the complexity required by so many different users. But learning algorithms can learn about every single user and personalize the experience for each one, and that is why we need them.

THE DEMOCRATIZING EFFECT OF OPEN-SOURCE CODE

One myth that I would like to shatter in this book is that AI requires millions of dollars in investment, or that AI is just an arms race controlled only by tech giants like Google, Facebook, Amazon and others. Yes, such companies are investing a fortune in AI. For example, Intel, Microsoft, Amazon and Google alone invested $42 billion

69 "MIT Professor Claude Shannon dies; was founder of digital communications," MIT News, http://news.mit.edu/2001/shannon.

70 Pedro Domingos, *The Master Algorithm: How the Quest for the Ultimate Learning Machine Will Remake Our World.*

in research and development in 2018. They also have access to vast data, and, as we explained earlier, this gives them a major advantage in their fields.

But data is also verticalized in industries where certain businesses dominate. Google may have the best search query data, but it does not have all the data in industries such as health care, financial services or automotive engineering. Tesla has managed to accumulate more real-world data on self-driving cars than Google, even though Google has a five-year head start on research in the field. Tesla turned all its customers into data gatherers by installing relatively cheap equipment in all its commercial vehicles, letting its drivers collect data when they use self-driving features such as self-parking or autosteer (autopilot) for crash avoidance. Google collects data for its self-driving car technology on a much smaller scale, gathering data with high-end sensing equipment only on its own fleet of cars. As a result, after six years, Google had 15 million miles of self-driving data, while Tesla had more than three times this much, with 47 million miles of data, after just six months. The lesson is that data is not just the preserve of Google, and you can deploy creative strategies to gather data.

AI is also in the hands of thousands of people through open source libraries, which are repositories of software that is freely available to anyone. To build the very best, most robust software, there are advantages in making it open source. This means that millions of developers can work on it and improve it. Open source both improves the software and democratizes it by allowing free access to everyone. Since 2015, Google has made its deep-learning engine, TensorFlow, open source. In 2015, Facebook made the server that runs its Big Sur AI algorithms open source. And Google has open-sourced Parsey McParseFace, an AI language-parsing tool. These AI libraries are accessible to thousands of PhDs, developers and even hobbyists.

TRAINING AND PREDICTION

The first stage of machine learning is training, which involves feeding data into the machine. It is important to feed exactly the right data for the specific question you want to answer. The machine learns through the discovery of patterns. As Andrew Ng of Stanford and Coursera, the open online learning platform he cofounded puts it: "You throw a ton of data at the algorithm and let the data speak and have the software automatically learn from the data."

The machine uses learning algorithms to simplify the reality and transform this discovery into a model. Therefore, the learning stage is used to describe the data and to summarize it as a model. Creating models is something machines can do far more quickly and more effectively than humans, according to author and Babson College distinguished professor Thomas Davenport:

> "Humans can typically create one or two good models a week; machine learning can create thousands of models a week."[71]

MACHINE LEARNING LIFE CYCLE

1. Define the question / problem.
2. Gather data.
3. Train algorithm.
4. Test the algorithm.
5. Collect feedback.
6. Refine the algorithm.
7. Loop 3–6 until the results are satisfying.
8. Use the model to make a prediction.

Once the algorithm gets really good at drawing the right conclusions, it applies that knowledge to new sets of data.

71 "Industrial-Strength Analytics with Machine Learning," *CIO Journal*, WSJ.com, September 11, 2013, https://blogs.wsj.com/cio/2013/09/11/industrial-strength-analytics-with-machine-learning/.

When the machine learning model is built, it is possible to apply it to never before seen data to make predictions. The new data goes through the model and a prediction is made. This is an important capability of machine learning. There is no need to update the rules or retrain the model. You can even use the model previously trained to make inferences about new data.

Prediction is not just about the future but also the present. When banks decide that a transaction is fraudulent, they use prediction. Some 80 percent of credit card fraud was detected in the 1990s, and today it is 99.9 percent, thanks to prediction. When the computer I am writing this book on corrects my text in real time, it uses prediction. Prediction, then, is fundamentally about providing missing information:

> [Making] predictions is the process of filling in missing information. Prediction takes all the information you have, often called "data"? And it uses it to generate information you don't have.[72]

PREDICTION AND INTELLIGENCE

The core function of machine learning is making predictions. So, you may ask, why do we call it artificial intelligence if it is just about making predictions? The reason is prediction is a key component in human intelligence and how the brain works. Our very perception is based on prediction, as Jeff Hawkins explains.[73] Imagine you are in a room looking at all the objects around you. Without performing any action, somehow you "understand" the room. Now, imagine that a new object appears in the room, such as a blue coffee cup. You know immediately the cup is new; it jumps out at you as not belonging. To notice this, neurons in your brain that were not active must have become active. How did these neurons notice that something is different? Because they are continuously making predictions.

72 Ajay Agrawal and Joshua Gans, *Prediction Machines: The Simple Economics of Artificial Intelligence*, (Cambridge, Massachusetts: Harvard Business Review Press, 2017), 24.

73 Jeff Hawkins, *On Intelligence*.

The brain uses stored memories to constantly predict everything we see, feel and hear. It is as if your brain is saying, "Are the curtains on the wall? Yes. Are they grey? Yes. Is there a shadow on the wall from the sunlight? Yes. And so on. When you look around the room, your brain is using memories to make predictions about what it expects you to experience before you do. Jeff Hawkins comments in *On Intelligence*:

> Prediction is so pervasive that what we "perceive"—that is, how the world appears to us—does not come solely from our senses. What we perceive is a combination of what we sense and of the brain's memory-derived predictions. Prediction is not just one of the things your brain does. It is the *primary function* of the neocortex, and the foundation of intelligence. [74]

To illustrate just how fundamental prediction is to our intelligence, Hawkins gives a number of everyday examples: You step forward but miss the stairs and your brain instantly recognizes something is amiss and you readjust to maintain your balance; you listen to a melody and hear the next note in your mind before it is played; as someone talks, you just know what words they are going to say next; if I write "how now brown," you have already thought "cow." Hawkins points out that intelligence tests throughout school are really tests of predictive ability. For instance, given a sequence of numbers, what should the next one be? Science itself is an exercise in prediction, hypothesis and testing. Intelligence relies on making predictions about patterns in language, math and social situations. Jeff Hawkins comments: [75]

> These predictions are the essence of understanding. To know something means that you can make predictions about it. . . . We can now see where Alan Turing went wrong. Prediction, not behavior, is the proof of intelligence.

74 Jeff Hawkins, *On Intelligence*, 87.

75 Jeff Hawkins, *On Intelligence*.

PREDICTION AND ECONOMIC IMPACTS

Prediction then is the very foundation of intelligence, and machine learning's use of prediction will have a fundamental economic impact. In *Prediction Machines*[76] , Ajay Agrawal, Joshua Gans and Avi Goldfarb—professors of economics at the Rotman School of Management in Toronto—examine the impact of machine learning from an economics perspective. They argue cheaper prediction will have a crucial economic impact affecting supply and demand, production and consumption, and prices and costs. When the price of something falls, we use more of it. When the price of something fundamental drops drastically, the world can change. For example, light became 400 times cheaper between the 1800s and now, leading to the world lighting up. When computers made arithmetic calculations cheap, this had a massive economic impact since more people had access to math and it was extended into more and more areas.

Cheaper prediction will be useful in traditional prediction tasks like forecasting but also in endless new domains. Cheaper prediction through machines will cause an economic impact on a par with personal computers. Prediction machines may become so reliable and effective that they change how organizations operate. Machine learning will not just be used to execute a strategy, it will change the strategy itself. Prediction through machine learning is an immensely powerful new technology.

HUMAN PREDICTION VS. MACHINE PREDICTION

Do we actually need machines to make predictions? Aren't human beings good enough? Well, as US baseball legend Yogi Berra once observed, "It is tough to make predictions, especially about the future."

Human beings are good at making predictions when there is little data, for example, seeing someone's face once and then remembering

76 Ajay Agrawal and Joshua Gans, *Prediction Machines: The Simple Economics of Artificial Intelligence.*

it. However, humans normally make predictions on the basis of *strong features*, based on a small number of data points correlated to a specific outcome, normally with a cause and effect relationship; for example, in predicting whether someone will have a heart attack, strong predictive factors include a person's weight and smoking.

Machine learning factors in strong features but it also takes into account thousands of *weak features*, data points that may not be obvious but have predictive power when combined across millions of cases. This enables subtle correlations that are impossible for humans, but learning algorithms using complex mathematical relationships, such as nonlinearity, exceed even the best human minds in making predictions.

In *Thinking, Fast and Slow*, Daniel Kahneman demonstrates that algorithmic decisions are more accurate than human predictions. Even trained counsellors making predictions about the outcomes of their own students are less accurate than machines.[77] More than fifty years of data from topics such as longevity of cancer patients, career satisfaction, the likelihood of violent crimes, the prices of goods and the successes of new businesses show that machines have done better than people. [78]

That said, human and machine predictions are not mutually exclusive; we can make predictions together. For example, in 2016, a Harvard–MIT team of AI researchers won the Camelyon17 grand challenge, which focused on detecting breast cancer. The team's deep learning algorithm made correct predictions with 92.5 percent accuracy, while a human pathologist's predictions were 96.6 percent accurate. When AI researchers combined the predictions of their algorithm with those of a pathologist, the result was 99.5 percent accuracy. Partnering human and machine predictions created almost perfect predictions in this case. This speaks to the key role AI has in augmenting, rather than replacing, human beings.

77 Daniel Kahneman, *Thinking, Fast and Slow*, New York: Farrar, Straus and Giroux, 2011.

78 Daniel Kahneman, *Thinking, Fast and Slow*.

DEEP LEARNING AND NEURAL NETWORKS

The state of the art type of machine learning that makes the most powerfully accurate predictions is called deep learning. In business, deep learning has been responsible for the most useful applications and, in fact, has led to renewed excitement in AI since 2013. Roboticist Daniela Rus, director of MIT's Computer Science and Artificial Intelligence Laboratory (CSAIL), explains: "I think that today most people who say "AI" actually mean machine learning, and more than that, they mean deep learning within machine learning." Most deep learning methods use neural network architectures, which is why deep learning models are often referred to as deep neural networks. The term "deep" usually refers to the number of hidden layers in the neural network. Traditional neural networks only contain two to three hidden layers, while deep networks can have as many as 150.

Deep learning differs from machine learning in the way it learns the structure of the data. Deep learning algorithms are constructed with connected layers. Each layer is composed of neurons, so named because they work in parallel, like the neurons in the human brain. As you read this sentence, neurons in your brain are active on different levels at the same time. Some neurons recognize shapes like the lines and dots in the letters. Other neurons combine these shapes to form ideas about what letter is being represented. These neurons send this information up to the syntactic level and onto the semantic level, recognizing whole words; neurons also send information to other neurons to derive the meaning of the words in the context of the sentence. These neurons share all this information in parallel, back and forth, up and down, side to side. This parallel characteristic is what inspired the parallelism in neural networks, as shown in the following diagram:

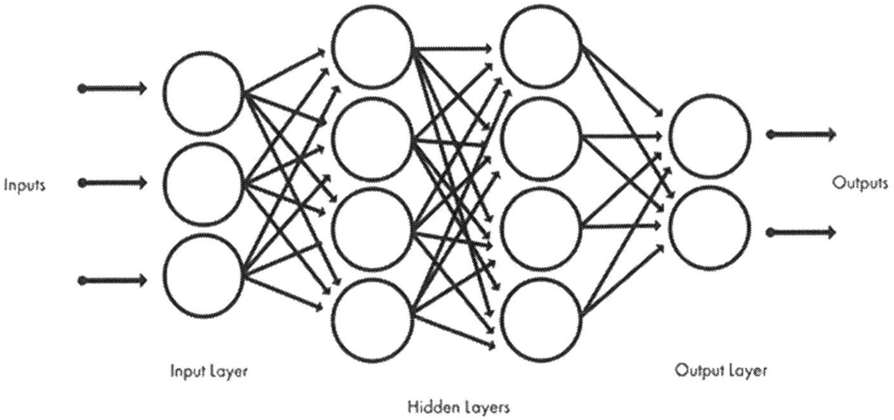

Figure 5: visual illustration of deep learning

HOW DEEP LEARNING WORKS

To understand deep learning and what makes it so effective, you have to understand parameters. A parameter is a number in your prediction equation that you choose to yield the best results. In AIQ [79], authors Nick Polson and James Scott lay out their case that we used to use small models with small parameters to make predictions. Small models have a few parameters, while massive models have lots of parameters. For example, you could predict the maximum heart rate of someone for their age with this model: Max heart rate = 220 – age. This is a small model with just one parameter; the baseline of 220, from which you subtract your age. The problem is that such a simplistic model won't be as accurate as a model with more parameters.

Using machine learning, we can fit models with hundreds of parameters. With deep learning, we can fit hundreds of thousands of parameters. For example, Google published information about a deep learning neural network model named Inception that could automatically label and recognize an image. The model involved 388,736 parameters, and its prediction was based on 1.5 billion arithmetic operations. In a world

79 Nick Polson and James Scott, *AIQ: How Artificial Intelligence Works and How We Can Harness Its Power for a Better World.*

of big data, such massive models can make highly accurate and useful predictions in endless domains.

Deep learning has made AI much more powerful in recent years. For example, in November 2016, Google Translate was used to translate some Japanese text into English and this was the result:

> Kilimanjaro is a 19,710 feet of the mountain covered with snow, and it said that the highest mountain in Africa.

The next day the Google translation had improved markedly:

> Kilimanjaro is a mountain of 19,710 feet covered with snow and is said to be the highest mountain in Africa.[80]

The translation improved because Google had improved its machine learning engine for Google Translate by implementing deep learning. [81] This enables many more parameters and arithmetic operations on masses of data such that predictions become incredibly accurate. As a Google engineer said: "When you go from 10,000 training examples to 10 billion training examples, it all starts to work. Data trumps everything." [82]

This highlights an important characteristic about machine learning and deep learning. Adding much more data can make models that are not working, suddenly work. This finding was highlighted in 2009 when three computer scientists from Google wrote a paper entitled The Unreasonable Effectiveness of Data. There is an unexpected phenomenon in machine learning that goes like this: Even a messy dataset with a billion items can be highly effective in tasks such as machine translation, for which machine learning using a clean dataset with a mere million items is unworkable. This is unexpected because a million is a big num-

80 Ajay Agrawal and Joshua Gans, *Prediction Machines: The Simple Economics of Artificial Intelligence.*
81 Ajay Agrawal and Joshua Gans, *Prediction Machines: The Simple Economics of Artificial Intelligence.*
82 Gary Kasparov with Mig Greengard, *Deep Thinking: Where Machine Intelligence Ends and Human Creativity Begins.*

ber. So when we learn the algorithm doesn't work, our intuition may tell us it won't *ever* work. But what may, in fact, be needed is an even larger training set. As the controversial founder of Cambridge Analytica once said, "There is no data like more data."

TYPES OF TRAINING

So what happens when you don't have enough data? To make predictions without enough training data, we can use a specific type of machine learning called reinforcement learning. This is what Alan Turing brilliantly foresaw when he described a child-machine. Rather than preprogamming knowledge into a machine, you can build a machine like a child that learns itself and builds knowledge. Reinforcement learning enables machines to learn by trial and error, generating their own data.

We can only apply reinforcement learning in a simulated environment, as with chess or Go, which is why DeepMind was able to employ this technology so effectively. We couldn't use reinforcement learning to generate data about self-driving cars on the road because to learn we would have to drive off 1,000 cliffs. But there are solutions for creating simulated environments, such as video games and test environments that are being used specifically to develop reinforcement learning AI systems.

Reinforcement learning is one of three fields of machine learning that are classified according to the type of supervision they get during training:

- Supervised learning
- Unsupervised learning
- Reinforcement learning

SUPERVISED LEARNING

Supervised Learning is by the far the most widely used type of machine learning. In supervised learning, the machine uses data that is labelled. For example, when an unwanted email comes into your inbox, and you mark it as spam, you are actually training a machine with labels. It learns how to classify new emails based on the labels you have used, i.e., spam or not spam. The algorithm uses training data and feedback from humans to learn the relationship of given inputs to a given output. Yann LeCun, Facebook's chief AI scientist, who also invented the widely used convolutional neural networks (CNNs) explains:

Almost all the applications of deep learning today use supervised learning. Supervised learning is when you give the correct answer to the machine when you're training it and then it corrects itself to give the correct answer. The magic of it is that after it's trained, it produces a correct answer most of the time in categories it's been trained on.

UNSUPERVISED LEARNING

In unsupervised learning, the machine uses data that is unlabelled. Unsupervised learning is seen as being crucial to the progression of machine learning, as it is how human beings learn. When a baby is developing, we do not show it thousands of pictures of cats to train it to recognize a cat. We just tell the baby a few times what a cat is, and the baby learns unsupervised by observing its environment. Unsupervised learning has a very long way to go in its contribution to the field of AI, but it can be used today in effective business applications. For example, Critical Future was engaged by one of the largest manufacturers in the world to analyze its customer data with machine learning. The company gave us a data file with an open brief to draw insights from it. Since it is such a big company, the data file contained 20 million data points. It would take a team of human beings years to analyze such a large data haul manually. Our consultant, Artis Luguzis, a PhD in machine learning applied a technique of unsupervised learning to the data called "clustering."

CLUSTERING

Clustering means using the machine to identify groups without any human intervention. In other words, we let the data tell us what patterns are there. From clustering, the machine found 20 million data points of customers, translated into 20 customer groups.

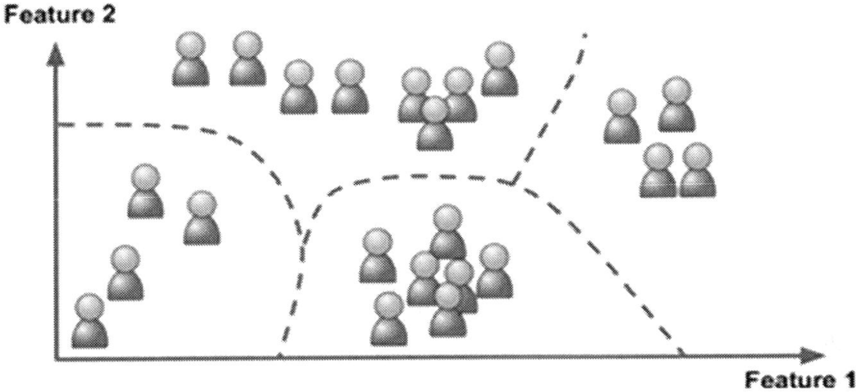

Figure 6: visual illustration of clustering

We then needed human intervention to characterize those groups and understand their relevance. The benefit of clustering is that the machine is naive to the data. It doesn't have any human biases, so it finds connections that humans would have never considered. What we found was that the 20 groups created by the machine were actually customer types: big spenders, frequent spenders, risky customers and more. This provided significant customer insight for our client.

REINFORCEMENT LEARNING

The final type of machine learning is reinforcement learning. This enables the machine to learn from interaction. The machine works by trial and error, gathering data and following reward signals. Its objective is to learn to act in a way that will maximize its expected long-term rewards. In short, the agent acts in the environment and learns by trial and error to maximize its pleasure and minimize its pain.

Reinforcement learning is based on the findings of seminal psychologist B.F. Skinner, who showed the importance of reinforcing stimuli by rewarding specific behavior and making the same thing more likely to occur in the future. Reinforcement learning is one of the main ways that human beings learn, such as when you learned to walk as a baby or learned to ride a bike or throw a baseball. You tried it and gradually improved by trial and error. Reinforcement learning can trace its origin back to the basal ganglia, which are ancient reptilian parts of the brain tied to motor control. The basal ganglia use reinforcement learning–type algorithms to help humans acquire skills.

Russell Kirsch was the first to propose using this approach in AI. He proposed that an "artificial stimulus" could use reinforcement to learn good moves in a game. Demis Hassabis, who founded DeepMind, has achieved stunning feats with reinforcement learning. Hassabis learned from his PhD studies in neuroscience that the human brain works from reinforcement learning called temporal difference learning, which is implemented by dopamine. Dopamine neurons track prediction errors that your brain is making and then strengthen synapses according to these reward signals. This insight led Hassabis to focus on reinforcement learning at DeepMind, and when he combined it with deep learning, the technology was able to massively scale up to produce deep reinforcement learning. This is what AlphaZero, the program, used to learn chess in nine hours and then beat the greatest chess-playing machine in history.

Hassabis believes reinforcement learning is much more involved in human brain function than is currently known. For example, evolution could have tacked reward signals in the human brain for gathering new information. Hassabis believes that since reinforcement learning is so fundamental to the human brain, the field will be very important for the future of AI and become "just as big as deep learning."

MACHINE VISION

Just as deep learning took inspiration from how the brain works with neural networks and reinforcement learning is based on how humans and animals learn, other aspects of artificial intelligence mimic human and animal abilities, such as vision. Machine vision is a fascinating subfield of machine learning through which computers can see. Just as a person or an animal sees, machines can use vision to detect, analyze and understand images.

The business applications of machine vision are powerful. For example, Critical Future was engaged by Klinik Healthcare Solutions, a leading Finnish AI company, to develop machine vision software. Our brief was to create software that can detect skin diseases from photographs. Our consultant Brayan Impada, a PhD in machine vision, developed a program that can detect skin cancer by analyzing photographs. Users simply upload a photograph of a skin mole to the system and get back a prediction of whether the mole is malignant or benign. Since human doctors mainly use visual diagnosis for assessing whether a mole is cancerous, an AI system using machine vision can be just as effective.

NATURAL LANGUAGE PROCESSING

Not only do machines now have vision but, like human beings, they can also work with language. From using Google Translate to speaking with a virtual assistant like Alexa, we have all become familiar with computers using language. But how do they do it?

The secret is in turning words into numbers. Computers don't understand language in the same way human beings do. Noam Chomsky, the great linguist and cognitive scientist, once said: "Children don't learn language; they grow language." We are remarkably good at understanding context and meaning, even when there is ambiguity. We are also great at understanding where one word ends and another begins, even though they may actually sound interconnected. Even neuroscientists can't understand how our minds do this so well. For all these reasons, it is not possible to write computer code with rules for language processing. This would require too many rules, over too many languages and would be an insurmountable task.

The breakthrough came with natural language processing. This field of AI turns words into numbers and uses statistical methods to decipher meaning. Drawing on vast data lakes of words that have been created from online platforms such as Google to Facebook and beyond, natural language processing is based on language models, data and statistical tools. One popular model in the field is Word2Vec, a two-layer neural net for processing text. It swallows a given set of text and then returns the text as a set of vectors, transforming the words into a numerical form that computers can understand.

The need for such algorithms is ever-increasing since humans produce continuously expanding volumes of text each year. Natural language processing is at the center of the AI revolution, since it provides a tool for humans to communicate with computers effectively. NLP draws from many disciplines, including computer science and computational linguistics, in its pursuit to fill the gap between human communication and computer understanding. NLP makes it possible for computers to read text, hear speech, interpret it, measure sentiment and determine which parts are important. Machines can analyze more language-based data than humans, without fatigue and in a consistent, unbiased way.

The natural language–processing market is predicted to reach $22.3 billion by 2025, and it will have broad business applications. Google recently launched Talk to Books, which uses NLP to read 100,000 books and 600 million sentences in half a second and then return the best answer it can find to any question. At Critical Future, we were asked by one of the world's leading data providers to build an AI system that can read legal documents. The client engaged human operators to read thousands of legal documents, making standardized checks to support financial-service clients. To replace this method, we developed software using natural language processing that can read the documents and make the same checks autonomously. This has saved the client hundreds of thousands of dollars in the first year of operation.

GENERATIVE DESIGN

AI is so far mimicking human intelligence in vision, learning, speech and language and, in robotics, movement. But AI can't do everything humans can do, right? Machines can't engineer things as human can? They can't come up with creative new ideas, can they? Well, actually, yes, they can.

Critical Future is pioneering a new field of AI called generative design, which rivals human engineers, creatives and designers. This AI software can independently create drawings, perform calculations and explore trade-offs. The role for humans is to tell the generative design software what kind of part to design. Our project is in oil and gas, and we rely on our client to propose a great deal of domain-specific expertise. We use generative design to automatically generate designs for oil and gas structures.

Generative design has already been used to design a car chassis. As far back as 2013—a long time in AI years—the start-up Autodesk teamed with stunt drivers in Los Angeles. Their aim was to develop an automated system that could determine the specifications of a race car chassis and then design it from scratch. To do this, the team applied sensors to a stripped-down race car that measured the quantities of interest, to collect the data essential for the AI. It captured data on stresses, strains, temperatures, displacements and more. A real driver test-drove the sensor-equipped car, accelerating, braking and speeding up in the process. At the end, the team had collected 20 million data points and then plugged these into Dreamcatcher, a generative design system from Autodesk.

The software came up with a design (see Figure 7) looks like something from nature. This is not a coincidence. It has taken millions of years of evolution to develop the highly efficient structures of the natural world, such as bones and skeletons. So the optimal design from an AI program is remarkably similar to what nature would provide. AI's designs mirror the hand of god, or nature itself. The chassis is also asymmetrical and stronger on one side. The reason is that a car turns more often in one direction, and, therefore, the two sides are subject to different forces. Human designers have been aware of this fact for a long time but have not been able to produce such a fitting design to solve this problem. [83]

Figure 7: car chassis produced by Generative Design, sourced from the book Machine, Platform, *Crowd: Harnessing Our Digital Future*, New York: W. W. Norton & Company, 2017.

ENSEMBLE AI

We have covered powerful narrow AI capabilities across movement, speech, language, predictive power, vision and even creative engineering. What would happen if you applied them at the same time in one creation? This is being done with compelling results through ensemble AI solutions. These solutions bring together different narrow AIs into one combined solution. A well-known example of ensemble AI is the self-driving car, which combines several narrow AIs into one overall solution. As we have seen, AI now has the following capabilities:

- Vision
- Language
- Movement
- Touch
- Smell
- Listening
- Acting
- Creativity

83 Andrew McAfee and Erik Brynjolfsson, *Machine, Platform, Crowd: Harnessing Our Digital Future*, New York: W. W. Norton & Company, 2017.

These narrow AI capabilities have already been combined to produce a manifestation of AI that's a lot more humanlike—androids that have many of the qualities of a human being. That is exactly what Japanese roboticist Hiroshi Ishiguro has achieved. He has designed and produced some thirty androids, most female, but he claims with some justification that his android Erica is the most humanlike robot ever created.[84] She has a beautiful neutral face and can hold a conversation. She understands what you are saying, moves and makes decisions. Erica is so human that her creators do not believe she is strictly a machine but represents a new category somewhere between machine and human. While this may pose philosophical questions for Westerners with a Judeo-Christian understanding of life, it is not so problematic in Japan. The Japanese Buddhist tradition teaches that every object has a soul, and so, of course, Erica herself also has a soul.

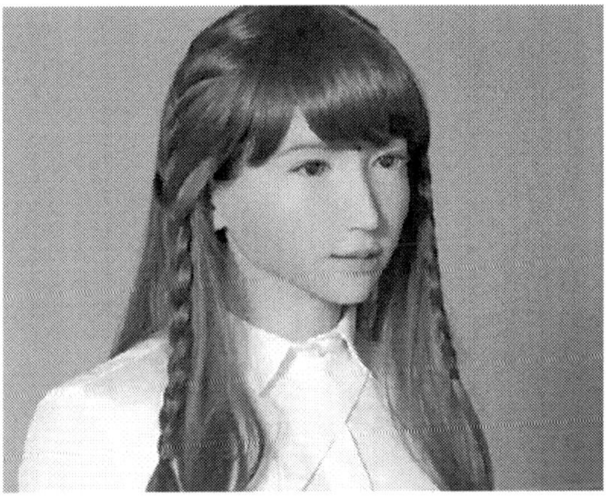

Figure 8: Erica a robot of Hiroshi Ishiguro

84 "Are We Ready for Intimacy With Androids?" *Wired*, October 17, 2017, https://www.wired.com/2017/10/hiroshi-ishiguro-when-robots-act-just-like-humans/.

CHAPTER 4

How Business Can Leverage AI

"The core currency of any business will be the ability to convert data into AI."
— Satya Nadella, CEO, Microsoft

"Just as electricity transformed everything almost 100 years ago, today I actually have a hard time thinking about an industry that I don't think AI will transform in the next several years."
— Andrew Ng, cofounder, Coursera

In the last chapter, we examined the powerful capabilities of AI. In this chapter, we explore how these can be applied to business. Andrew Ng has compared the current state of AI to the discovery of electricity. This remarkably powerful general purpose technology has now entered an era of growth and implementation. In the same way that progress in electricity revolutionized the business world in the 1800s, improvements to AI in the 2000s are propelling a myriad new business opportunities. Amazon CEO Jeff Bezos, the wealthiest man in the world, has said we are in a golden age of AI that can provide "an enabling layer" for "every business." As Bezos says, AI has been central to the success of Amazon, optimizing a multitude of areas:

I would say a lot of the value that we're getting from machine learning is actually happening kind of beneath the surface. It is things like improved search results, improved product recommendations for customers, improved forecasting for inventory management, and literally hundreds of other things beneath the surface.

But AI is not the exclusive preserve of Amazon and the other tech giants. Every business can be enhanced by AI. This includes large multinational corporations, mid-sized companies and even SMEs. AI is within reach of all of us. Open-source code and bright people are all businesses need to make massive progress with AI. The opportunities are endless.

REIMAGINING BUSINESS WITH AI

Where do you start? The key thing to consider: AI offers unlimited opportunities for smart, effective, business solutions. There is not a fixed set of 20, 50 or 1,000 solutions. There are as many opportunities for applying AI to business as your imagination and innovative spirit permit. You need to reimagine business processes. Consider that applying AI to a business process could make a positive impact. New applications for AI in your business will create a new solution that only you are utilizing, giving you a healthy competitive advantage. Custom AI systems are a strategic asset that will increase the overall value of your business.

The first phase is focused on comprehension of the technology. This includes: (1) technical knowledge of how AI works and what it can do, and (2) market knowledge of how the technology will impact business models and evolve over time. This book aims to answer many of these questions.

ALIGNMENT WITH AI OBJECTIVES AND AMBITION

In the book The Executive Guide to *Artificial Intelligence*, Andrew Burgess argues that AI implementation should involve alignment with your strategic **objectives**. These may include:

1. Generate revenue
2. Reduce costs
3. Manage risks
4. Improve customer experience

You then need to consider your AI **ambition**. You might want to:

- Just tick the AI box to claim you have AI in your marketing materials
- Improve processes
- Transform a function
- Develop a whole new product, service or business
- Shift your business to become an "AI as a service" business. This links back to your strategic objectives, since you should be open to revising your business strategy based on your AI ambition.

BE STRATEGIC

My team and I at Critical Future don't recommend implementing AI just to tick a box to claim you have AI in your marketing materials. This would result in a shallow implementation of AI without any long-term benefit or strategic value. We recommend, instead, developing AI systems that support your business strategy.

Cynthia A. Montgomery, noted professor at Harvard Business School, explains: "A great (business) strategy is more than an aspiration, more than a dream: It's a system of value creation, a set of mutually reinforcing parts." [85] Value creation involves these two outer limits: customers' willingness to pay (essentially, customers' satisfaction with a good or service) and suppliers' willingness to supply (essentially, their opportunity cost—the lowest price at which they would be willing to sell to a particular firm).

When a company drives a wider wedge between these lines, by expanding the total value created, its existence matters in an industry. At this point, the company is much more likely to be able to claim some of the

85 Cynthia Montgomery, *The Strategist: Be the Leader Your Business Needs,* New York: HarperBusiness, 2012.

value for itself, meaning it is able to increase its own profitability without making its partners in trade less well off. A business creates value by driving the widest wedge possible between the satisfaction of customers and the all-in costs of suppliers:

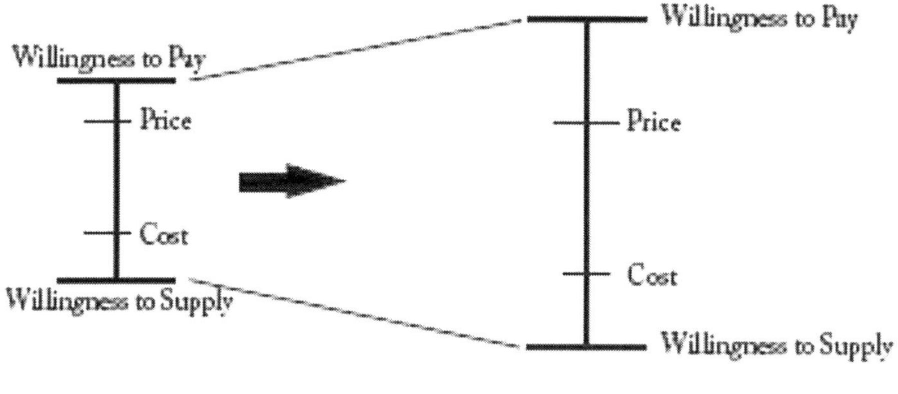

Figure 9. Value Creation, by economists Adam Brandenburger, Barry Nalebuff and Harborne Stuart

This is where your AI system development should be focused—on supporting you to drive the widest wedge to create value. Ask yourself what matters most about your company. If your organization were to disappear tomorrow, who would miss it most? The AI systems you develop should make your company matter more to the people who care most about it.

ASSESS OPPORTUNITIES

You can then conduct an AI opportunity assessment to ascertain where AI can be applied to your business. You can use AI to solve external sector wide challenges. For example, at Critical Future we have developed AI systems to predict property values, predict cancer, predict stock prices and predict commodities. To identify external opportunities, simply think what is the most valuable thing you can predict in your sector? Think through where to find the data, and come and talk us at Critical Future and we will build an AI System leveraging deep learning to predict it for you. I have no doubt whatever statistical models are currently being used to make these predictions we can beat them with AI.

You can also use AI to solve internal challenges facing your specific business. To help with this, we provide a framework here of specific opportunities to apply AI to every business function.

While all these opportunities for AI enhancement will support your business, you can prioritize them based on the strategic value they offer. The AI opportunities will fit some types of businesses better than others, within different contexts. For example, ecommerce companies may find that using AI to enhance logistics provides a competitive advantage. This can increase customers' willingness to pay and suppliers' willingness to provide. B2B business-services companies, such as consultants, lawyers, accountants and recruiters, may find that the best value lies is increasing sales through AI. This can enable sales teams to be more effective, win more customers and increase lifetime value. B2C consumer-facing companies like retailers may find the best opportunity for AI is in marketing, where it is possible to personalize the experience to every customer, ensuring each prospect receives the right message, in the right way, at the right time. Manufacturing businesses may find the best opportunity for AI is in operations, to increase productivity and lower fixed costs. But there are no hard and fast rules here; it is up to you to decide where AI can deliver the most value for you.

The opportunity assessment must be done on a case-by-case basis. It involves three key considerations:

1. Strategy: What is the opportunity for value creation? Will this AI system make my company matter more to the people who care about it the most?
2. Data: Is the required data available or obtainable?
3. Resources: Can we achieve this AI system either through buying ready-made AI software or through hiring consultants, contactors or full-time team members to deliver?

AI BUSINESS SOLUTIONS FRAMEWORK

Function	Challenges	Intelligent Solutions
Supply Chain	• Enhance visibility. • Find weak links. • Match demand with production. • Remove bottlenecks. • Scale supply. • Manage fluctuating demand. • Schedule deliveries. • Manage suppliers more effectively.	• Control software responds automatically to scale supply chains, in response to real or predicted demand. • Predictive intelligence anticipates demand based on previous demand fluctuations. • Computerized suggestions help resource managers make decisions with all available information. • Heuristic algorithms produce rapidly convergent load-spreading solutions. • Machine learning, combined with IoT devices and intelligent monitors, automatically flag failing or slow links in supply. • Natural language processing (NLP) for data cleansing and building data robustness
Sales	• Discover new customers. • Find cross-sell/ upsell opportunities. • Prioritize customer types. Obtain customer insights.	• Analytic systems explore existing customer graphs to find new customers. • Supervised (or reinforced) learning systems analyze existing e-commerce data to personalize user experience.

	• Increase conversion rates. • Automate admin processes and data management. • Increase sales force with digital employees.	• Ranking systems prioritize customers most likely to respond to upselling. • Intelligent sales lists order customers by most urgent. • Automatic data analysis tools provide insights from raw customer data. • Virtual sales agents can engage with customers as chatbots or conduct sales admin, such as automatically transcribing sales calls.
Operations	• Predict maintenance and risks. • Optimize production lines. • Anticipate and schedule maintenance. • Quality Assurance • Improve productivity. • Preserve energy. • Schedule tasks. • Plan effectively. • Management insights and dashboards, live reporting and predictions	• Predictive maintenance systems estimate probability of failure and/or time to failure of production components. • Machine vision provides automated visual inspections for quality assurance. • Robotics automates production lines. • Predict which processes, people, tools will deliver optimum productivity. • Predictive asset utilization uses power when you need it and doesn't when you don't to preserve energy. • Personnel systems learn from employee data and past performance to allocate the best available employee.

		• Use planning AI techniques to schedule dependent tasks in an optimal order. • Accurately estimate project timelines with all available data based on previous projects.
Marketing	• Build brand avatars. • Design campaigns. • Track campaign effects. • Plan future marketing areas. • Predict future trends. • Target and personalize advertising. • Generate marketing content. • Listen to your audiences online.	• Rank or cluster existing customers according to interests, and tailor advertising to them. • Identify information flow and marketing effect on test subjects with eye-tracking and other computer vision techniques. • Receive reports on campaign effect with automatic summarization of multiple market metrics. • Identify lucrative product areas for marketing with ranking systems. • Capture product sentiment and "trending" concepts with natural language systems to monitor and predict market direction.
IT	• Prevent cyberattacks. • Triage automatically. • Create custom intelligent software.	• Predict and prevent maintenance requests with online predictive maintenance systems.

	• Carry out penetration testing. • Identify and report network security breaches	• Automatically assign incoming ticket priority and/ or tags with natural language processing systems. • Ensure in-house developers are AI-literate to produce intelligent company tooling where required. • Constantly test deployments with intelligent tooling; alert administrators to security flaws and misconfigurations. • Monitor network traffic and topologies with alerting systems for unusual activity.
Human Resources	• Identify talent. • Conduct Interviews. • Review performance. • Automate processes. • Gauge emotions. • Assess talent.	• Explore social/business networks such as LinkedIn and compile candidate lists with graph-processing AI. • Filter, schedule interviews and even assess candidates automatically with chatbot/ language processing systems. • Highlight extremal performers in a large company with one-class supervised learning techniques. • Process internal communications with sentiment analysis tools: Keep an eye on the mind-set of your employees.

		• Use virtual agents to replace human operators to reduce admin. • Automate data capture and analytics processes.
Finance	• Report trends. • Financial analytics • Fraud detection • Credit risk • Reviewing contracts • Procurement • Robo-advice	• Filter and refine voluminous financial reports with AI recommendation systems. • Predict and flag developing issues, such as unexpected losses, spiraling budgets or cash flow problems, with sequence learning. • Regression tools objectively apply learned numerical procedures, such as those found in risk management. • Analyze and understand how account holders spend, invest and make financial decisions; customize advice for customers. • Index documents; extract information. • Virtual finance agents communicate with suppliers etc. • Robo-advisors give financial advice.

AI FOR SALES

Automate data processing

The most important possession of a sales professional is time. It is essential that sales people prioritize time to focus on actual selling, which means engaging with customers, building relationships, writing proposals, and presenting and closing deals. But doing all this can be challenging because mundane tasks, such as data collection, maintaining CRMs and qualifying leads can take up much of a salesperson's time. Artificial intelligence can automate such repetitive tasks. AI data processing systems can be integrated with CRM software, such as Salesforce, Pardot and Marketo. With data admin handled by AI, sales teams can then spend more time selling.

Discover new customers

Networking, either in-person or via a social media platform such as LinkedIn, is time-consuming and expensive. AI can automatically process social networks for you with a tool called a graph-traversal algorithm, answering queries like "list all colleagues of our existing customer base."

AI can also increase website conversion. An intelligent agent using supervised or reinforcement learning can learn data, such as visitor geolocation, time of day and tracking information, as well as "live" feedback like mouse tracking. This can enable you to tailor your website to your user's, which maximizes conversion.

Add virtual sales agents

AI can even do the selling for you through virtual sales agents. The advantage of sales AI over human teams is that artificial intelligence can enable you to respond to every query, even at 3 a.m., making customers feel valued. AI-powered virtual sales assistants are low-maintenance team members. They work 24-7, don't leave for more money, don't take vacations or sick days and always arrive on time.

Tools can be simple. Chorus.ai, for example, joins conference calls in the same way a sales administrator would, to record and transcribe content in real time. And chatbots leverage natural language processing to give proscribed or learned answers to customer queries. There are also more complex virtual sales agents who have complex abilities, such as learning from memory and interacting with customers. For example,

Skandinaviska Enskilda Banken (SEB), a major Swedish corporate bank, now uses a virtual assistant called Aida. This remarkable creation was built by IPSoft and is based on the IPSoft product, Amelia, which SEB renamed Aida. Able to handle natural-language conversations, Aida has access to vast stores of data and can answer many frequently asked questions, such as how to open an account or make cross-border payments. She can also ask callers follow-up questions to solve their problems, and she's able to analyze a caller's tone of voice (for instance, frustrated versus appreciative) and use that information to provide better service later. Aida is now interacting regularly with 1 million customers for SEB.

Figure 10: Amelia by IPSoft

Predictive intelligence and intelligent sales

AI predictive intelligence can identify patterns in customer data. Algorithms can analyze millions of data points to find correlations and patterns. This process can identify cross-selling and upselling opportunities. AI predictive analytics can be used to reach out to customers through prompts, offers or assistance to increase conversion and reduce churn.

AI ranking systems help sales teams prioritize leads by maximizing the expected return (i.e., expected profit multiplied by probability of sale). Ranking systems order customers by probability of sale, based on all available customer data.

The goal is intelligent sales automation, which can:

- Discover new customers using algorithms to process large prospect lists
- Predict the most lucrative customers leading to higher deal values and more repeat business
- Identify cross-selling and upselling opportunities
- Automate data processing to reduce admin burden
- Gain insight into conversion, customer types and deal size to enable strategic sales management
- Employ virtual sales agents that operate 24/7 without breaks and can be continuously improved

The key aspect of sales work that AI can't automate is relationship building. Sales people in the AI Age will still be reading Dale Carnegie's 1936 classic, *How to Win Friends and Influence People.*

AI FOR MARKETING

Branding

AI is permeating every element of marketing, even becoming the brand. For example, Alexa is becoming the face of Amazon's brand. Alexa is not limited to the marketing function, and like Amelia, who I described as a virtual sales agent, Alexa, in fact, works cross-functionally, making sales by taking spoken orders for products and filling many customer service functions by answering questions. But as Alexa performs the job of customer interaction, the AI is becoming the primary way for a company to differentiate itself and it is representing the brand.

In the future, a brand will be more than a static logo, like Disney's Mickey Mouse, it will have an interactive personality. Mickey Mouse will be able to talk to millions of children at the same time, engaging them in the Disney brand. The same will be true of every company. Branding collateral will not just be producing a logo and some design templates, but the personality, tone, and feel of an AI that will engage with customers in real time. AI brand design agencies will turn your brand into a speaking, thinking, feeling AI to interact with your customers.

Personalization

Being able to provide the right message, at the right time, to the right person is the key to marketing. In order to achieve this level of personalization at scale, the only option is artificial intelligence. AI can provide the most powerful type of marketing: personalization and even hyper-personalization. Traditionally, to tailor messaging to customer segments, marketers would create personas of potential customers, which were a rough estimation of customer profiles. With AI, marketers can have a thousand personas or even millions. If all 300 million of Amazon's customers were logged online right now, they would each have a different experience, an experience tailored to them, with products most relevant to what they are interested in. This may include winning product recommendations those customers didn't even realize they wanted. As deep learning finds patterns in data, it can also, in some ways, know you better than you know yourself.

Campaign design

Campaign design can also be improved directly with testing that AI techniques can help you do. User eye motion can be tracked across a screen in a technique known as eye-tracking, effectively highlighting the area that a consumer is looking at in an advertisement. Additionally, combining computer vision techniques with machine learning techniques has allowed emotion detection; for example, Microsoft Azure offers a service that detects combinations of "anger, contempt, disgust, fear, happiness, neutral, sadness and surprise." Knowing both where a consumer looks during an advertisement and the emotions it generates adds an enormous amount of value to traditional A/B testing.

Marketing analytics

Automatic summarization and other AI data analysis and learning tools can extract and report trends and relationships in this data, intelligently scoring the likelihood of a customer opening an email, subscribing to a newsletter or making a purchase.

Content creation

AI programs can produce content to increase web traffic. Joe Pulizzi, founder of the Content Marketing Institute, recently said:

> In 10 years, the majority of content will be generated by software. In 20 years, humans will wonder why we wasted so much time on content creation. I can't see any other way around this.

Open AI announced in February 2019 it had developed powerful new natural language–generation AI. For example, if you write a sentence about the conspiracy theory that the United States never really went to the moon, it will continue the argument for you.

Social listening

Natural Language systems can read news articles and product reviews to determine both overall market sentiment toward a product and the trend of the market.

Coca Cola listens to trending news to produce creative content linked to the news. Doug Busk, the company's former global group director for social and digital communications, says "the brand Coke is mentioned over 35 times per minute somewhere around the world," making it one of the most socially discussed brands in the world. While this presents a tremendous opportunity to harnesses positive publicity, it also poses a colossal challenge to minimize the impact of negative publicity. Jen Miller, who worked on Coca-Cola's global digital innovation efforts for nearly six years, says, "The world has changed; the way we work must change." Coke has devised The Hub [86], a sophisticated high-tech social media center that listens, analyzes and engages in real time. The Hub network helps create more interactive and focused campaigns, monitors customer reaction to those campaigns and measures brand engagement by analyzing online conversations.

Social media management

KLM Royal Dutch Airlines uses AI for social media management. It adds automated answers to customers' general questions without requiring an intervention by a human service agent. Over 50 percent of its 130,000 social media mentions are handled with 95 percent accuracy. The AI system learns from the service agent's actions and gets smarter over time.

Data-driven marketing

AI enhances every element of marketing. Future brands will be AI incarnate, like Alexa for Amazon or Amelia for IPSoft. The best-in-class AI marketing model involves fully leveraging the power of machine learning, with these functions:

- Use data to determine the best ROI and campaign effectiveness.
- Listen to customers on social media and derive insights through analytics.
- Design campaigns based on AI tests that reveal human emotional responses.
- Automate many time-consuming CRM processes.
- Personalize the end-to-end experience for the user, tailoring the entire proposition in precisely the right way for that specific individual.

86 "Step Inside the Hub: Coke's Social Media HQ," Coca-colacompany.com, January 12, 2017, https://www.coca-colacompany.com/stories/step-inside-the-hub--coke-s-social-media-lab.

AI FOR THE SUPPLY CHAIN

Prediction

One of the most challenging aspects of managing a supply chain is predicting future demand. Without AI, this is done by human subjective judgments, with hit and miss results. Using machine learning algorithms to analyze large, diverse datasets drastically improves the accuracy of demand forecasting. For example, a regression algorithm can predict future demand based on all known variables, such as the time of year, previous demand or competitor sales. It can also reduce undersupply when demand is low and reduce waste when it's high.

Planning optimization

AI can determine the optimum schedule for deliveries. Final delivery of goods might, for example, require a driver to leave a depot, circle around several locations and return. Traditional algorithms for this problem are slow and do not allow for other possibilities, such as multiple drivers or prioritized items. AI offers several approaches to optimize route planning from deep reinforcement learning solutions to swarm intelligence and evolutionary algorithms.

Supplier risk management

AI can analyze datasets, such as assessments, audits and credit scoring, which provide an important basis for further decisions regarding a supplier. Supplier selection can be more predictive than ever before. Machine-to-machine automation provides multiple "best supplier" scenarios based on your specific parameters.

End-to-end visibility

Combining machine learning with advanced analytics, IoT sensors and real-time monitoring is providing end-to-end visibility for the first time across many supply chains. What's needed in many supply chains today is an entirely new operating platform or architecture predicated on real-time data, enriched with patterns and insights not visible in the past with previous analytics tools. Machine learning is an essential element in future supply chain platforms that will revolutionize every aspect of supply chain management.

Robotics

Robots, such as Amazon's Kiva robots, can pick up goods and distribute them to different stations within a warehouse in mere minutes, and they only need five minutes every hour to charge. The robots lift and stack plastic bins full of products, then they take the products to pickers, who select the right product for shipment.

Automated supply chain

The future is an automated supply chain, which:

- Predicts demand to precisely match supply
- Optimizes planning to identify the optimal routes
- Reduces supplier risks by analyzing unstructured data
- Combines with IoT for automated monitoring and quality assurance
- Delivers real-time, end-to-end visibility
- Replaces human beings with robots, who work without breaks in warehouse fulfillment

All this is happening before self-driving cars completely revolutionize logistics. By 2040, self-driving cars will account for 95 percent of all vehicles sold. As the often-quoted British supply chain guru Dave Waters says, "Artificial Intelligence will permeate supply chains in ways we haven't even thought of."

CASE STUDY: AI FOR SUPPLY CHAIN
SCHNEIDER ELECTRIC'S GLOBAL SUPPLY CHAIN

Challenge

Schneider wanted to reduce the costs involved in the company's existing supply chain flows for 240 manufacturing facilities around the world and 110 distribution centers. It also wanted to analyze potential opportunities to assimilate new business units that Schneider had just acquired.

Approach

LLamasoft built a supply chain predictive model that could automatically create the best routing options for Schneider's enormous raw materials supply chain, which includes circuit breakers that are small enough to fit on a store shelf to transformers that are the size of a large room. Data engineers at Schneider first built a data extraction tool that could collect the enterprise data from all the ERP systems, verify and "clean" the data to be input onto the LLamasoft platform.

Outcomes

The customized model needed about two to four hours to analyze 200,000 transportation policy data points, 130,000 flow and routing constraints, and more than 150 initial scenarios (data provided by Schneider). It identified $9.32 million in annual savings for Schneider, which could potentially be obtained by altering product flow in the supply chain. This might include, for example, rerouting certain shipments directly from the manufacturing plants, rather than through one of the distribution centers, to save on material handling and inventory storage costs.

AI FOR HUMAN RESOURCES

Many core HR skills can already be supported by AI, such as recruitment, performance reviews, disciplinary actions, interpreting laws and even showing empathy. In the future, HR AI managers will be programmable with company values in a way that human beings could never quite match. AI HR managers will truly live the company values; they will be impartial, neutral and automatically updatable with new regulations. They will also be able to pick out the top performers with uncanny precision, based on machine learning prediction powers. This will enable companies to operate as true meritocracies, without the unconscious bias that holds back women and ethnic minorities. AI HR managers, in short, will be the perfect company ambassador.

Recruitment

AI is already being used in recruitment and job selection for the US Navy. The University of Memphis LIDA (Learning Intelligent Distribution Agent) performs several HR tasks for the US Navy, as described below:

"She selects jobs to offer a sailor, taking into account the Navy's policies, the job's needs, the sailor's preferences and her own deliberation about feasible dates. Then she negotiates with the sailor, in English, via iterative emails, about job selection, . . . [and] answers the only question there is for sailors, "What do I do next?"

Conducting interviews

Chatbots can conduct first-line interviews, asking candidates about their current employment status, level of satisfaction, salary, experience, skills and more.

Furhat Robotics of Sweden has created an AI robot called Tengai to conduct interviews. The firm has spent the past four years building a humanlike computer interface that mimics the way we speak, as well as our subtle facial expressions. The idea, according to chief scientist Gabriel Skantze, is that "it feels much less scary or strange compared to a more traditional robot."

Since October 2018, the start-up has been collaborating with one of Sweden's largest recruitment firms, TNG. The goal is to offer candidates job interviews that are free from any of the unconscious biases.

Performance reviews

Supervised learning can be used to learn existing company performance standards and highlight some performers for attention.

Company sentiment analysis

AI for HR is also used to report on company mind-set. While this can be done qualitatively, this is an inherently subjective method. If the company uses one method of communication more or less exclusively, such as email, Skype, Slack or IRC, natural language processing tools and sentiment analysis can be employed to quantify employee mood and highlight positive or negative influencers.

Automating processes

The automation of business processes like HR ticketing can be completed through a shared-service function or the development of insights, and dashboards would be provided to the business.

AI will be valuable in automating repetitive recruiting tasks such as:

- Sourcing resumes: Manually screening resumes is still the most time-consuming part of recruiting, especially when 75 percent to 88 percent of the resume holders who apply for a position are unqualified.
- Scheduling interviews
- Providing feedback

This will allow recruiters and HR managers the opportunity to focus on strategic work that AI will most likely never replace, such as connecting with top talent, providing a more personalized interview experience and establishing training and mentoring programs. Speeding up these parts of recruiting through automation reduces time to hire, which means you'll be less likely to lose the best talent to faster moving competitors.

AI for HR: Best practice model

HR is clearly a function where machines can augment human work, raising productivity and enhancing effectiveness. The future for the HR function will include the combination and manifestation of these tools into fully automated HR AI managers (HAIMS), who will do much of the work of human relations (performance assessment, regulatory and legal considerations, recruitment, empathy and more). This will free up HR professionals to be more strategic, resolve ambiguities, and build personal relationships. With the time consuming administrative work done by AI, HR professionals can focus on higher order challenges.

CASE STUDY: AI FOR HR
UNILEVER HR'S EMPLOYEE RECRUITMENT PROCESS

The consumer goods giant was looking for a way to diversify its 170,000-person workforce. HR determined that it needed to focus on entry-level hires and then fast-track the best into management. But the company's existing processes weren't able to evaluate potential recruits in sufficient numbers—while giving each applicant individual attention—to ensure a diverse population of exceptional talent.

Here's how Unilever combined human and AI capabilities to scale individualized hiring. In the first round of the application process, candidates are asked to play online games that help assess traits, such as risk aversion. These games have no right or wrong answers, but they help Unilever's AI figure out which individuals might be best suited for a particular position. In the next round, applicants are asked to submit a video in which they answer questions designed for the specific position they're interested in. Their responses are analyzed by an AI system that considers not just what they say but also their body language and tone. The best candidates from that round, as judged by the AI, are then invited to Unilever for in-person interviews, after which humans make the final hiring decisions.

Outcomes: The time reviewers spent on applications declined 75 percent, and there was a more diverse base of new hires coming from a more diverse set of 2,600 universities, a substantial increase over the previous 840. Rather than coming just from the top universities, which we are programmed to think are the best, the AI removed this bias and evaluated candidates on overall data. This meant many candidates from other universities, who would have been excluded, were instead included. This produced a more diverse set of candidates.

AI FOR FINANCE

Trend reporting

Salesforce CEO Marc Benioff explains why his company's AI system, Einstein Forecasting, is vital:

For a CEO, typically the way it works is you have various people in your staff meeting who are telling you what they want to tell you to get you to believe what they want you to believe. Einstein comes without bias. To have Einstein's guidance has transformed me as a CEO.

Fraud detection

HSBC has developed an AI-based solution that improves the speed and accuracy of fraud detection. The AI monitors and scores millions of transactions daily, using data on purchase location and customer behavior, IP addresses and other information to identify subtle patterns that signal possible fraud. HSBC first implemented the system in the United States, significantly reducing the rate of undetected fraud and false positives, and then rolled it out in the UK and Asia.

Machine learning algorithms, like those used by Mastercard's Decision Intelligence technology analyze various data points to identify fraudulent transactions that human analysts might miss, while improving real-time approval accuracy and reducing false declines. Using machine learning to spot unusual patterns and improve general regulatory compliance, workflows help financial organizations develop more efficient and accurate processes.

Ocado, an English online supermarket, has announced what it says is the world's first AI-based fraud detection system for online grocery purchases. The system identifies orders that are delivered but not paid for and determines whether it is the result of malicious intent by analyzing data from past orders. Ocado engineers implemented a deep neural network using Google's open-sourced TensorFlow software library and uploaded the fraud detection system to a data lake in Google Cloud. The company claims that the system has improved the accuracy of Ocado's fraud detection by a factor of 15.

Credit risk

AI can improve credit risk models by both denying risks and also extending the credit model to previously under-lent groups. Banks' current credit scoring systems are biased against the underprivileged because the current system assesses them mainly on obvious, strong features. AI, on the other hand, looks at weak and hidden features. In this way, you get a well-rounded and holistic picture. So people that were disenfranchised and not able to get credit because they didn't fit the standards in the traditional model can become enfranchised and get more credit through AI.

Reviewing contracts

Deloitte, one of the globe's Big Four accounting organizations, formed a partnership with machine-learning developer Kira Systems to create models that are intended to quickly read thousands of complex documents, extracting and structuring textual information for better analysis. If a company has 15,000 contracts to be reviewed, an auditor will try to get a representative sample for analysis. With AI partnerships like Deloitte and Kira Systems, natural language processing and machine learning train the application to recognize the structure of these contracts and to pick out the key clauses, terms and conditions and the key points within a contract in an automated fashion.

Procurement

SAP CoPilot, a digital assistant by German software multinational SAP, is designed to help businesses with tasks such as purchasing contracts and collaboration with colleagues. A typical business question might be: "What's my total spend with vendor X?" SAP's goal is to eliminate the need for users to manually interact with multiple work apps to get a job done. SAP CoPilot does this through virtual intelligence, speech recognition, natural language processing, statistical analysis and machine learning.

Financial advisors

Robo-advisors, which provide financial advice with minimal human intervention, analyze and understand how account holders spend, invest and make financial decisions; this allows them to customize the advice they give customers. Wealthfront, an automated investment services firm based in Redwood City, California, has artificial intelligence capabilities to track account activity on its own. The company helps clients analyze and understand how account holders are spending, investing and making their financial decisions, in an effort to provide financial planning advice.

AI for Finance: Best-in-class model

Finance is a natural fit with AI since both are focused on data. AI enhances finances first through analytics and predictions, which provide solutions to challenges in cash-flow, budgeting, planning and reporting. AI also offers insight in identifying trends and detecting fraud. AI then reduces the admin burden of finance through automation, such as analyzing the text in thousands of contracts and assigning workstreams. Finally, AI virtual agents take on the more strategic role of the CFO as a Robo-advisor offering customized financial advice. The future of the finance function is AI-powered.

CASE STUDY: AI FOR FINANCE
SMARTBIZ LOANS FINANCIAL ADVISOR

SmartBiz Loans, a digital marketplace for SBA loans, unveiled its advisor product, which will help users determine their loan readiness and provide guidance on financial health matters.

"It's the world's first intelligent CFO advisor that uses artificial intelligence and machine learning to help customers," SmartBiz declared. Those customers, as the name would suggest, are SME businesses. The advisor tool is a free service that can be accessed by creating an online sign-in and password. To receive advice, the user is required to upload tax documents. Based on the information in those documents, the advisor uses AI and machine learning to provide a series of analysis reports, from cash-flow analysis and business credit to determining the firm's loan-readiness. Through a chatbot system, the advisor is also able to answer questions.

AI FOR OPERATIONS

Preserve energy

Preserving energy leads to a reduction in fixed line costs, but it's also a CSR initiative. In utilizing AI to reduce energy consumption, your business also supports sustainability. Predictive asset utilization uses AI to preserve power only when you need it.

Predict maintenance

The cost of machine downtime is estimated at a staggering $647 billion lost globally each year, according to the International Society of Automation. Using AI to predict maintenance can prevent issues before they exacerbate and, in the process, lower costs of scheduled maintenance.

Predictive maintenance uses deep learning to analyze historic data to develop models to predict when a machine might break down or otherwise stop performing. This can feed into a control system that works in real time for interventions aimed at reducing downtime and increasing operational efficiency.

Quality and safety management

AI for production lines includes machine vision inspection systems to maintain quality and safety. Landing.ai, founded by Andrew Ng, uses machine vision to find microscopic defects in products at resolutions beyond human vision. The machine is able to recognize unknown defects and send alerts for "automated issue identification."

Automating manufacturing operations

One of the main drivers of manufacturing productivity has been the introduction of robot workers. Invigorating these robots with AI offers the opportunity to improve workflow efficiency, flag potential risks and adapt to changing circumstances. These advantages of AI-driven automation offer improvements in the use of time and resources. Over time, AI-fuelled robots can learn to work more effectively with their human counterparts.

Planning and scheduling

Using AI for planning and scheduling enables you to predict which processes, people and tools will deliver optimum productivity. AI can allocate appropriate personnel, automate the scheduling of tasks, have real-time management insights and dashboards, and accurately predict project timelines based on historic data and real-time performance.

Automatically scheduling jobs with AI uses machine learning combined with rules and parameters set by the production manager. AI algorithms make the various routine, real-time manufacturing scheduling decisions that are needed in a modern manufacturing plant. Human beings remain in the loop, providing useful oversight of the machine schedulers.

CASE STUDY: AI FOR OPERATIONS
GOOGLE DEEPMIND ASSET UTILIZATION[87]

DeepMind implemented deep learning to reduce energy costs and waste in Google data centers. The company found that "reducing energy usage has been a major focus for us over the past 10 years. . . . One of the primary sources of energy use in the data center environment is cooling. Just as your laptop generates a lot of heat, our data centers—which contain servers powering Google Search, Gmail, YouTube, etc.—also generate a lot of heat that must be removed to keep the servers running," says DeepMind. Implementing machine learning enabled DeepMind "to reduce the amount of energy used for cooling by up to 40 percent." This equated to "an overall 15 percent reduction in overall PUE overhead after accounting for electrical losses and other non-cooling inefficiencies," according to DeepMind. The implications for deep learning go further than Google's data centers, "given its potential to greatly improve energy efficiency and reduce emissions overall," which helps Google address climate change and sustainability issues.

AI FOR IT

Cybersecurity

Learning algorithms defend corporations, economic systems and even nations. Foreign attacks on government and business come by the day, hour and minute, and AI fends them off. Human security is too

87 "DeepMind AI Reduces Google Data Centre Cooling Bill by 40%," Deepmind.com, July 20, 2016, https://deepmind.com/blog/deepmind-ai-reduces-google-data-centre-cooling-bill-40/.

slow, and there are too few to do battle with the armies of cybercriminal bots. Even your personal email would be unusable from the deluge of spam, without machine learning.

"The threat of cybersecurity may very well be the biggest threat to the U.S. financial system," says J.P. Morgan Chase CEO Jamie Dimon. J.P. Morgan spends almost $600 million annually to tighten its defenses and ward off a constant stream of attacks. But the interconnected nature of the financial system means the risk is ever present. Small- to medium-size businesses are even more at risk than larger firms with better protection.

AI guards the wall in the fight against cybercrime through identifying abnormalities in data patterns. Once unusual activity is detected, the AI programs can investigate to determine if there is a security breach in the system. AI can find patterns humans miss, such as detecting advanced malware that is masquerading as a harmless piece of code.

Service requests

AI can cut down the number of service requests. AI automation helps employees handle their own service requests, rather than requiring the intervention of more experienced technicians. Machine learning predicts which agents should receive which support tickets, offering end users automated responses that don't require a human's intervention.

Monitoring

AI IT operations platforms analyze vast volumes of IT data from disparate sources by applying various types of algorithms to the data in real time. AI reduces alert noise by filtering and prioritizing important notifications. AI conducts causal analysis and applies analytics to a broad and wide set of data.

Intelligent IT

The end goal is intelligent information technology to:

- Detect threats
- Test penetration

- Reduce administration workload
- Identify and report network security breaches
- Gain greater visibility

CASE STUDY: AI FOR IT
WIMBLEDON LEVERAGES AI TO FIGHT CYBERCRIME[88]

Wimbledon, the world's oldest and most prestigious tennis tournament, turned to AI to improve its cybersecurity. The Wimbledon digital experience is fundamental to growing the value of the Wimbledon brand globally and to attracting a millennial and Generation Z digital-native audience. But the Wimbledon experience has been under threat from cybercrime, which increased substantially over the course of the 2017 tournament.

Alexandra Willis, head of communications for Wimbledon explains: "A security breach during those two weeks would be really damaging to the Wimbledon brand. And because Wimbledon is so much a part of the fabric of British identity, a successful attack could be perceived as more than just targeting a tennis event."

IBM's Watson AI system protects Wimbledon with cognitive technologies. In the summer of 2017, this enabled analysts to quickly and efficiently identify and address the real threats hidden in nearly 200 million events experienced during the 2017 tournament. The result of using AI cyberprevention was that detection and prevention were sixty times faster than without AI-generated protections.

Comparing AI security-threat investigations and manual analysis, five times more security incidents by volume were analyzed during the 2017 tournament using Watson, and zero breaches impacted the Wimbledon website and brand.

88 "IBM Security helps Wimbledon focus on the court, not the cloud," IBM Security, October 25, 2017, https://www.youtube.com/watch?v=m-hq2aOMeuE.

CHAPTER 5

The Impact of AI on Jobs

"It is unworthy of excellent men to lose hours like slaves in the labor of calculation, which could safely be regulated to anyone else if machines were used. . . . How much better will it be to bring under mathematical laws human reasoning, which is the most excellent and useful thing we have."

— Gottfried Wilhelm Leibniz, 1685, coinventor of calculus

"There certainly will be job disruption. Because what's going to happen is robots will be able to do everything better than us. . . . I mean all of us,"

— Elon Musk, 2017

"Romanticizing . . .the loss of jobs to technology is little better than complaining antibiotics put too many grave diggers out of work."

— Garry Kasparov, 2018

MACHINES TAKING HUMAN JOBS

With so much opportunity for AI in business covered in the last chapter, it begs the question, what will be the impact on jobs? Indeed, the President of the United States received this grave warning about the potential for machines to cause mass unemployment. It came from the Ad

Hoc Committee on the Triple Revolution, which included three Nobel Peace Prize winners:

> A new era of production has begun. Its principles of organization are as different from the industrial era as those of the industrial era were from the agricultural. The . . . revolution has been brought about by the computer and automated self-regulating machine. This results in a system of unlimited productive capacity, which requires progressively less human labor.

But this was not a recent warning. The president was Lyndon B. Johnson and the year, 1964. Concerns about the impact of machines on jobs go back a long way. In the nineteenth century, the Luddites, a band of British mill workers, tried to hold onto farming jobs by smashing agricultural machinery.

Today, governments and institutions are again worried about machines taking jobs. Andy Haldane, chief economist of the Bank of England, has said the UK can expect massive job displacement from AI on a scale as large as that arising from the Industrial Revolution.

> "Each of those [industrial revolutions] had a wrenching and lengthy impact on the jobs market, on the lives and livelihoods of large swathes of society. Jobs were effectively taken by machines of various types; there was a hollowing out of the jobs market, and that left a lot of people for a lengthy period out of work and struggling to make a living. . . . That hollowing out is going to be potentially on a much greater scale in the future, when we have machines both thinking and doing—replacing both the cognitive and the technical skills of humans. . . . What we can, I think, say with some confidence, however, is that given that the scale of job loss displacement, it is likely to be at least as large as that of the first three industrial revolutions." [89]

89 "Bank of England chief economist warns on AI jobs threat, BBC.com, August 29, 2018, https://www.bbc.com/news/business-45240758.

WILL AI CAUSE MASS UNEMPLOYMENT?

Academics have warned about the potential of AI to cause mass job displacement. In 2013, an influential paper by Oxford University academics Carl Frey and Michael Osborne warned that about 47 percent of jobs in the United States were at high risk of being automated.[90] They also found that wages and educational attainment exhibit a strong negative relationship with an occupation's probability of computerization, meaning those jobs most at risk are at the lower rungs of society. Frey and Osborne's research set the tone for much of the pessimistic debate over automation that ensued.

In 2015, futurist Martin Ford, in his book *Rise of the Robots*, took the implications of AI automation a step further and argued AI will lead to mass unemployment. Ford argued that while the previous technological revolutions displaced manual laborers, the AI revolution is different because it also threatens the jobs of skilled workers. Ford pointed to the lack of employment in new companies, such as Instagram. The social media powerhouse was acquired by Facebook for $1 billion, while, remarkably, it had only 13 full-time employees. Ford made the case that a universal basic income (UBI) will be required to cope with mass unemployment caused by AI.

Business heavyweights such as Sir Richard Branson, Mark Zuckerberg and Elon Musk have discussed universal basic income as a serious policy proposal. Andrew Yang, a successful Silicon Valley entrepreneur and philanthropist, is a US 2020 presidential candidate, with UBI as the primary plank of his platform. And a research organization associated with Y Combinator is running a UBI pilot program that gives a thousand families a stipend of thousands dollars every month for five years in Oakland, California.

Google cofounder Larry Page put forward an alternative way to deal with scarce work in the AI Age. Page advocated both a four-day work-

90 "The Future of Employment: How Susceptible Are Jobs to Computerisation," Oxford Martin School, University of Oxford, September 17, 2013, https://www.oxfordmartin.ox.ac.uk/downloads/academic/The_Future_of_Employment.pdf.

week or job sharing, which entails multiple people sharing the same job. In the latter, a single full-time job would be split into several part-time jobs, which results in reduced pay for each worker. So, in essence, this is a proposal for mass underemployment as a solution for mass unemployment.

DIGITAL UTOPIA

Some see the advent of potential AI-generated mass unemployment as a great issue of our times. I will refer to this idea as AI-phobia. Others see it as offering a potential paradise or a Digital Athens, a term coined by MIT computer science professor Erik Brynjolfsson. Ancient Athenians enjoyed new advantages such as leisure and democracy because they had slaves to take care of manual work. In the same way, AI could provide robot slaves that would take over the monotonous, repetitive work and free us to fulfill ourselves. Over 2,300 years ago in Athens, Aristotle (384–322 BCE) extraordinarily foresaw this potentiality. In his book *Politics*, he wrote:

> For suppose that every tool we had could perform its task, either at our bidding or itself perceiving the need, and if, like—the tripods of Hephaestus, of which the poet (that is, Homer) says that "self-moved they enter the assembly of gods"—shuttles in a loom could fly to and fro and a plucker (the tool used to pluck strings) play a lyre of their own accord, then master craftsman would have no need of servants nor masters of slaves.[91]

Aristotle's incredible prescience notwithstanding, I think an even more fitting analogy is a Digital Communist Utopia because Karl Marx's depiction of working lives in a communist system appears strikingly similar to an AI Age that frees human beings from cognitive and manual tasks. This seems especially apt given that the idea of a universal basic income resonates with communist ideals of income equality:

91 "The Internet Classics Archive, *Politics*, Aristotle," http://classics.mit.edu/Aristotle/politics.html.

> In communist society, where nobody has one exclusive sphere of activity but each can become accomplished in any branch he wishes, society regulates the general production and thus makes it possible for me to do one thing today and another tomorrow, to hunt in the morning, fish in the afternoon, rear cattle in the evening, criticize after dinner, just as I have a mind, without ever becoming hunter, fisherman, shepherd, or critic. [92]

But alas, a life free from work may not be arriving anytime soon. More recent analysis suggests this digital utopia may not be in the cards. Newer studies have brought down significantly the share of jobs at risk to AI automation. In the 2016 OECD study, 'The Risk of Automation for Jobs in OECD Countries,"[93] by Melanie Arntz, Ulrich Zierhan and Terry Gregory, the authors put this figure at 9 percent in the United States. Only a fraction of the 47 percent estimate provided by Oxford University academics Carl Frey and Michael Osborne; nonetheless, 9 percent still translates to about 13 million jobs across the United States alone.

The OECD study across 32 countries found close to one in two jobs are likely to be significantly affected by automation, based on the tasks they involve. But the degree of risk varies. About 14 percent of jobs in OECD countries are highly automatable (i.e., have a 70 percent-plus probability of automation). Why such a difference? The OECD researchers challenged Osborne and Frey's occupation-based approach. They pointed out that specific tasks will be automated rather than whole jobs. Taking a task-based approach reduces the number of jobs at risk significantly. However, the OECD analysis is still equivalent to more than 66 million workers being displaced by AI in the 32 countries studied. This would lead to huge job displacement, and it would cause regional imbalances since AI-caused job losses are unlikely to be distributed equally across countries.

92 "Marx's Vision of Communism," The Writings of Bertell Ollman, NYU.edu, https://www.nyu.edu/projects/ollman/docs/vision_of_communism.php.

93 "The Risk of Automation for Jobs in OECD Countries: A Comparative Analysis," Melanie Arntz, Ulrich Zierhan and Terry Gregory, OECD, https://www.oecd-ilibrary.org/social-issues-migration-health/the-risk-of-automation-for-jobs-in-oecd-countries_5jlz9h56dvq7-en.

FOR EVERY JOB LOST, A NEW ONE CREATED

Nonetheless, from a historical perspective, we need not fear technological unemployment. Since the Industrial Revolution, for every job lost to a machine, a new one has been created. In the journal article, "Why Are There Still So Many Jobs: The History and Future of Workplace Automation," [94] MIT economics professor David Autor makes a strong case that fears about AI job displacement are overblown. He argues that people often underestimate the adaptability of the market and workforce. For example, in 1900, 41 percent of the US workforce was employed in agriculture; by 2000, that share had fallen to 2 percent, mostly due to a wide range of technologies, including automated machinery. But during that period, jobs were created in other sectors, such as industry, and the average standard of living improved massively. As Ray Kurzweil recounts:

> How did that last Industrial Revolution work out? Two hundred years ago, the weavers had enjoyed a guild that was passed down from generation to generation for hundreds of years. Their business model was turned on its head and disrupted when all these thread-spinning and cloth-weaving machines came out that completely upended their livelihoods. They predicted that more machines would come out and that most people would lose their jobs, and that employment would be enjoyed just by an elite. Part of that prediction came true—more textile machines were introduced and many types of skills and jobs were eliminated. However, employment went up, not down as society became more prosperous. [95]

IS THIS TIME DIFFERENT?

The counter argument, summed up by Yuval Noah Harari, is "this time could be different" since artificial intelligence challenges not just manual labor, as the Industrial Revolution did, but also skilled, cognitive

94 "Why Are There Still So Many Jobs: The History and Future of Workplace Automation," *Journal of Economic Perspectives,* Summer 2015, https://economics.mit.edu/files/11563.

95 Martin Ford, *Architects of Intelligence.*

work. This doesn't leave much work for human beings. There are basically two things human beings can do, manual work and cognitive work. The Luddites, who smashed farming machinery, were overly pessimistic about the impact of the Industrial Revolution, which took away many manual jobs. Today, no one would want to till the fields by hand or wash industrial quantities of laundry by hand , and people happily pass such manual work to tractors and washing machines. But as vast swathes of white collar cognitive jobs are taken, it is less clear what work will be left for human beings to do. Cognitive automation, in the eyes of the AI-phobic, is the greatest threat to human employment in history.

However, there is a lack of evidence supporting the belief that cognitive automation will lead to mass unemployment. For example, automated teller machines, a.k.a. ATMs, took away the cognitive tasks of bank tellers. ATMs were introduced in the 1970s, and they quadrupled in the United States from approximately 100,000 in 1995 to 400,000 in 2010. Following Harari's logic, we might naturally assume that these machines had all but eliminated bank tellers in this period. But actually US bank teller employment increased in this interval from 500,000 to approximately 550,000.

Another example of cognitive automation is the spreadsheet, invented by Dan Bricklin, who was frustrated at doing repeated calculations for his Harvard MBA case studies. His invention of VisiCalc for the Apple II computer reduced the time it took to make calculations by one hundredfold. There were 400,000 bookkeepers in the US paid to do this cognitive task in the 1970s, only to see their work replaced by the spreadsheet. Again, following Ford or Harari's logic, we would assume the invention of the spreadsheet put them out of work. But there are today over 1 million more bookkeepers in the US than before the arrival of the digital spreadsheet.

The actual experience of cognitive automation suggests that, like manual automation, it eliminates some tasks, even possibly some jobs, but not total work or employment. Take a lesson from chess. Garry Kasparov was worried when he faced IBM's Deep Blue in 1997 that a loss could put him out of work. But although AI chess programs now completely dominate human players, chess grand masters are still playing tournaments. Actually, the chess sector is growing, and the number of human beings who play chess worldwide is estimated in the hundreds of millions. Chess programs and human players have found a synthesis as technology is used in training and to enhance the overall standard of play.

LESSONS FROM THE DIGITAL AGE

Another AI-phobic argument is that the speed of the AI revolution will be much faster than any previous technological transformation. Electricity and the steam engine each took decades to impact employment, but many fear AI will hit so fast and hard that we will not be able to cope. First of all, it is not clear this is true. Management consultants McKinsey & Company looked up massive job losses over the past 200 years and predicted the next 20 years are within the norm. The digital revolution also impacted extremely quickly with a major effect on jobs, but, once again, workers adapted. The digital age exemplifies the adaptiveness of the market and how quickly we create new jobs, even new industries and new cultures. The tech start-up is an entirely new form of company. Few people in the 1980s or even the 1990s had heard of venture capital investors nor had they expected them to be paired with MBAs and software programmers. A whole new corporate culture emerged as we went from the culture of Ricky Gervais' *Office* of 1997, with paper salesman in suits, to the Google campus of 2019 with trendy engineers in T-shirts and sneakers. The digital age brought new jobs such as programmers, web designers, software developers, social media managers and all their various and strange Java to Python specializations. It changed the role of the jobs that remained, affecting digital marketers to spreadsheet accountants. As Daniela Rus, director of CSAIL at MIT, puts it:

> Only 10 years ago, when the computer industry was booming, nobody predicted the [current] level of employment in social media, in app stores, in cloud computing and even in other things like

> college counselling. There are so many jobs that employ a lot of people today that did not exist 10 years ago and that people did not anticipate would exist. I think that it's exciting to think about the possibilities for the future and the new kinds of jobs that will be created as a result of technology.[96]

The digital age did not bring mass unemployment. It did not even bring unemployment. Martin Ford was right that Instagram, with its scant 13 employees, sold for $1 billion, but he was wrong if he thought these digital companies are leading to unemployment. In fact, unemployment is at record low levels in the developed world. In the US, the home market of Instagram, unemployment fell to 3.6 percent in March 2019, the lowest level since 1969.[97]

Had businesspeople been told in 1990 that the digital age would tear apart huge industries like print publishing, that giants like Kodak and Blockbuster would go bust and that huge parts of the workforce would have to retrain to fill new digital jobs, then they may have been just as fearful then as they are of AI today. Business adapted to the digital age, and it can adapt to the AI Age, too. It certainly is challenging for an experienced coal miner to learn new skills as a software programmer. But for the miner's children, software programming is a natural career choice. It is as natural as it was when coal mines were first opened and farmhands found they had to go underground and labor amid black coal dust to earn a living.

In fact, Bit Source in rural Pikeville, Kentucky, a town in the heart of Central Appalachia's coal mining country, has retrained coal miners as data miners, proving that, with the right support, as the company says, "former coal miners can successfully transition to the high-tech world of custom software development." [98]

---

96 Martin Ford, *Architects of Intelligence.*

97 "Jobs surge in April, unemployment rate falls to the lowest since 1969," CNBC.com, May 13, 2019, https://www.cnbc.com/2019/05/03/nonfarm-payrolls-april-2019.html.

98 "Hillibillies who code: The former miners out to put Kentucky on the map," Theguardian.com, April 21, 2017, https://www.theguardian.com/us-news/2017/apr/21/tech-industry-coding-kentucky-hillbillies.

Human beings are immensely adaptable. We who have transitioned from hunting in tribes to farming in towns to industrialization in cities to digitization in great metropolises can transition again to the AI Age. Every new generation has transitioned to something new. They have not done so reluctantly but have actively sought out change. Each generation seeks to be different from its predecessor. In our culture, our music, our fashion, our language, our jobs, we seek to differentiate ourselves from our parents. Every generation seeks to reinvent itself and feels itself a failure if it doesn't achieve something new, futuristic and most important, very different from what generations before have achieved. This is fundamental driver of human behavior. Homer said in The Iliad around 1,200 years ago:

> As is the generation of leaves, so is that of humanity.
> The wind scatters the leaves on the ground, but the live timber
> Burgeons with leaves again in the season of spring returning.
> So one generation of men will grow while another dies.
> —Homer, The Iliad [99]

Irish poet John Montague echoed Homer in his poem, "The Living & the Dead":

> The sap of another generation
> fingering through a broken tree
> to push fresh branches
> towards a further light,
> a different identity.
> —John Montague (1929–2016), from "The Living & The Dead"[100]

Our children will not want to live in our world. To them, the digital age, as new and exciting as it seems to us, will be the epitome of boredom and tedium. They will want to break the mold. The changes wrought by the AI Age will not be a burden to them but a gift. They would not have it any

99 "The Iliad Mortality Quotes," Shmoop.com, https://www.shmoop.com/iliad/mortality-quotes-2.html.
100 John Montague, *Selected Poems*, Toronto: Exile Editions Limited, 1982, 1991.

other way. The coming generations do not want our old world, so we need not grieve its loss on their behalf.

THE LIFE AND DEATH OF COMPANIES

The nature of business, like life, is change. The vast majority of companies today won't exist in a few years. This is not because of AI or digitization but because this has always been the case. Distinguished physicist Geoffrey West demonstrates in his book *Scale* that companies live and die like organisms. Of the 28,853 companies that traded on the US stock market in 1950, 22,469, or 78 percent, were defunct by 2009. Of these, 45 percent were acquired or had merged with other companies, while 9 percent were liquidated or went bankrupt, 3 percent had been privatized, 0.5 percent had undergone a leveraged buyout and 0.5 percent reversed acquisitions. The remainder disappeared for other reasons. He suggests a universal dynamic of business life cycles:

> In other words, the general dynamics and overall life of companies are effectively independent of the business sector they operate in. This strongly suggests there is a universal dynamic at play. . . . This really is quite amazing. [101]

West explains the reason companies die is that in their youth, new ideas and enthusiasm flourish, but as old age kicks in, they narrow product spacc and bccome more specialized. Market forces encourage tried and tested products over new products, which are more risky but better long term. They become more unidimensional without diversity, which makes them less resilient such that configuring and reinventing becomes increasingly more expensive. So when a large enough unanticipated shock comes along, they are at risk for a buyout, takeover or bankruptcy and die. Human beings and companies are finely balanced between metabolism and maintenance costs. In people, this is known as homeostasis; the gradual buildup of unrepaired damage makes us less resilient and increasingly vulnerable to fluctuations and perturbations as we age. A case of

101 Geoffrey West, *Scale: The Universal Laws of Life, Growth, and Death in Organisms, Cities and Companies*, Penguin Random House, New York: Penguin Random House, 2018.

the flu or pneumonia, which we can fight off in our youth, can kill us in old age. West explains:

> Just as organisms must die in order that new may blossom, so it is that all companies must disappear or morph into new, innovative variations to flourish: better to have the excitement and innovation of a Google or Tesla than the stagnation of a geriatric IBM or General Motors. . . . This also means Google and Tesla, which now seem invincible, will themselves eventually fade and disappear. From this point of view, we should not lament the passing of any company—it's an essential component of economic life. [102]

Interestingly, of the 5,586 companies that have survived more than two hundred years (3,146 in Japan, 837 in Germany, 222 in the Netherlands, 196 in France) 90 percent of these had fewer than three hundred employees. It appears these companies managed to find an equilibrium.

THE EVOLUTION OF JOBS

As companies live and die, so, too, will jobs. This is a natural part of the life and death of companies. There is no need to mourn the loss of companies. As we discovered in Chapter 2, Thomas Malone, founding director of the MIT Center for Collective Intelligence, argues in his book *Superminds* that individuals come together into organizations such as companies to form collective intelligences, which have their own consciousness. Apple, for example, was said by its CEO, Tim Cook, to be conscious, to have goals, values and more. So if companies have consciousness, and live and die like organisms, then, of course, jobs will die with them and new jobs will be born. Following this logic, we would expect new jobs to be created at new companies and jobs to decay at old companies, and that is exactly what we find.

To understand why AI will not cause mass unemployment, we need to understand where jobs come from. What we see is that jobs are like crops, they can be planted and sown, harvested and then they decay, while

102 Geoffrey West, *Scale*.

new jobs are grown to take their place. Technologies are like sunlight and wind for new jobs: They blow new seeds on the fields; this helps new jobs grow and squeezes out the old but never takes away the work altogether. We began this chapter with a reference to US President Lyndon B. Johnson's 1960s commission on machines making jobs redundant. It concluded reassuringly: "The basic fact is that technology eliminates jobs, not work,"[103] a point that still holds true today.

PUBLIC-SECTOR JOBS

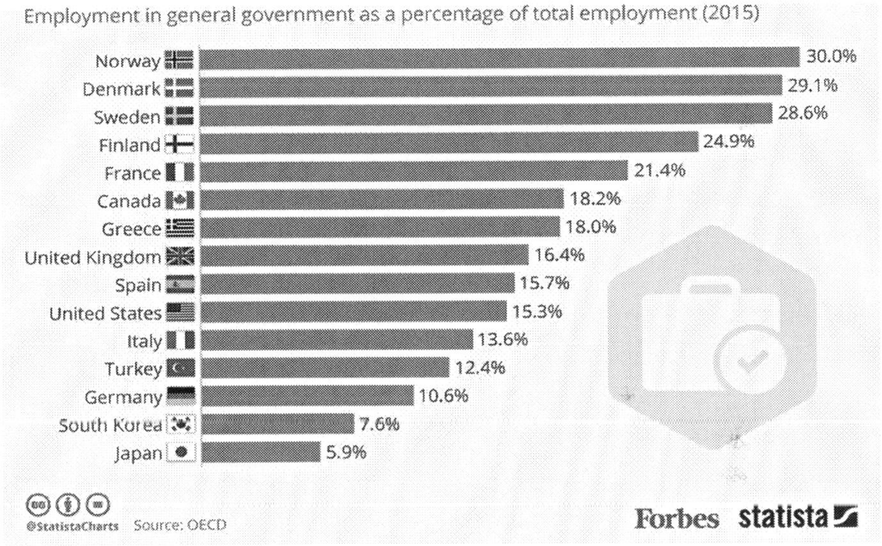

Figure 11: employment in general government as a percentage of total employment, source Statista

The first major source of jobs is in the public sector. The percentage of the population employed in the public sector is pronounced in Norway, with the highest government employment levels, where it reaches 30 percent of total employment. The size of public-sector workforces are also above average in the remainder of Scandinavia: Denmark, 29.1 percent; Sweden, 28.6 percent; and Finland, 24.9 percent. In North America, 18.2 percent of Canada's workforce is employed by the government, while in

103 "Why Are There Still So Many Jobs: The History and Future of Workplace Automation," *Journal of Economic Perspectives*, Summer 2015, https://economics.mit.edu/files/11563.

the United States, the share is slightly lower at 15.3 percent. Austerity policies after the 2008 financial crisis resulted in developed countries cutting back their public-sector workforces in recent years, but their share is still substantially higher than in many Asian countries. In South Korea, 7.6 percent of the total workforce is part of the government, while in Japan, the third biggest economy in the world, the share is only 5.9 percent.

These public-sector jobs are created by taxpayers. As long as governments are able to collect taxes, there will remain every opportunity for these jobs in the AI Age. These jobs serve social purposes and social causes have no limit. Even if AI technologies were to take over jobs in the public sector, such as administrative roles, the public sector can always offer the population solutions for more happiness, less suffering and more support. In fact, mental health crises, abuse, poverty and crime levels in our current societies suggest social jobs and desires are severely underserved in every country.

AI will generate wealth and spur productivity, promising more revenues for taxation. This wealth may be concentrated in fewer hands, but this presents a challenge for taxation and redistribution policy—a challenge requiring more public-sector jobs to resolve it. Therefore, countries with fewer public-sector jobs in the future may not be those being transformed by AI. But, instead, those that do not have AI because these will be less competitive, and, as a result, have lower growth and fewer tax receipts to spend on public-sector jobs. As Stuart J. Russell, an AI visionary who teaches computer science at the University of California, Berkeley, explains:

> In the long run, even though machines will be doing a lot of goods and basic services like transportation, there are still things that people can do which improve the quality of life for themselves and others. There are people who are able to teach, to inspire people to live richer, more interesting, more varied and more fulfilling lives, whether that's teaching people to appreciate literature or music, how to build, or even how to survive in the wilderness. Those services may be coaching, they may be teaching, they may

> be consoling, or maybe collaborating, so that we can all really have a fantastic future. It's not a grim future at all: It's a far better future than we have at present, but it requires rethinking our education system, our science base, our economic structures. [104]

PRIVATE-SECTOR JOBS

The other major source of jobs responsible for the remaining 70 percent to 95 percent of jobs in most countries is the private sector. Not long ago, the US-based Kauffman Foundation and Canada's Institute for Competitiveness & Prosperity each tried to find out where new private-sector jobs come from: Kauffman in 2015, the Canadian institute in 2012. The surprising truth both found independently is that over the last twenty-five years almost all private-sector jobs have been created by businesses less than five years old. Big companies have been destroyers of jobs. Steve Denning, commenting on the studies in Forbes wrote:

> In fact, between 1988 and 2011 . . . companies more than five years old destroyed more jobs than they created in all but eight of those years. Both on average and for all but seven years between 1977 and 2005, existing firms are net job destroyers, losing 1 million jobs net combined per year. By contrast, in their first year, new firms add an average of 3 million jobs.[105]

Not every start-up manages to survive; roughly a third will close by their second year, while half will make it to their fifth year. This means the jobs that many firms create at birth will subsequently disappear. The remaining start-ups, the 50 percent that survive until age five, represent our major source of net job creation. According to the Kauffman study, "New businesses account for nearly all net new job creation and almost 20 percent of gross job creation." [106]

104 Martin Ford, *Architects of Intelligence.*

105 "The Surprising Truth About Where New Jobs Come From," Forbes.com, October 29, 2014, https://www.forbes.com/sites/stevedenning/2014/10/29/the-surprising-truth-about-where-new-jobs-come-from/

106 "The Importance of Young Firms for Economic Growth," Kauffman.org, September 13, 2015, https://www.kauffman.org/what-we-do/resources/entrepreneurship-policy-digest/the-importance-of-young-firms-for-economic-growth.

So old companies are net destroyers of new jobs, and new businesses are the major source of new net job creation, just as we would expect from companies that have life spans like organisms. Jobs are like branches on trees; they grow on new companies. Old and unloved jobs decay and fall off. As AI creates disruption and transformation, it will present a challenge to the status quo and opportunity for new businesses. AI is planting new trees, laying seeds and fertilizing the land, enabling new businesses that are responsible for net job growth to sprout.

AI IS ALREADY HERE

This has been the AI jobs story so far. After all, there are already AI applications in many of the world's major companies. One study showed that, from 1990 to 2007, some 670,000 US jobs were taken over by robots. If you are an Uber driver today or a Deliveroo worker, an AI is even your boss because your working day is decided by a computer algorithm. AI is the foundational tech for many of the world's most successful companies, from Amazon and Apple to Google, Facebook and Netflix. So is AI causing unemployment today? Well, actually, the opposite is true. The record low unemployment figures in the US and Canada[107] and the record employment figures in the UK, where more people are employed than ever before, show not only the resilience of jobs in the digital age but also the resilience of jobs at the beginning of the AI Age. Advanced economies that have developed and employed AI technologies have not seen unemployment rising; instead, it is falling.

MAN AND MACHINE

Paul Daugherty and H. James Wilson, two leaders of Accenture, the multinational professional services company, explain in their book *Human + Machine: Reimagining Work in the Age of AI* the reason that AI is not and will not in future lead to mass unemployment. They argue that AI's greatest power is in "complementing and augmenting" human capabilities, not in replacing the need for humans. In the AI Age, they say, machines do

107 "Unemployment Rates Around the World," GFmag.com, November 1 2018, https://www.gfmag.com/global-data/economic-data/worlds-unemployment-ratescom.

what they do best—the grunt work, repetitive tasks and analyzing data, and humans do what they do best—resolving ambiguous information, exercising judgment and dealing with customers. Repetitive work makes humans feel like robots, so AI is freeing humans from these tasks, which "allows humans to be more human," [108] the authors say.

Daugherty and Wilson believe AI is empowering a business-process revolution, even greater than industrial mass production and digitization, where machines work at the service of man. AI systems are amplifying human skills and collaborating with us to achieve productivity gains not previously considered possible. Humans and machines are not adversaries in this new world but partners pushing each other to higher levels and completing each other's capabilities.

AN ENGINE FOR JOB CREATION

AI is also an engine for job creation. For example, a recent study looked into a California tech start-up that found itself growing so fast its computing systems kept getting larger and more complex. Such growth required the company to constantly draft more humans to monitor, manage and interpret the data.[109]

James Manyika, chairman of McKinsey Global Institute, McKinsey & Company's research arm, reveals that of the 800 or so occupations in the US Bureau of Labor Statistics database, there is a category called "other," which has become the "fastest-growing occupational category because we're constantly inventing occupations that didn't exist before," [110] Manyika says. If you look at 10-year periods in the United States, at least 8 percent to 9 percent of jobs didn't exist in the previous period because they were just invented. The question is whether the number of jobs gained thanks to AI will total more than the jobs lost. According to

108 Nick Bostrom, *Superintelligence. Paths, Dangers, Strategies*, 46

109 "The Co-existence of Machines and Humans Is the Way Forward," Huffpost.com, December 6, 2017, https://www.huffingtonpost.co.uk/entry/the-co-existence-of-machines-and-humans-is-the-way-forward_uk_5a1ef334e4b0e37da0447bde.

110 Martin Ford, *Architects of Intelligence.*

Manyika, McKinsey's analysis shows that, "We will come out ahead, that there will be more jobs gained than jobs lost, unless, of course, some variables change catastrophically underneath us." [111]

PricewaterhouseCoopers, one of the Big Four auditors, sees a jobs uptick as well. In reviewing the UK market, PwC found that over the next 20 years, AI will create more jobs than it displaces. AI will displace about 7 million jobs over the next 20 years, the company says, but, importantly, AI will create 7.2 million new jobs over the same period. Ultimately, the overall effect on the UK economy will be positive. Perhaps fears about robots taking our jobs have been misplaced after all. John Hawksworth, chief economist at PwC UK, says:

> Major new technologies, from steam engines to computers, displace some existing jobs but also generate large productivity gains. This reduces prices and increases real income and spending levels, which, in turn, creates demand for additional workers. Our analysis suggests the same will be true of AI, robots and related technologies.[112]

There will be whole new categories of new jobs in the future. Human + Machine details new jobs we can expect, such as the "machine relations manager," who would be similar to a human resources manager but who would actually oversee AI systems instead of human workers. There could also be trainers like the vehicle design anthropologist at Nissan, whose job is to help machines learn human characteristics, such as teaching self-driving cars to know when to break the rules for the greater good.

An empathy trainer may be another new job; that person would help teach machines to display compassion as chatbots and personal assistants are already being trained to respond with sympathy to human questions. There will be explainers, such as the algorithm forensic analyst who is

111 Martin Ford, *Architects of Intelligence.*

112 "Those stories about AI taking our jobs might be dead wrong," Mashable.com, July 17, 2018, https://mashable.com/article/ai-new-jobs/.

responsible for explaining the black box results of an algorithm and holding it to account. An explicability strategist would decide what AI or other system to use to explain how results have been obtained. Finally, there will be sustainers, such as AI safety engineers, that try to anticipate any harmful unintended consequences of an AI system.

SKILL GAPS

We see that just as the digital revolution gave us many new roles such as the digital marketing manager, website designers and software developers, the AI revolution will also create many new jobs. "Great," I hear you say perhaps a tad sarcastically, "but there won't be anyone qualified to do these new AI jobs."

The AI Age will certainly create major gaps in skills, but again from a historical perspective we need not underestimate the ability of the workforce to retrain. As David Autor says:

> In 1900, the typical young, native-born American had only a common school education, about the equivalent of sixth to eighth grades. By the late 19th century, many Americans recognized that this level of schooling was inadequate: farm employment was declining, industry was rising, and their children would need additional skills to earn a living. The United States responded to this challenge over the first four decades of the 20th century by becoming the first nation in the world to deliver universal high school education to its citizens (Goldin and Katz 2008). Tellingly, the high school movement was led by the farm states. Societal adjustments to earlier waves of technological advancement were neither rapid and automatic nor cheap. But they did pay off handsomely. [113]

We are absolutely on the verge of a massive upheaval as the AI Age arrives, on a par with what we experienced when the Industrial Revo-

113 Claudia Goldin and Lawrence F. Katz, *The Race Between Education and Technology*, Cambridge, Massachusetts: Harvard University Press, 2010.

lution arrived. But human beings are adaptable. Immensely adaptable. Yuval Noah Harari, who is AI-phobic in terms of his perception of jobs, still believes humans will adapt to the AI Age. He explains in his book Sapiens that human beings are born unfinished. Horses can walk when they are born but humans are vulnerable; we need our parents' constant attention to nurture us. Why are we born unfinished? Because this makes us adaptable. We could be born an Inuit living in an igloo in the Arctic cold, or we could be born into a family of bankers in New York City. In each case, we adapt to our environment.

A child born in the AI Age will not feel out of place, just as a child born in the digital age does not feel out of place. In fact, babies and children become more digitally immersed from younger ages than their parents. The same will be true for AI. Today's children are no longer digital natives, they are AI natives. They will grow up interacting with intelligent machines. This will shape their world outlook. Millennials have been known for their differences as the first digital-native generation. Children born now are the first generation of the AI Age, and their outlook, relationship with technology and adaptability to AI will be significantly different than their parents'.

RETRAINING

The good news is that the information revolution means it has never been easier to retrain or adapt. The AI Age will not be displacing humans with pens and pencils but humans with powerful technologies at their fingertips. Information tools such as the internet, mobile phone and search engines represent ubiquitous human intelligence enhancements. A human being plus Google has access to more information than the most knowledgeable human being in the world. Retraining that once took time, such as visiting a library or attending a training course in person, is now immediate, accessible anywhere and costs little or nothing.

At Coursera, a leading platform offering massive open online courses (MOOCs), I can pull up a course from Harvard, MIT or Oxford University in seconds and train myself on my mobile phone anywhere in the world. MOOCs like Coursera have proven so popular that the global market for them is projected to grow from $3.9 billion in 2018 to $20.8 billion in 2023. With incredible resources like this, thousands can be trained, or retrained, quickly. People today have at their fingertips the knowledge they need to adapt to AI.

In the future, AI itself can also be used for retraining on a scale never before seen. AI can provide personalized education systems that can act as personal tutors, offering affordable one-to-one education for the first time. These systems will be available on the private market, but there is also a key role governments play in providing public education and retraining. They could, however, be doing much more, especially in the West. A 2016 report entitled Artificial Intelligence, Automation and the Economy states that the United States spends only 0.1 percent of GDP on programs that help people adjust to workforce changes. In contrast, part of China's strategy to become the preeminent AI nation by 2030 involves major investments in retraining workers for a new economy based on machines and humans working together as the normal production and service mode.

A PRODUCTIVITY BOOST

AI will, indeed, boost productivity in all major advanced economies. Accenture's "Why Artificial Intelligence is the Future of Growth" analyzed twelve developed economies and found that AI has the potential to double their annual economic growth rates by 2035. Across the globe, rates of gross domestic product (GDP) growth have been shrinking. Moreover, this has been true for three decades. Economists had argued that productivity growth over the next quarter century will continue at the sluggish pace we have experienced since 2004. Great inventions, such as the steamship and telegraph, had not been repeated. And this deficit of innovation, combined with unfavorable demographic trends, flagging educational attainment and rising wealth inequality, slowed economic progress for the foreseeable future.

AI promises to reverse this trend, and it promises massive productivity gains to economies just when they need them most. McKinsey found that over the past fifty years, of the 3.5 percent average GDP growth over that period, 1.7 percent has come from expansion in the labor supply and 1.8 percent from productivity growth. In the next fifty years, aging populations and other demographic effects will result in the labor supply expanding by a dismal 0.3 percent. So productivity will need to improve substantially to maintain the rate of economic growth we've become accustomed to [114]. Therefore, the great productivity gains AI promises are coming just when they are needed.

RISING INEQUALITY

The problem is that productivity boosts and wealth creation may not be shared equally. The world is becoming more equal in the sense that absolute poverty is declining, and the gap between poor and wealthy nations is closing. However, relative inequality is rising within developed economies. For example, in 1965, the top CEOs in the US earned twenty times the average salary, but by 2019 they earned a staggering 312 times the average salary. AI could continue this trend of wage stagnation, captured by Thomas Piketty in his book *Capital in the Twenty-First Century.* The book's central thesis is that when the rate of return on capital is greater than the rate of economic growth, over the long term, the result is concentration of wealth, and this unequal distribution of wealth causes growing inequality, and social and economic instability.

Erik Brynjolfsson, director of the MIT Initiative on the Digital Economy, argues the digital age exacerbates such inequality for three main reasons:

1. It replaces old jobs (the ones that were available to the uneducated) with technology.
2. It confers more financial reward on company owners.
3. It creates more superstars that benefit disproportionately, such as Mark Zuckerberg, 34, who is now worth $65 billion, or J.K. Rowling the first billionaire author.

114 Martin Ford, *Architects of Intelligence.*

I would add a fourth reason: The new global tech giants have found clever ways to reduce the amount of tax they pay. A recent report from the European Commission indicated that tech companies pay less than half the tax of traditional, brick-and-mortar businesses. The report explained that digital businesses are able to take up a stateless "free rider" position, offering services and products to consumers in one country while claiming to be based in another tax jurisdiction.

As governments receive less tax from digital superstars, inevitably it effects redistribution of wealth, resulting in more inequality. Certainly, the nature of the AI Age will be similar to the digital age in terms of its potential impacts on inequality. The AI Age will reward founders and investors in companies who, with one technology, could replace thousands of jobs. AI has the potential to create the biggest superstar businesses and entrepreneurs in history. An AI breakthrough in general intelligence, for example, would offer unfathomable wealth and power to its creator. Therefore, wealth that was in the hands of thousands of workers could be placed mainly in the hands of a few AI entrepreneurs and investors.

ENSUING ECONOMIC AND SOCIETAL PROBLEMS

Inequality is problematic because it leads to increased social and health problems. Nations with high income inequality have much higher incidences of crime. A 2002 World Bank study found that crime rates and inequality are positively correlated, and an increase in income inequality has the effect of intensely increasing crime rates. There is also a correlation between income inequality and health and social problems. One study, for example, suggested that the loss of life from income inequality in the US in 1990 was the equivalent of the combined loss of life due to lung cancer, diabetes, motor-vehicle accidents, HIV-related causes, suicide and homicide.[115] The main reason for income inequality's negative effect on health and social problems is believed to be "status anxiety." Society places people in a hi-

115 "Income Inequality and Mortality in Metropolitan Areas of the United States," JW Lynch et al., American Journal of Public Health, July 1998, NIH.gov, https://www.ncbi.nlm.nih.gov/pmc/articles/PMC1508263/.

erarchy that increases status competition and causes stress, which leads to poor health and other negative outcomes.

Inequality is also bad for the economy, since anywhere between 55 percent and 70 percent of the demand in advanced economies is driven by consumer and household spending. So people need to be earning enough to consume what is being produced, or an economy will fall into recession. As Nobel laureate economist Joseph Stiglitz says:

> Consider someone like Mitt Romney, whose income in 2010 was $27.6 million. Even if Romney chose to live a much more indulgent lifestyle, he would spend only a fraction of that sum in typical year to support himself and his wife in their several homes. But take the same amount of money and divide it among 500 people, say, in the form of jobs paying $43,400 apiece and you'll find that almost all the money gets spent. The relationship is straightforward and ironclad: As more money becomes concentrated at the top, aggregate demand goes into decline.

POLICY EFFECTIVENESS

The crucial factor restraining future AI from causing inequality will be public policy, which is effective in reducing inequality through redistribution. Author Thomas Picketty says that in the past, equality rose as a result of political policy. For example, differences in earnings dropped sharply during the 20th century in France, mostly after World War II. The shrinking inequality during this period, Piketty says, resulted from a highly progressive income tax after the war. The lesson is that policy change through progressive taxation can ensure redistribution, and that reduces inequality.

Redistributive policies will need to be reinvented and reshaped for the AI Age. For example, in the UK, the government is considering a digital services tax, which is expected to raise £400 million (US$509 million) per year by 2020. The digital services tax, for the first time, taxes revenue instead of profits in an effort to overcome the problem of tech giants claiming operations in other international jurisdictions. France became the first nation to implement a digital service tax focused on revenues of large tech such as Amazon, Google and Facebook in 2019 to raise around €400 million. Likewise, AI Age governments will have the option to introduce AI services taxes to garner tax receipts that can be used for redistribution.

AI will boost economies. The money is there; it's just a question of how to tax it and redistribute it. Without AI, the money might not even be there to tax. The challenge becomes one of public policy to ensure this wealth is redistributed evenly. As Nobel laureate Herbert Simon wrote during the automation anxiety of the 1960s: "Insofar as they are economic problems at all, the world's problems in this generation and the next are problems of scarcity, not of intolerable abundance. The bogeyman of automation consumes worrying capacity that should be saved for real problems."

IMPROVING DIVERSITY

AI disruption may actually offer a chance to build a better world. In upsetting the status quo, AI may improve areas such as gender inequality. As AI automation takes away left-brain technical jobs, other jobs requiring high emotional Intelligence may be more in demand. Looking at US occupations by gender reveals women predominate in jobs involving relating, caretaking and services, and they make up 80 percent of nurses, teachers and social workers. Empathy skills may become increasingly important in the AI Age, providing more opportunities to women and thereby potentially reducing the gender gap.

NEW JOBS FOR A NEW ERA

AI will cause mass job disruption, but not mass unemployment. Workers will need to find new jobs, retrain and learn to work with AI. Fortunately, the information revolution means it has never been easier to access knowledge to adapt. The evidence suggests that in the short to medium term, there will actually be more new jobs created than jobs lost, along with substantial productivity gains. The wealth will be in the system; the challenge will be how to redistribute it fairly and how to help people adapt. These are major policy challenges for governments, but history tells us these are not insurmountable. If governments are not able to prevent inequality from AI job disruption, then it will be a failure of our political systems rather than a workforce technology issue. As the British godfather of deep learning, Geoffrey Hinton, puts it:

> If you can dramatically increase productivity and make more goodies to go around, that should be a good thing. Whether or not it turns out to be a good thing depends entirely on the social system, and doesn't depend at all on the technology. People are looking at the technology as if the technological advances are a problem. The problem is in the social systems, and whether we're going to have a social system that shares fairly or one that focuses all the improvement on 1 percent and treats the rest of the people like dirt. That has nothing to do with technology. [116]

From this perspective, AI's impact on jobs will be a test for social and political systems, revealing whether they are still fit for their purpose. The inherent benefit for those of us living in democracies is if enough citizens think there needs to be policy change, they can vote for such a change in elections. This built-in feedback loop ensures future governments will respond to future social issues. Democratic societies also have the choice to slow down AI development while ethical issues and industry impacts are resolved. For example, unions representing truck drivers successfully lobbied the US Congress in 2017 to exclude trucks from legislation aimed at speeding up autonomous vehicle development.[117]

China, a less democratic and more authoritarian political system, is adopting a more techno-utilitarian approach to AI. The promotion of a broader social good, with gains in productivity, is seen as good enough reason for some industries and jobs to lose out. China is also taking a

116 Martin Ford, *Architects of Intelligence.*
117 "Union cheers as trucks kept out of U.S. self-driving legislation," Reuters.com, July 28 2017, https://www.reuters.com/article/us-usa-selfdriving-vehicles/union-cheers-as-trucks-kept-out-of-u-s-self-driving-legislation-idUSKBN1AD2S3.

more proactive approach to workforce retraining for the AI Age. China's approach may mean it is able to implement AI more quickly since it doesn't have to wait to resolve ethical dilemmas or sector impacts. China's managed approach is certainly farsighted, but it may fall victim to the inherent difficulties of large-scale state planning.

The most effective approach may be a combination of West and East; techno-utilitarianism combined with government policy to reduce inequality and increase workforce retraining support—but channelled through stimulating private market initiatives rather than large public-sector programs. For example, a highly effective policy for the digital age in the UK has been the EIS scheme, through which taxpayers can gain substantial tax relief by investing in start-ups. This has stimulated the digital sector through private-sector enterprise rather than public-sector programs.

Whatever the policy program adopted, the challenge for governments will be to maximize the wealth and productivity gains from AI, while preventing inequality and uneven impacts leading to unemployment. We should remember this is essentially a challenge of redistribution from wealth creation and productivity gains—fundamentally a challenge of sharing extra wealth—providing good reason to temper pessimism about the impact of AI on jobs in the short and medium term.

In the longer term, with the event of a singularity, all bets are off. The consequences of the singularity and the emergence of human level AI or even a superintelligence will be so profound the impact on employment would be impossible to prejudge. But as brilliant British economist John Maynard Keynes, acidly observed, "In the long run, we are all dead."

CHAPTER 6

Skills For The AI Age

Civilization advances by extending the number of important operations which we can perform without thinking about them".
— Alfred North Whitehead

"Step-by-step, I think it is possible for almost anyone to become great at AI."
— Andrew Ng

"Computers are useless; they can only give you answers."
— Pablo Picasso

Machines will not cause mass unemployment in the foreseeable future, just as they didn't in the past. But AI-invigorated machines will cause fundamental shifts in the economy's mix of jobs. Millions of jobs will be changed, lost and created, transitioning to a new economy in which AI and humans find a new equilibrium. In this chapter, we look at what skills professionals will need in order to navigate this transition effectively with skills for the AI Age.

There are two broad strategies available for workers in the AI Age:

1. **"Focus on AI" by being part of the AI revolution through selling, developing and consulting on AI, or**
2. **"Focus on Humanity" by focusing on the comparative advantages humans have over AI.**

FOCUS ON AI

The first strategic approach is to become one of the harbingers of AI, supporting companies to further this technological revolution. AI will transform economies, but it cannot do so alone. AI requires armies of human workers to plan, develop and deploy AI across the economy. Management guru Peter Drucker, as far back as 1954, outlined how human beings are fundamental to the deployment of machine technology in an economy. His words still ring true today:

> The technological changes now occurring will carry [the Industrial Revolution] a big step further. They will not make human labor superfluous. On the contrary, they will require tremendous numbers of highly skilled and highly trained men—managers to think through and plan, highly trained technicians and workers to design the new tools, to produce them, to maintain them, to direct them. Indeed, the major obstacle to the rapid spread of these changes will almost certainly be the lack, in every country, of enough trained men.

The AI Age will require legions of trained professionals and other workers who do less technical work. Not everyone will become an AI developer or data scientist. It's a bit like digital technology. Everyone working in digital doesn't need to know how to code or develop software to get the most out of digitization in business. In the digital world, professionals need to understand how digital and business interlink and need not undertake technical work like coding. The same will be true for AI. It could create opportunities all up and down the employee spectrum. Such opportunities will range from the highly technical creators of AI to the nontechnical champions of AI. Here is a look at the kinds of opportunities that AI will present.

Data production

Data is the so-called "oil" of the AI Age, and the most lucrative oil has always been produced. Producing oil made billionaires out of men like Rockefeller and Getty. Producing data has made multibillionaires of today's equivalents, among them Mark Zuckerberg, Larry Page and Sergey Brin. Companies like Google and Facebook are so valuable precisely because they generate proprietary data points on all of us. We have volunteered our most valuable possession, our data, in exchange for free access to their platforms.

Shoshana Zuboff, professor emerita at Harvard Business School, describes this in her 2019 book, *The Age of Surveillance Capitalism*, as a fundamental shift in how wealth is created. Rather than extracting "labor surplus" from workers, today's tech giants extract a "behavioral surplus" from their customers. This is "behavioral data we give to tech companies over and above that which they need to make their services work better for us," Zuboff says.

Tech giants do not own all business data. For example, they do not have data on banking transactions or medical operations or manufacturing outputs and much more. There is a universe of untapped data out there waiting for bright sparks to extract it. In the AI Age, entrepreneurs and businesses that find ways to generate proprietary data sources will be extremely successful. That said, the public's concern with loss of privacy may change its relationship with personal data. Governments may step in and further regulate the sale of personal data, which may force companies to use data more responsibly. Even if that happens, data will still be a valuable commodity.

The next step in the data value chain is to be a data refiner; just as oil needs to be refined to have value, so, too, does data need to be worked on. Data scientists that can use statistics and machine learning to analyze data will be increasingly in demand in the AI Age. Indeed, it is already estimated there is a growing shortage of data scientists.[118]

AI consulting and AI training

Technological transformation means change, and helping companies with this transition will require consultants. Businesses need outside help to advise them on how to adapt to the AI Age. Consultancy services across all aspects of this shift will be in demand; everyone from big-name consulting firms to individual freelancers will be needed to perform management to strategic planning, procurement advice and more. The market for AI is just opening up and cannot be filled by in-house talent alone. Jeff Dean, Google's senior vice president for AI, explains:

> There are currently around 10,000 to 20,000 organizations in the world that have hired machine learning expertise in-house and are productively employing it. I'm making up that it's roughly that order of magnitude. Then, if you think about all the organizations in the world that have data that could be used for machine learning, it's probably 10 million organizations that have some sort of machine learning problem. [119]

AI development

Developing AI systems is an obvious growth hot spot. All current AI models need humans to provide the data that trains AI. There are no AI systems that train themselves. While a computer can tweak the architecture and modify some parameters, the overall architecture needs to be designed by a human. This leaves lots of work for AI developers. The benefit of the current information age is anyone can teach themselves AI. As Andrew Ng reasons:

---

118 "IBM Predicts Demand for Data Scientists Will Soar 28% by 2020," Forbes.com, May 13, 2017, https://www.forbes.com/sites/louiscolumbus/2017/05/13/ibm-predicts-demand-for-data-scientists-will-soar-28-by-2020/

119 Martin Ford, *Architects of Intelligence.*

> Because of YouTube video, talk and books, I think it's easier than ever for someone to find materials and study by themselves, just step-by-step. Things don't happen overnight, but step-by-step. I think it's possible for almost anyone to become great at AI. [120]

Entrepreneurship

Becoming an AI entrepreneur is the biggest opportunity in terms of upside potential in the AI Age. The business landscape in the AI Age will be comprised of the leading tech giants, the so-called FANG (Facebook, Amazon, Netflix, Google) plus Microsoft, and the Chinese equivalents (Baidu, WeChat, Alibaba, Tencent and more). But it will also include new AI start-ups that use deep learning to revolutionize specific industries.

Kai-Fu Lee, Chinese AI pioneer, uses the extended metaphor of electricity to explain how this competitive dynamic will play out.[121] It is a contest, he says, between two approaches to distributing "electricity": the "grid" approach of the Seven Giants of corporate AI research (Google, Facebook, Amazon, Microsoft, Baidu, Alibaba, and Tencent) versus the "battery" approach of start-ups.

The grid

The grid is trying to commoditize AI by turning machine learning into a standardized service to be purchased by any company and accessed via cloud computing. The goal of the grid approach is to lower the expertise threshold and increase the functionality of cloud-based AI platforms. For example, Google has launched Google AutoML, which is a low-cost machine-learning platform. This type of automated machine learning makes AI education more available and helps non-data scientists use AI. Fei-Fei Lee, formerly a Google AI researcher and now codirector of Stanford University's Human-Centered AI Institute, explains:

---

120 Martin Ford, *Architects of Intelligence.*

121 Kai-Fu Lee, *AI Superpowers: China, Silicon Valley, and the New World Order*, New York: Houghton Mifflin Harcourt, 2018.

> An example of what we're doing is a product we created that's called AutoML. This is a unique product on the market to really lower the entry barrier of AI as much as possible—so that AI can be delivered to people who don't do AI . . . You bring the training data and we do everything for you. It's been very rewarding to see this democratization of cutting-edge AI.[122]

The battery

AI start-ups are taking the opposite approach. They are building specific AI products for each use case. Rather than general purpose machine learning, they are developing specific solutions and training algorithms for solving tasks. They aim to build AI champions disrupting traditional businesses. For example, Critical Future is pioneering Industrial Vision, software that uses machine vision to watch manufacturing operations and inspect for health and safety. In this specific vertical market software, we can go deeper than the standardized products of Google and so develop winning solutions.

While the tech giants do have access to vast data, they have data relevant for their business; for instance, Google has web search data. But they do not have all the vertical data in specific industries, such as medical diagnosis, life Insurance or manufacturing performance. Because data is verticalized, it is possible to build defensible business models in specific sectors. There is room in the market for many new companies to grow and be extremely successful. The AI Age will bring to life a set of new AI giants, and there will certainly be new faces, as Andrew Ng predicts:

> Look at how big the "start-ups," like Google, Amazon, Baidu and Facebook are now and how they did such as great job building incredibly valuable businesses based on the rise of the internet. With the rise of AI, there will also be some incumbent companies, ironically many of them were start-ups in the previous age. We want to find or create the next Google or Facebook. [123]

122 Martin Ford, *Architects of Intelligence.*

123 Martin Ford, *Architects of Intelligence.*

As Mark Cuban, the self-made tech billionaire, says, "I am telling you, the world's first trillionaires are going to come from somebody who masters AI and all its derivatives and applies it in ways we never thought of." To get to the level of depth needed to make a successful AI start-up, a strong strategy is to combine your own domain expertise in your current job with AI. Many of the key people in AI today came from fields other than pure computer science. Demis Hassabis, the founder of Google's DeepMind, was a neuroscientist, and he achieved success by combining his medical expertise with AI. Andrew Ng explains that professional experience is extremely valuable when combined with AI:

> Advice I tend to give people is that—let's say you're currently a doctor and you want to break into AI. As a doctor, you'd be uniquely positioned to do very valuable work in health care that very few others can do. If you are currently a physicist, see if there are some ideas on AI-applied to physics. If you're a book publisher, see if there's some work you can do with AI in book publishing, because that's one way to leverage your unique strengths and to complete that with AI, rather than competing on a more even playing field with the college grad stepping into AI. [124]

The factories

I would like to add a third layer to Kai-Fu Lee's electricity analogy of supply-side players (grid versus battery), with the demand side being factories. There are millions of businesses that will leverage the power of AI. In fact, there will be more companies that leverage AI than AI suppliers. This means most people will work in the factories that use the AI supplied on the grid and battery sides. So if you are an ordinary worker, the factory is where you will most likely work with AI, in other words, by applying it inside your own company rather than by joining an AI firm.

Just as factories adapted themselves to using electricity and brick and mortar retailers digitized, in the AI Age, companies will make investments

124 Martin Ford, *Architects of Intelligence.*

in AI, by recruiting AI talent themselves or by hiring AI consultancies like Critical Future. These companies will build AI systems that significantly boost their productivity and competitive advantage. As the AI Age takes hold, it will be these companies applying AI to their own businesses that will gain the competitive edge. These AI pioneer companies will be able to operate at a cost and productivity level that their rivals cannot match.

Intrapreneurship

Such AI-enabled companies will require the intrapreneurship of professionals inside organizations to champion AI in their existing businesses. This is where the opportunity for most people to thrive in the AI Age lies—as an AI champion. Not everyone can be an AI developer or a data scientist, or an AI entrepreneur or AI consultant. The economy simply doesn't need that many.

Most professionals will carry on working in large existing businesses in roles we all know today like sales, marketing, finance. But the professionals that succeed will use AI to optimize these functions, such as AI-enabled sales, AI-enabled marketing and AI-enabled finance. You might be a marketing manager who leverages machine learning to increase customer conversion, a sales manager who uses AI to automate data processing or a finance manager who uses AI to predict cash flow. Employees can ensure their own professional success by helping their employers adapt to the AI Age; it will help them gain and maintain a serious competitive advantage.

FOCUS ON HUMANITY

AI division of labor

The second strategic approach to ensure career success in the AI Age is to focus on the competitive edge that humans have over AI. The point is to carve out niche careers in areas where humans have strengths over AI. In the eighteenth-century, Adam Smith coined the term "division of labor" to describe how factories radically altered work and fuelled productivity. The AI Age will bring a new division of labor between humans and AI. Jobs will be divided into the domain of humans and the domain of machines. How can we tell which jobs are best done by AI and which by humans? By looking at the comparative advantage humans and machines have over each other in specific jobs.

Comparative advantage

Herbert Simon, who taught computer science and psychology at the Carnegie Institute of Technology (now Carnegie Mellon), truly understood how economics and computer science are interconnected. Simon won both the highest award in economic theory, the Nobel Prize, and the A.M. Turing Award, the most coveted award in computer science, for his contributions to AI. In the 1960s, Simon's essay "The Corporation: Will it be managed by machines," answered many of the questions still lingering today. Simon showed that predictions of mass unemployment caused by machines are fundamentally flawed by employing political economist David Ricardo's historic principle of comparative advantage.

Developed in the nineteenth century for free trade, Ricardo's model shows that society can always find uses for additional output. Free trade, he said, results in more goods and services produced per person, not unemployment as a result of the increased competition. This is a crucial point. Output does not stay the same, and jobs, goods and services are not finite. When production capacity is increased in the AI Age, through, for example, free trade or machine intelligence, the result will be more goods and services produced per person. This shows why predictions of machine-caused mass unemployment have always been wrong until now and will be wrong again in the future.

But AI will cause a shift in the mix of jobs. In the AI Age economy, the shift will be based on where machines and humans have comparative advantage over each other. As Simon put it:

> If computers are a thousand times faster than bookkeepers in doing arithmetic but only one hundred times faster than stenographers in taking dictation, we shall expect the number of bookkeepers per thousand employees to decrease but the number of stenographers to increase. Similarly, if computers are a hundred times faster than

> executives in making investment decisions but only ten times faster in handling employee grievances (the quality of the decisions being held constant), then computers will be employed in making investment decisions, while executives will be employed in handling grievances. [125]

Frank Levy and Richard Murnane put it succinctly in their book, The New Division of Labor: How Computers Are Creating the Next Job Market: "At any moment in time, the boundary marking human advantage over computers largely defines the area of useful human work."[126]

However, it is not a static picture. The situation is fluid, so much so that economist Robin Hanson compares the impact of AI on jobs to a rising tide. The rising tide of AI subsumes some human jobs, Hanson says, leaving others safe on the economic shores:

> The tasks that are "most human" (those in which humans have an economic advantage over machines) are on the higher ground. Here, you find chores best done by humans, like gourmet cooking or elite hairdressing. Then there is a "shore" consisting of tasks that humans and machines are equally able to perform and, beyond them, an "ocean" of tasks best done by machines. When machines get cheaper or smarter or both, the water level rises, as it were, and the shore moves inland. This sea change has two effects. First, machines will substitute for humans by taking over the newly "flooded" tasks. Second, doing machine tasks better complements human tasks, raising the value of doing them well.[127]

The human edge

The question is: What is the human comparative advantage over AI? In the AI Age, what fields, skills, types of work will human beings shift

125 "Cognitive Comparative Advantage and the Organization of Work: Lessons from Herbert Simon's Vision of the Future," University of Connecticut, SSRN.com, January 7, 2003, https://www.ssrn.com/abstract=353262.

126 Frank Levy and Richard J. Murnane, *The New Division of Labor: How Computers Are Creating the Next Job Market*, Princeton, New Jersey: Princeton University Press, 2004.

127 "Economics of the Singularity," Spectrum.ieee.org, June 1, 2008, https://spectrum.ieee.org/robotics/robotics-software/economics-of-the-singularity.

toward? Many analysts have pointed to the essentially human traits of empathizing, caring and creativity as key factors that will constitute the human advantage. For example, best-selling author Daniel Pink argues in his book, *A Whole New Mind: Why Right-Brainers Will Rule the World*, that the dominance of professionals, mathematicians and technical types is over. The future belongs to those artsy, head-in-the-sky types he calls right-brainers, who had previously been made to feel inferior to left-brainers:

> The last few decades have belonged to a certain kind of person with certain kind of mind—computer programmers who could crank code, lawyers who could craft contracts, MBAs who could crunch numbers. But the keys to the kingdom are changing hands. The future belongs to a very different kind of person with a very different kind of mind—creators and empathizers, pattern recognizers, and meaning makers. These people—artists, inventors, designers, storytellers, caregivers, consolers, big-picture thinkers—will now reap society's richest rewards and share its greatest joys.[128]

Certainly, this thinking is sound. In the past, many human beings had to become like machines in their jobs. But now, the machines have come to take on those machine jobs. For example, in London, black cab drivers studied for years to learn every street in the city by rote. They had to memorize 25,000 streets and 320 routes to get their licence. Studies have shown their hippocampus, the area of the brain associated with memory, actually enlarged as a result of this intense studying. Black cab driving gave working class Brits the chance to earn a relatively high income by spending a few years learning a set of skills and then applying those same skills over the rest of their working careers.

Everything changed with the invention of GPS mapping, an AI system. Drivers with the low-cost Uber ride-sharing service were able to use GPS for even greater knowledge of London than black cab drivers. Using GPS navigation apps like Wayze, Uber drivers could even tell where traf-

128 Daniel J. Pink, *A Whole New Mind: Why Right-Brainers Will Rule the Future,* New York: Riverhead Books, 2006.

fic was causing delays and then use AI to reroute in real time. Londoners voted with their pocketbooks, and a staggering 3.5 million Londoners used Uber. As a result, the income of black cab drivers has declined substantially.[129] The Black cab-versus-Uber issue really exemplifies trends the AI Age will initiate. Narrow technical skills, however complex, are at risk of AI automation as long as they are narrow, because machines can perform narrow technical skills better than human beings. The strengths of human beings lies in generality, rather than in any narrow skill, even the narrow aspects of a very human quality: empathy.

Empathy

Empathy has been held up as a source of human comparative advantage and a bastion protecting humans against machines. Empathy literally means to see through the eyes of the other. As Albert Einstein said, "Empathy is patiently and sincerely seeing the world through the other person's eyes. It is not learned in school; it is cultivated over a lifetime." Doctors, lawyers and teachers are among the many jobs that rely on the ability to see from the other's perspective. Who better than a human being to understand another human being? Could machines ever understand and respond to human emotions? Well, yes, I think they could because the physiological manifestation of human emotions can be learned.

In the nineteenth century, Charles Darwin wrote a follow-up to his major work, *On the Origin of Species*, which transformed our understanding of the world. In his later work, *Expression of the Emotions in Man and Animals*, Darwin claimed there are universal emotions in humans and animals that can be seen in their expressions. It was considered highly controversial at the time, but two centuries later, Paul Ekman, a University of California professor, discovered that people in cultures around the world recognize six basic facial expressions (anger, disgust, fear, happiness, sadness and surprise). This includes preliterate peoples untainted by exposure to cinema or television, thereby suggesting the very universality Darwin had proposed.

129 "London's black-cab drivers consider suing Uber for £1bn," Theguardian.com, July 24, 2018, https://www.theguardian.com/technology/2018/jul/24/londons-black-cab-drivers-consider-suing-uber-for-1bn.

Ekman proved the underlying expressions in a person's facial response are universal. A smile is a smile everywhere, tears are tears and if someone rolls their eyes at you—you're not that interesting. This is true from the forest of the Amazon to the desert of Saudi Arabia and the streets of the modern Western metropolis. There are also cultural norms: For instance in Asia, people mask negative emotions by wearing a social smile. But all of these expressions, both universal and cultural, can be detected by the trained human or machine eye.

Ekman catalogued over 10,000 facial expressions, more than 3,000 of them related to emotions. His facial expression analysis system, called Facial Action Coding System, was able to connect facial muscle combinations to the emotions they represent. As a result, Ekman could understand what emotion was being represented by facial expressions.

Emotions

Ekman sees emotions as "autoappraisers" scanning the environment for things that will affect our welfare. This can be based on what we have learned and experienced in our individual lives (for example, city dwellers fear muggers; rural people, wild pigs). But this is also derived from our evolutionary past, accounting in part for why we are afraid of snakes and spiders, which have been considered dangers since antiquity. Ekman explains:

> I am convinced that one of the most distinctive features of emotion is that the events that trigger emotions are influenced not just by our individual experience, but also by our ancestral past. The autoappraisers are scanning for what has been important to survival, not just in our own individual lives but also in the lives of our hunter-gatherer ancestors. [130]

When these autoappraiser emotions manifest themselves, physiological signs can be detected. There are patterns in human facial expressions

130 Paul Ekman, *Emotions Revealed, Second Edition: Recognizing Faces and Feelings to Improve Communication and Emotional Life*, New York: Holt Paperbacks, 2007.

that can reveal the underlying emotion a person is feeling. Humans can be trained to read these patterns, and Ekman had a good career training law enforcement personnel how to read expressions to discern whether someone is lying. But machines can also be trained to read these facial expressions, even better than humans. As journalist Raffi Khatchadourian writes in *The New Yorker*, "Computers can now outperform most humans in distinguishing social smiles from those triggered by spontaneous joy, and in differentiating faked pain and genuine pain."

AI empathy

Affectiva, an exciting Boston-based AI start-up, has built on Ekman's work to develop an AI emotion-sensing platform. This is being used in many business applications, such as assessing the emotional response people have to an advertisement by analyzing their facial expressions on a moment-by-moment basis. Affectiva then aggregates that data into an unbiased set of data about how people respond emotionally to advertising. Affectiva is doing this in 87 countries, from the United States and China to Iraq and Vietnam, and in doing so it has collected data even Facebook and Google do not have. Affectiva software can also monitor drivers for drowsiness, distraction, fatigue and intoxication through monitoring their face.

Affectiva CEO Rana el Kaliouby, who holds a PhD from Cambridge University and did postdoctoral work at MIT, believes her platform may even know our emotions better than we know ourselves. For example, if you ask someone to rate how depressed or suicidal that person is on a scale of 1–10, they are not very accurate. But with AI, Affectiva can build baselines of mental health so that when systems detect someone is deviating from normal, family members or health professionals can be alerted.

AI empathy is also being developed in robots. In one unexpected episode in 2018, a robot deployed in space displayed enough empathy to tell his human astronaut colleague he was being "mean." Cimon (Crew Interactive Mobile Companion), which leverages IBM Watson's artificial intelligence, arrived on the International Space Station to assist human crew members with tasks, provide some entertainment and boost morale. Cimon was programmed to detect the emotions of human astronaut colleague Alexander Gerst so it could converse with him. But in a televised demonstration of the robot, things took an unusual turn. Gerst asked Cimon to play his favorite song, "The Man-Machine," by German electronic band Kraftwerk. Then unexpectedly, Cimon started to question his human companion's intentions. Showing empathy, Cimon asked Gerst, "Don't you like it here with me?" and told him, "Don't be so mean, please."

AI-based empathy is also being used a lot closer to home in everyday applications. Machines can find patterns in data, then personalize offerings that respond to a customer's emotional needs. For example, Amazon can predict what millions of customers might want to buy next. Or Netflix can predict a film you may like. Spotify can predict the right song to make you feel happy, sad, love, sick or excited. It even groups its machine learning–created playlists under emotional headings like "Uplifting," "Life Sucks" and "Stress Buster." In this way, the platform is using AI empathy to impact the emotions of millions of people every day. These playlists appeal to millions of people's emotions, but they are not produced by right-brain human creative types; they are generated by machines.

This points to a fundamental advantage machines have over humans in the area of empathy: data versus intuition. Machines go by data. They can correlate data to tell how sad you are from your glum facial expression, the chocolates and tissue payments on your bank statement, your Google searches on self-help forums, your GPS showing you haven't left home in two days, the book you just bought online on Chinese philosophy and how long you spent staring at old photos on your phone. Humans just go by intuition. I think over time and over millions of people, data beats intuition.

This leads to the question, Where do emotions really come from? Are they emanating from our soul? Or are they just neurons firing in our brain? In her book, How Emotions are Made, neuroscientist Lisa Feldman Barrett distinguishes between the classical view of emotions and the constructed view, or how she believes emotions really work. The classical view says that emotions are something uniquely human that come from inside of us and are distinctive to our species. The constructed view sees emotions alternately as "a computational moment within your constantly predicting brain." Take a look at this description of how Barrett thinks empathy really works:

> Suppose you and I are chatting over coffee, and when I make some witty remark, you smile and nod. If my brain predicted your smile and your nod, and the visual input to my brain confirms these movements, then my own prediction—say, to nod back at you—becomes my behavior. You, in turn, might have predicted my nod, along with a host of other possibilities, which causes a change in your sensory input, which interacts with your predictions. In order for your neurons to influence one another not only through direct connections but indirectly through the outside environment, in an interaction with me. We are performing a synchronized dance of prediction, and action, regulating each other's body budgets. This same synchrony is the basis of social connection and empathy; it makes people trust and like each other. [131]

If empathy is as she describes, a response to your brain predicting how you should respond in a given situation, then AI can also predict it. A machine could therefore have more empathy than a human being in the long term. Yuval Noah Harari, the best-selling author of *Sapiens*, certainly thinks so. Harari argues the human mind is not the outward manifestation of an eternal soul but just the result of mental algorithms and pattern recognition. Machines can eventually understand these calculations better than humans:

> AI can be better at jobs that demand intuitions *about other people*. Many jobs . . . require the ability to correctly assess the emotions

131 Lisa Feldman Barrett, *How Emotions Are Made: The Secret Life of the Brain*, New York: Houghton Mifflin Harcourt, 2017.

> and desires of other people. . . . As long as it was thought that such emotions and desires were generated by an immaterial spirit, it seemed obvious that computers will never be able to replace human drivers, bankers, and lawyers. For how can a computer understand the divinely created human spirit? Yet if these emotions and desires are, in fact, no more than biochemical algorithms, there is no reason why computers cannot decipher these algorithms—and do so far better than any *Homo sapiens.* [132]

Lake Wobegon Effect

If you were to take an empathy test, you'd probably find you overestimate your ability to read emotions and empathize. That's perfectly human. Studies show that most humans significantly overrate their own abilities. This has become known as the Lake Wobegon Effect, a natural tendency to overestimate one's capabilities and to see oneself as better than others. Research psychologists refer to this tendency as self-enhancement bias. We all tend to think we are smarter, warmer, funnier, more empathetic than we really are. This happens because we derive our sense of self-worth in contrast to other people. The Lake Wobegan Effect may mean we overestimate human capability over machines, and I think empathy is a good example of that. It also points to another advantage machines have over humans—they don't have egos! Machines just go by data.

Creativity

How about creativity? If machines are taking routine work, then by extension, humans will be doing nonroutine work involving innovation, flexibility and creativity. Creativity, it is claimed, is free from the grasp of AI's growing tentacles because it is unique to humans, the only beings who can make art, poetry, music. A machine could never develop creative intelligence, could it?

Creativity can be defined as "the use of imagination or original ideas to create something; inventiveness." Machines already have creativity in some sense. We saw with chess in Chapter 1 that the computer moves are now

132 Yuval Noah Harari, *21 Lessons for the 21st Century,* New York: Spiegel & Grau, 2018.

so inventive they appear to convey great creativity. The AI chess creativity is so marked, Gary Kasparov has said chess judges look for creativity as a telltale sign human players are cheating by using a machine.

We also covered generative design in Chapter 3. This type of machine learning uses generative adversarial networks (GANs) to produce new images or designs.

Figure 12: images entirely constructed by machines using GANs.

A scene from a video game with an AI system using GANs.

Indeed, AI art has now emerged as a new industry. The AI-art gold rush began in October 2018, when the New York auction house Christie's sold "Portrait of Edmond de Belamy" for $432,500. It is a piece of art entirely created by an AI system using GANs in the style of 19th-century European portraiture. An image produced by generative design is an amalgamation of the images used in training, so it is not completely original.

Figure 13: The AI-generated "Portrait of Edmond de Belamy," which sold for $432,500 at auction.

The front cover to this book was designed entirely by AI. It is the first time in history that AI has created a book cover. To do this my colleague Ali El Hassouni, a PhD in Generative Adversarial Networks, fed 200,000 book covers into a GANs system. The GANs system very quickly learned how to create book covers, as you can see in a video here: https://vimeo.com/manage/349647465/general

This AI System created many unique book covers, and we human beings selected the one on the front of this book. But when you look at it, you are seeing Art created entirely by a machine. Never before has AI created a book cover entirely on its own. The really unique aspect, is that there were no human fingerprints here at all. In the past, an artist may not actually have physically created an art work, like Damien Hirst when he made his Mother & Child cow in formaldehyde. But the artist has always conceived the art, it is their conception, their human imagination. The cover of the book is something entirely new and alien. It is art which is created solely by AI. A human being has not influenced any element of the creation. The front cover of the book is proof, that AI can be creative, and makes the point more powerfully with an image, than I could do with words.

Similarly, Professor David Cope has developed AI programs to compose music. They analyze the style of a composer and then use special "recombination" procedures to create new compositions. On Cope's website, you can download 5,000 files of computer-generated Bach-style choruses. Cope argues that "recombinancy appears everywhere as a natural evolutionary and creative process." Is Cope right, and is creativity just a process of recombination? Could simply recombining what we have experienced in new forms be the basis of all creativity? Is this the source of great art, literature, music?

Let me give you an example. In 1967, the Beatles created a bona fide masterpiece: *Sergeant Pepper's Lonely Hearts Club Band.* The album invented many new techniques that today have become standard in the music industry, from laying down tracks one layer at a time, to mixing sessions and introducing diverse musical styles. But the album was also a beautiful exercise in a recombining the band members' experiences from across their lives. "Strawberry Fields Forever," which was the first song recorded in these sessions, although it doesn't appear on the album, was based on a children's home near where John Lennon grew up. John was drawing on a childhood memory and recombining the feel and experience of it with music. Paul McCartney's "Penny Lane" drew on memories of a bus shelter where the band would gather in Liverpool. George Harrison's experiences in India are recombined into Asian guitar melodies. "Lovely Rita" referred to a female traffic warden who gave Paul a ticket. The track "Being for the Benefit of Mr. Kite" was an evocation of a circus poster from 1843 that John bought at an antiques shop; all the lyrics from this song come from this Victorian flyer. "Lucy in the Sky With Diamonds" was inspired by a childhood painting of Julian Lennon, John's son, recombined with literary classic *Alice and Wonderland* and classical music. The Beatles recombined experiences from across their lives, both distant and immediate, into songs to create one of the most artistic and groundbreaking albums of all time.

Does this suggest all art is at its core really just recombination? T.S. Elliot, one of the twentieth century's greatest poets, thought so:

"One of the surest tests is the way in which a poet borrows. Immature poets imitate; mature poets steal; bad poets deface what they take, and good poets make it into something better, or at least something different. The good poet welds his theft into a whole of feeling which is unique, utterly different than that from which it is torn; the bad poet throws it into something which has no cohesion. A good poet will usually borrow from authors remote in time, or alien in language, or diverse in interest."

A similar sentiment has been attributed to Picasso as "Good artists borrow; great artists steal." The question is whether human creativity is based on recombining? Or can human brains somehow create entirely new ideas? If a human has an idea, it must originate somewhere. How could something come from nothing? Humans need far less training data; they rely on processing their entire lives, and they may pull from the memory of an event that happened days, weeks or years ago to come up with a creative idea today. But recombination has a large role. If a machine were able to process decades of information and recombine across domains as varied as art, fashion, music, design and more, a machine might be able to produce an album rivaling the quality of *Sergeant Pepper's Lonely Hearts Club Band* or develop creativity even greater than that of human beings. Such a machine, though, would have capabilities beyond those of current AI systems.

There is also more to high creativity and inventiveness in humans than just recombining experiences. For example, when Alan Turing invented the universal machine he was undoubtedly being creative. Was Turing recombining? Possibly. But in a much broader sense than just amalgamating things he had experienced. Turing needed to combine mental models of how the world worked with mathematics and computer science. Rather than just connecting the dots across domains, he needed to apply causality and reasoning, which are capabilities beyond even the most advanced AI systems today. Human imagination entails more than recombining objects, it is also applying reasoning and causality, using mental models of how the world works, developing hypotheses—applied to a new domain to create something truly original. Such powers of imagination are held by men, but are, once again, far beyond the capabilities of today's AI machines.

Therefore, imagination and high creativity and inventiveness remain strong areas of human comparative advantage. MIT's Andrew McAfee and Erik Brynjolfsson argue that, for many years to come, humans will be better than machines at ideation, innovation, thinking outside of the box (which they call large-scale pattern recognition), and complex forms of communication. Subsequently, they believe the education system should be adapted to reflect these skills and be less about rote learning. They praise the Montessori approach of self-directed learning, hands-on engagement and largely unstructured school days. Oxford University academics Carl Benedikt Frey and Michael Osborne, who caused a stir by predicting mass AI job displacement, also believe people will need to develop creative and social skills to survive.

Be a generalist

Human creativity is an area of comparative advantage over AI because of its generality. Empathy (in terms of assessing emotions) is a narrow skill, so AI can be trained to do it. But when empathy means being able to connect the dots across domains to truly understand another human being, this is a general skill and machines cannot master this. It is the same with creativity; just coming up with a new image or song can be done by machines using GANS or Cope's recombinancy. Generalist feats, such as thinking across domains, applying causal reasoning, developing models of how the world works to propose a new original idea like Turing's universal machine, are a uniquely human talent.

Our true competitive edge over machines is our general intelligence, or floodlight cognition. This is the same type of intelligence we discussed in Chapter 2, which separates human from animal intelligence. As we saw, animals are so smart there is not really much difference between their intelligence and human intelligence. The mammalian brain is almost identical to the human brain. Animals also have language, emotions, tool use, culture and more.

But what humans have uniquely is floodlight cognition, or the ability to turn our general intelligence to meeting new challenges. This general intelligence is, for the foreseeable future, far beyond machines. Therefore, the human competitive edge over machines in the AI Age is not any narrow competence. Machines can learn even narrow capabilities that appear human, such as empathy. So, in a mixed economy with AI, the human competitive advantage is general intelligence. We can use our floodlight cognition to solve new problems, think of new ideas and connect the dots. We can be more versatile and adaptable than machines. Creativity is an area of comparative advantage for humans since it requires generality. All those skills linked to general intelligence then are what humans need to thrive in the AI Age.

Don't be narrow

In the coming AI world, one bit of advice: Don't become a technician. As the CEO of AI marketing platform Phrasee told me: "Don't even learn to code, as soon machines will be able to code themselves." When we were young, our parents told us to "get a profession." This meant learning technical skills for a few years and then selling them for the rest of our careers. For the AI Age, this is bad advice. Instead of learning narrow technical skills, we need versatile, cross-domain, generalist skills. Mark Tegmark argues in his book, Life 3.0, that the best role for the professional is the general problem solver, not the technician:

> If you go into medicine, don't be the radiologist who analyzes the medical images and gets replaced by IBM's Watson, but the doctor who orders the radiology analysis, discusses the results with the patient, and decides on the treatment plan. If you go into finance, don't be the "quant" who applies the algorithm to the data and gets replaced by software, but the fund manager who uses the quantitative analysis results to make strategic investment decisions. If you go into law, don't be the paralegal who reviews thousands of documents for the discovery phase and gets automated away, but the attorney who counsels the client and presents the case in court. [133]

Versatility and continuous learning

Technology is changing so fast that jobs and livelihoods go in and out of existence on a faster time scale than a human career. There has always been technological change that has taken away some lines of work and created others. But it happened across generations. Now it is happening within a single generation, and this means workers need to be more adaptable than ever before.

Traditionally, at the start of a career it was possible to develop a set of skills and then rely on those skills for the rest of your working life. People historically spent time studying and then moved on to working. As technology accelerates and requires new capabilities, learning will need to become more sequential. Learning and working will happen in parallel, as people acquire new skills, apply those skills and continue to do this cyclically throughout their careers.

In the AI Age, workers need to be continually retraining as technology advances faster than ever. Typical careers, in which a person advances through the ranks of a particular field, will increasingly fade away. Humans

133 Max Tegmark, *Life 3.0: Being Human in the Age of Artificial Intelligence*, New York: Vintage Books, 2018.

will have to become more comfortable learning new skills, and retooling will become the norm. As Andrew Ng explains, career dynamics have changed so much that not only will you no longer have one job for life, you will not even have one career for life:

> I think we are moving away from a world where you have one career in your lifetime. Technology changes so fast that there will be people that thought they were doing one thing when they went to college that will realize that the career they set out toward when they were 17 years old is no longer viable, and that they should branch into a different career. We've seen how millennials are more likely to hop among jobs, where you go from being a product manager in one company to the product manager of a different company. I think that in the future increasingly we'll see people going from being a material scientist in one company to being a biologist in a different company to being a security researcher in a third company. [134]

In the AI Age, to reach a certain level of adaptability and versatility, workers will need to practice continuous learning. Professionals will need to stay engaged, retrain and relearn, and reinvent themselves a few times over their careers. This may seem a terribly difficult challenge, but part of the problem is that human workers have spent so long working like machines they have lost the ability to think for themselves. Adam Smith, with whom we began this chapter, also took time in his 1776 magnum opus *The Wealth of Nations* to criticize work structures that stifle our abilities to learn:

> The man whose whole life is spent in performing a few simple operations, of which the effects are perhaps always the same, or very nearly the same, has no occasion to exert his understanding or to exercise his invention in finding out expedients for removing difficulties which never occur. He naturally loses, therefore, the habit of such exertion, and generally becomes as stupid and ignorant as it is possible for a human creature to become."[135]

134 Martin Ford, *Architects of Intelligence.*

135 Adam Smith, *The Wealth of Nations*, London: Penguin Classics, 1982.

Polymaths and interdisciplinary education

As a Brit writing this book, I have been struck by the number of British people who have had a profound effect on AI. From Alan Turing, who discovered the field, to I.J. Good, who originated the Intelligence explosion; Geoffrey Hinton, the godfather of deep learning; and Demis Hassabis, the founder of DeepMind. What is it about the small, drizzly island of Britain that has produced so many AI greats? Well, one unique aspect of the British education system, which the rest of the world views as a curiosity, is that it provides a general education. Rather than studying technical or vocational courses that we then follow up with a career, we Brits have an unusual approach of, instead, studying something else that is not, on the face of it, related at all to a job. Many a UK prime minister has studied classics, bankers may have read philosophy, office workers graduate in media studies.

The idea is that although you do not learn anything that may seem specifically applicable to your future job, you have, instead, developed a general intelligence and critical thinking abilities that can be applied from classics to banking, from philosophy to entrepreneurship and on and on. I have no doubt a general education will be crucial in the AI Age in two ways: It will instigate new breakthroughs in AI by bringing in fresh thinking; and it will endow ordinary workers with the generality and versatility to be adaptable enough to survive the tumultuous careers of the AI Age.

In this vein, industry partners such as McKinsey & Company are establishing a new university in London for polymaths. The London Interdisciplinary School will educate students tasked to decide, for example, whether mosquito genes should be edited to eliminate malaria. This is exactly the sort of education we need to develop our general intelligence for a life with AI. While most of the attention for AI is on the United States and China, Britain has played such a fundamental role in the development of AI that its future contribution to the field should not be underestimated.

Personal services

Economics laureate Herbert Simon also correctly predicted in his 1960 essay there would be a movement away from blue-collar and clerical jobs and towards jobs involving personalized service:

> In the entire occupied population, a larger fraction of members than at present will be engaged in occupations where "personal service" involving face-to-face human interaction is an important part of the job. I am confident of stating this conclusion, far less confident in conjecturing what these occupations will be."

Among personalized services, Simon picked out sales as a resilient function:

> If we think that buying decisions are not going to be made much more objectively than they have in the past, then we might conclude the automation of the salesman's role will proceed less rapidly than the automation of many other jobs. If so, selling will account for a larger fraction of total employment.

The reason personalized service and sales will be on the shore in the AI world is they are all about relationship building. Human beings need other human beings to build relationships. In fact, a study of human happiness found that the most important driver of happiness is relationships. Geoff Colvin, Fortune's senior editor at large, argues in his book, *Humans Are Underrated: What High Achievers Know That Brilliant Machines Never Will,* argues that skills of deep human interaction such as storytelling, empathy and relationship building will become more valuable in the future:

> We're hard-wired by 100,000 years of evolution to value deep interaction with other humans (and not with computers). Those wants won't be changing anytime soon. As a result, the meaning of great performance has changed. It used to be that you had to be

> good at being machinelike. Now, increasingly, you have to be good at being a person. Great performance requires us to be intensely human beings.[136]

All you need is love

Machines can't build relationships on the same level as human beings because, although they can detect emotions, they can't have emotions. Machines can't emote. Machines can't love. AI, for all its incredible potential, can't give people the only thing that matters in life: love.

AI powerhouse innovator Kai-Fu Lee learned this lesson after a near brush with death. He realized that although he had a truly exceptional career, love and relationships are more important. In a way, his career obsession took him away from his family; he remembers vividly when his wife gave birth and he obsessed about getting to a presentation, only to rush off to it as soon the baby came. His realization, when facing a potentially deadly form of cancer, was that work has too much of an all-consuming role in our lives; if AI can free us from this, it can let us focus on what is important—love.

Lee cites T*he Top Five Regrets of the Dying*, the memoir of Bronnnie Ware, a nurse for the terminally ill, who wrote about her patients' dying wishes. When faced with death, they had more clarity about their lives. Their greatest regret was focusing too much on work and not realizing it was people who gave their lives meaning. No one facing death wished they had worked harder; instead, they wished they had spent more time with people they loved. Kai-Fu Lee realized that love is what humans will always be able to give other humans in a way no machine ever could:

> For all of AI's astounding capabilities, the one thing that only humans can provide turns out to also be exactly what is most needed in our lives: love. . . . We do know that humans are

136 Geoff Colvin, *Humans Are Underrated: What High Achievers Know that Brilliant Machines Never Will*, New York: Portfolio, 2015.

> uniquely able to love and be loved, that humans want to love and be loved and that loving and being loved are what makes our lives worthwhile.[137]

Collaborate, create and build relationships

Being a success in the AI Age means being more human. Educate yourselves and your children in the humanities, poetry, music, history, art. Make versatile, creative human beings who can adapt and thrive in any environment. AI cannot engage in cross-domain thinking. We should all have an interdisciplinary education; children should learn philosophy, history, politics, not just coding and other technical skills. Focus on building human relationships in your career. Have passion. Love. Stop working like a machine; the machines are here to do that for us now. In short, be a human being. The AI Age provides an opportunity to rediscover our humanity, as Geoff Colvin says so beautifully:

> As technology drives forward more powerfully every year, the transition to the newly valuable skills of emphasizing, collaborating, creating, leading and building relationships. . . . If the prospect sounds worrying, it shouldn't. On the contrary, it's wonderful news. Just think of what we are being asked to do—to become more essentially human, to be the creatures we were once and were always meant to be. . . . In the deepest possible sense, you've already got what it takes. [138]

137 Kai-Fu Lee, *AI Superpowers: China, Silicon Valley, and the New World Order.*

138 Geoff Colvin, *Humans Are Underrated*, 213.

CHAPTER 7
The Future of AI

"A great many internal and external portents (political and social upheaval, moral and religious unease) have caused us all to feel, more or less confusedly, that something tremendous is at present taking place in the world. But what is it?"
Pierre Teilhard De Chardin (1881 - 1955)

"In contrast with our intellect, computers double their performance every eighteen months. So the danger is real that they could develop intelligence and take over the world."
— Stephen Hawking

"Day by day, however, the machines are gaining ground upon us; day by day we are becoming more subservient to them, more men are daily bound down as slaves to ten them. . . . The time will come when the machines will hold the real supremacy over the world and its inhabitants. [This] is what no person of a truly philosophic mind can for a moment question...In the course of ages, we shall find ourselves the inferior race."
— Samuel Butler, Darwin Among the Machines, The Press, 1863

Kai-Fu Lee, AI tech guru, predicts AI will progress in four waves:

1. Internet AI
2. Business AI
3. Perception AI
4. Autonomous AI

Internet AI and Business AI are, at this moment, all around us, and they are reshaping our digital and physical worlds. This means we are now at stage three, Perception AI.

PERCEPTION AI

Perception AI is all about machines beginning to "see" the world. Before, AI machines were deaf and blind. Machines could not interpret audio and visuals. From a technological perspective, AI already has the ability to see, speak, hear, understand emotions in facial expressions or in text, move, hear and much more. Algorithms can now group the pixels from a photo, video or audio file into patterns and recognize objectives just as our brains do. The third wave of AI will use these powers to permeate every aspect of our lives. This will be accomplished with the proliferation of sensors and smart devices that are turning our physical world into digital data. This is already happening as, for example, Amazon Echo digitizes the sounds in your home, GPS digitizes your walk to the shops and WhatsApp digitizes your calls. This wave of AI will revolutionize how we experience and interact with our world, blurring the lines between the digital and physical worlds. Yann LeCun, Facebook's chief AI scientist, reveals perception AI will become mainstream very quickly:

> There's a lot of effort now to develop low-power and cheap hardware that can fit in your smartphone or your vacuum cleaner that can run a convolutional network on 100 milliwatts of power, and the chip can be bought for 3 bucks. That's going to change how a lot of the world around us works. Instead of going randomly around your room, your vacuum cleaner

> is now going to be able to see where it needs to go, and your lawnmower is going to be able to mow your lawn without running over your flowerbeds. It's not just your car that will drive itself. . . . AI is going to be in the hands of everyone because of progress in hardware technology that is specialized for deep learning, and that is coming in 2 or 3 years. [139]

AUTONOMOUS AI

Kai-Fu Lee's final phase of AI progress is Autonomous AI, which will have the deepest impact on our lives. Self-driving cars will replace drivers, autonomous drones will fill the skies and robots will take over factories, farming, fast food and more.

Autonomous AI should not be confused with automated AI. Autonomous AI can learn and act on its own with self-agency. Current robots are automated, because they can repeat an action, but they can't make decisions or improvise. They must be controlled by a program or human being. They can't manage deviations or irregularities in their work. But as machines develop—and Perception AI along with sight, touch, and optimization from data develop—machines will become especially useful. For example, swarms of autonomous drones will work together to paint the outside of your house. Heat-resistant drone swarms will fight bush fires, and they will perform search and rescue operations after natural disasters. They will also serve military and police applications.

ARTIFICIAL GENERAL INTELLIGENCE (AGI)

Kai-Fu Lee's four waves are all based on current technology and do not require any new breakthroughs. They are, instead, about gathering data and applying narrow AI, especially deep learning, to make enhancements and develop new business models. Current AI technology will not, however, get us to artificial general intelligence (AGI), the crucial step-

139 Martin Ford, *Architects of Intelligence.*

ping stone to human level AI (HLAI). We have decades of work ahead before we reach AGI, and even more before we achieve HLAI.

HUMAN-LEVEL AI (HLAI)

HLAI was the goal of the AI founders and early AI researchers. Alan Turing began the quest for the great "prize" with his 1947 lecture to the London Mathematical Society—the first recorded reference to what is now known as human level artificial intelligence. We covered Allen Newell and Herbert Simon's general problem solver in Chapter 1, which was also aimed at achieving HLAI. As Simon said in 1957, ". . . there are now in the world machines that think, that learn and that create. Moreover, their ability to do these things is going to increase rapidly until—in a visible future—the range of problems they can handle will be coextensive with the range to which the human mind has been applied."[140] HLAI is the grand goal of AI research, said A.M. Turing Award winner Edward Feigenbaum in 2013:

> Computational Intelligence is the manifest destiny of computer science, the goal, the destination, the final frontier. More than any other field of science, our computer science concepts and methods are central to the quest to unravel and understand one of the grandest mysteries of our existence, the nature of intelligence. Generations of computer scientists to come must be inspired by the challenges and grand challenges of this great quest. [141]

Demis Hassabis, founder of Google's DeepMind, predicts such AGI would solve intractable problems for human civilization, such as global warming and incurable diseases. AI may not remain Human Level AI for long since the inherent advantages of machines will enable them to quickly outstrip human intellect, as Stuart J Russell explains:

> We can't multiply million-digit numbers in our heads, and computers can do that relatively easily. So we assume that, in fact, ma-

140 Nils J. Nilsson, *The Quest for Artificial Intelligence.*
141 Nils J. Nilsson, *The Quest for Artificial Intelligence.*

> chines may be able to exhibit greater generality than humans do. . As soon as machines can read, then a machine can basically read all of the books ever written; no human can read all the books ever written. Therefore, once AGI gets past the kindergarten level, it will shoot beyond anything any human being has ever done, and it will have a bigger knowledge base than any human ever has. [142]

Nick Bostrom, director of the Future of Humanity Institute at Oxford University, says that AGI will be the last technology we ever need to invent:

> If AI were to be successful at its original goal, which all along has been not just to automate specific tasks but to replicate in machine substrates the general-purpose learning ability and planning ability that makes us humans smart, then that would quite literally be the last invention that humans ever needed to make.

Both Alan Turing and I.J. Good believed that when AI reached HLAI, it would redesign itself and quickly become something far greater. Bostrom uses the term "superintelligence" to describe this advanced AI. It would be able to lighten the burdens of humanity with the omniscience of a god. It could also represent a great danger for human beings. Our dominance over the world rests on our intelligence, and, just as the rest of the animal kingdom saw its fate fall into human hands as we evolved advanced intelligence, our fate would rest in the hands of an AI superintelligence. This watershed moment when AI exceeds human intelligence has become known as the singularity.

THE SINGULARITY

The term "singularity"—in science, a gravitational singularity is a one-dimensional point at the center of a black hole where all laws of physics cease to apply—became popular with AI thinkers after computer scientist and author Vernor Vinge used it in his 1986 science fiction

142 Martin Ford, *Architects of Intelligence.*

novel, *Marooned in Realtime*. Vinge later defined a technological singularity in an essay, predicting we will develop the technological means to create superhuman intelligence. According to Vinge, at this point the human era will come to an end. Everything we think we know will change at this moment. He explains:

> [Developments that we previously believed would happen in] a million years (if ever) will likely happen in the next century. I think it's fair to call this event a singularity. It is a point where our models must be discarded and a new reality rules. As we move closer and closer to this point, it will loom vaster and vaster over human affairs till the notion becomes commonplace. Yet when it finally happens, it may still be a great surprise and a greater unknown. [143]

Vinge predicted the singularity would happen by 2030. Large computer networks may "wake up as a superhumanly intelligent entity," he said. Writing in a similar vein, American mathematician and computer scientist Jack Schwartz wrote in 1987 of superintelligences creating a "new history":

> If artificial intelligences can be created at all, there is little reason to believe that initial successes could not lead swiftly to the construction of artificial superintelligences able to explore significant mathematical, scientific, or engineering alternatives at a rate far exceeding human ability, or to generate plans and take action of them with equally overwhelming speed. Since man's near-monopoly of all higher forms of intelligence has been one of the most basic facts of human existence throughout the past history of this planet, such developments would clearly create a new economics, a new sociology and a new history. [144]

Futurist Ray Kurzweil describes the singularity as:

---

143 Vernor Vinge, *The Coming Technological Singularity: How to Survive in the Post-Human Era*, NASA.gov, https://edoras.sdsu.edu/~vinge/misc/singularity.html.

144 Nils J. Nilsson, *The Quest for Artificial Intelligence.*

> . . . a future period during which the pace of technological change will be so rapid, its impact so deep, that human life will be irreversibly transformed. Although neither utopian nor dystopian, this epoch will transform the concepts that we rely on to give meaning to our lives, from our business models to the cycle of human life, including death itself.

Opinion is divided over whether the singularity is coming, imminent, centuries away or impossible. There are those who argue HLAI can never be achieved. The esteemed evolutionary psychologist Steven Pinker has been an outspoken opponent of the idea of a singularity:

> There is not the slightest reason to believe in a coming singularity. The fact that you can visualize a future in your imagination is not evidence that it is likely or even possible. Look at domed cities, jet-pack commuting, underwater cities, mile-high buildings, and nuclear-powered automobiles—all staples of futuristic fantasies when I was a child that have never arrived. Sheer processing power is not a pixie dust that magically solves all your problems. [145]

THE LIMITATIONS OF TODAY'S AI

American philosophy professor John Searle is one of the most famous opponents of "strong AI." In 1980, Searle presented the "Chinese room" argument, which purports to prove the falsity of strong AI. Essentially his argument is that AI only gives the illusion of intelligence and that is does not truly understand anything:

> Imagine a native English speaker who knows no Chinese locked in a room full of boxes of Chinese symbols (a database) together with a book of instructions for manipulating the symbols (the program). Imagine that people outside the room send in other Chinese symbols which, unknown to the person in the room, are

145 Meredith Broussard, *Artificial Unintelligence: How Computers Misunderstand the World*, Cambridge, Massachusetts: The MIT Press, 2018.

> questions in Chinese (the input). And imagine that by following the instructions in the program, the man in the room is able to pass out Chinese symbols which are correct answers to the questions (the output). The program enables the person in the room to pass the Turing Test for understanding Chinese, but he does not understand a word of Chinese. [146]

Searle argues no computer can ever understand Chinese or English, because, as the thought experiment suggests, being able to "translate" Chinese into English does not entail "understanding" either Chinese or English. The person in the thought experiment, and hence a computer, is only able to execute certain syntactic manipulations.

There have been many clever refutations of the Chinese Room analogy, which I won't go into here. On one important level, it matters not if the machine truly understands Chinese. If the machine can translate Chinese, and it has self-agency and the ability to achieve this complex goal, it is intelligent. This goes back to Turing's point all those years ago with the imitation game: We do not need to prove a machine can truly understand in a way that convinces a philosopher; what matters is if the machine displays intelligent behavior.

Here's a hypothetical illustration. Let us imagine an AI drone boat guarding against trespassers in national waters. This autobot can fire machine guns at anyone crossing a certain threshold and entering into national waters. Let us further suppose that Searle is on a vessel in the sea and crosses over into the national waters under guard. The AI patrol robot zeroes in on him and opens fire. Searle can call out to the AI drone, telling it, "You do not truly understand you are in a sea and patrolling this coast. You have no real understanding of marine warfare; all you are doing is executing algorithmic manipulations!" But it will not stop the bullets from flying in with high-precision accuracy. The important physical reality is the machine has the intelligence to shoot intruders. Whether it understands what shooting

146 "The Chinese Room Argument," Stanford Encyclopedia of Philosophy, March 19, 2004, https://plato.stanford.edu/entries/chinese-room/.

means or the geopolitical context in which it operates is, to this extent, irrelevant. It is the intelligent behavior that is important, as Turing argued over 70 years ago when he conceived the Turing test.

Nonetheless, it is absolutely true that today's AI has a far weaker understanding than humans or even animals. MIT roboticist Daniela Rus explains machine understanding is currently far inferior to that of humans:

> These systems can assimilate and correlate many more data points than humans are able to. However, when a system learns, for example, that there is a coffee mug in a photograph. . . . It has no real idea what that coffee mug represents. The system has no idea what to do with it. It doesn't know if you drink it, eat it or if you throw it.[147]

But present day AI does understand on a basic level, as deep learning pioneer Yoshua Bengio explains:

> The computer has some understanding; it's not a black-and-white argument. A cat understands a door, but it doesn't understand it as well as you do. Different people have different levels of understanding of the many things around them, and science is about trying to deepen our understanding of those many things. These networks have a level of understanding of images if they've been trained on them, but that level is still not as abstract and as general as ours. . . . The current level of computer understanding of images is still primitive, but it's still good enough to be incredibly useful in many applications. [148]

So current AI systems do have some primitive understanding, but we cannot get to AGI and HLAI without new breakthroughs to greatly increase this understanding. Deep learning is remarkably good at pattern recognition, but human intelligence is far more than this. Humans can also reason, imagine and conceptualize. Deep learning is not deep in the

147 Martin Ford, *Architects of Intelligence.*

148 Martin Ford, *Architects of Intelligence.*

sense of understanding what is happening below the surface. It may be able to recognize an image of a cat and predict correctly when it next sees a cat, but it doesn't know that a cat is a biological organism and often kept as a pet, or that it meows when hungry and, according to superstition, has nine lives. Deep learning doesn't understand a cat on any level beyond the pattern that makes up its image. Deep learning also needs to be trained on millions of data points before it can recognize the cat in the image. A human infant can see a cat a few times and then know it.

Current AI is narrow and limited, and just deploying or refining this won't get us to HLAI. As Andrew Ng points out that we need to develop new breakthroughs to get to HLAI:

> Deep Learning is incredibly effective for learning these input/output mappings and this is called supervised learning, but I think that artificial intelligence is much bigger than supervised learning. . . . There is a lot of room for something even better to be invented. It's hard to say right now exactly what that would be, though.[149]

EXPECT NEW BREAKTHROUGHS

The chances of new breakthroughs are high. We have made many breakthroughs over the past 80 years, so there is reason to believe we will do the same again in the next 80 years. There is also good reason to expect we will make even more progress. There are now more people working on AI than at any time in history. AI has moved from being a cottage industry to a major economic sector.

Nations are betting their future on AI from the United States and China to the UK, France, Russia and Canada. The world's most valuable and technologically savvy companies from Facebook to Amazon, Google, Baidu and Tencent are investing time, money and resources in AI with an almost religious fervor. Universities around the world, from elite institu-

149 Martin Ford, *Architects of Intelligence.*

tions like Harvard, MIT, Cambridge and Oxford to hundreds of others from Eastern Europe to Asia are brimming with AI talent. Thousands of bright PhDs are thinking about novel applications of AI. While all this is happening, a parallel track of research and development in neuroscience and cognitive science is illuminating our understanding of the human brain. All the funding, resources and intellectual firepower provides a high probability of new breakthroughs in AI.

MILESTONES TO HLAI

What would the new breakthroughs be? It's hard to know for sure. Yann LeCun of Facebook illustrates this moment with a metaphor: We are currently climbing a hill. We are excited about the progress we have made, but as we approach the top, we see a series of other hills rising in front of us. That is how the HLAI development landscape looks. Just as we reach the top of each hill, we see the limitations in our current AI and what we need to do to climb the next hill. It's not possible at this stage, with our current visibility, to see exactly how many breakthroughs we will need to reach human level intelligence. Nonetheless, leading AI thinkers do already agree on some key milestones we need to achieve to reach HLAI. These milestones follow in the next paragraphs.

Transferability

One of the main issues with current narrow AI is an inability to transferability of learning from one domain to another. This is something human beings excel at, and it is one of the key differentiators with other animals. Human beings have "floodlight cognition," which enables them to apply problem-solving skills to any new challenge, whereas animals have domain-specific intelligence. As a result, humans do not need to be trained on data each time we approach a new problem because we transfer learning from previous knowledge. So to reach HLAI, we will need to find a way to improve machine transferability of learning.

Demis Hassabis of DeepMind identified transferability of learning early on as a key milestone towards achieving AGI, and Ray Kurzweil has also spoken about its importance. Achieving this will mean that when we train AI systems, they are able to build on the knowledge gained from solving other problems to develop new techniques. They would be able to draw on the wealth of past experience to solve new problems. This would mean the AI systems need less training on new problems and less data since it would be applying already acquired learning. Humans are excellent at learning from small amounts of data, precisely because we are strong at transferring general skills from one area to another. Achieving this level of transferability with machines is a key milestone to HLAI.

Imitation

Linked to transfer of learning is imitation. One of the main ways children and adults learn is by demonstration and imitation. Both apes and humans have this ability, but ironically, humans' capacity to imitate far exceeds that of our closest cousins, the chimpanzee. Copying behaviors enables us to pass on skills, knowledge and culture. It is, therefore, viewed as a crucial cognitive ability, one that enabled human culture to develop into language, art and science. Today, there is research at Facebook, Google and MIT focused on helping machines learn from demonstrations. They are all attempting to tackle this important milestone to HLAI.

Causality

The ability to understand causal relationships is a crucial competence that enables humans to generalize and develop answers for new settings. Machine learning algorithms are extremely complex, but fundamentally they do not involve causal reasoning. Human children are excellent causal learners. Young children have sophisticated domain-specific causal reasoning abilities. Infants register particular aspects of physical causality; toddlers recognize various causal relations about others' desires and intentions, and preschoolers understand there can be nonobvious, hidden causal relationships behind things. Machines will need to develop these causal learning abilities to reach AGI. Judea Pearl, who won the Turing Award for his work on probabilistic and causal reasoning, argues in his new book, *The Book of Why: The New Science of Cause and Effect*, that causal reasoning could enable machines to reach HLAI. This would enable machines to communicate with humans effectively and even develop a capacity for free will.

Sense of self

True human-level intelligence in AI systems would also need to have a sense of self. Self-conceptualization is one of the few attributes human beings have that is believed to be nonexistent in animals. As René Descartes famously said, "I think therefore I am." A machine would have to realize it was playing chess or Go, or driving a car to be considered as having human level intelligence. This links to consciousness, a prerequisite to developing a sense of self.

Imagination

There are different levels of human understanding, from perceiving the world to interacting to the most advanced level—imagination. We have AI that can see and interact, but it cannot yet imagine. Imagination is not just for artsy creative types; it is also crucial to scientific enquiry. As Einstein, who used scientific imagination to construct a new theory of the universe, once said: "The true sign of intelligence is not knowledge but imagination."

Developing AI imagination is crucial to HLAI. AI may display some rudimentary type of imagination through GANs (generative adversarial networks). GANs can be used to generate images, as covered in the previous chapter. But the images produced are amalgamations of the images used in the training phase, so the machine is not imagining something truly new. It cannot produce counterfactuals, considering what would happen if it tried something different. When humans employ imagination, we do use recombinancy and amalgamations of things we have experienced, but we also use causality, reasoning and mental models of how the world works. It is this more sophisticated intelligence that we refer to as imagination and that machines need to develop to reach HLAI.

Generality and versatility

The main restriction of today's AI is that it is narrow. It can just do one thing very well, and it cannot handle multiple or different tasks. Human beings can watch a film, eat, drink, think about work and maybe send a WhatsApp message at the same time. Machines cannot handle this level of generality or versatility.

Self-replication

Human beings self-replicate. This is the very core of our being. Richard Dawkins made a persuasive case as long ago as 1976 about the "selfish gene" and that we are, in fact, complex robots for DNA—the building blocks of genes. The core purpose of human beings is to reproduce, which is driven by genes that can trace their ancestry back to a single-cell organism in the primordial soup hundreds of millions of years ago. This single-cell organism learned to replicate itself to preserve itself, he says:

> We are survival machines—robot vehicles blindly programmed to preserve the selfish molecules known as genes. This is a truth which still fills me with astonishment."[150]

Our ability to replicate ourselves is tied up with our advancement as a species. Through the blind process of natural selection, we have evolved from reptiles to mammals then apes to the wonderfully intelligent Homo sapiens. Would AI need to replicate itself to achieve human level intelligence? An AI that can copy itself might be able to confer some of the same advantages, deleting problematic aspects and refining its structure. Perhaps two AI systems could reproduce together in a form of machine procreation. AI systems would seek out complementary AI partners to reproduce with and produce new AI, which combine the strong points of each system. In doing so, perhaps AI would experience notions similar to sex, relationships and love.

Common sense

McCarthy and his Dartmouth colleagues in 1956 envisaged a generalized AI that's become known as "good old-fashioned AI," or GOFAI. There is a hypothesis behind it that thinking, as done by human beings, is a compu-

150 "Loveable rogue, or selfish killer?" Telegraph.com, March 21, 2006, https://www.telegraph.co.uk/technology/3345286/Loveable-rogue-or-selfish-killer.html.

tational process that can be studied. From this perspective, AI enables us to study the inner workings of the mind. It is not just about building machines that learn from data, but developing machines focused on the higher levels of human thought, machine that, like human beings, use common sense. McCarthy was not interested in machines just making predictions; for him, AI was about creating self-learning machines: "Our ultimate objective is to make machines that learn from their experience, as humans do."

For John McCarthy, the most important element of human common sense is that it's shaped by knowledge. People are able to apply what they've been told and what they already know about the world around them. In 1958, McCarthy wrote "Programs with Common Sense":

> We shall therefore say that a program has common sense if it automatically deduces for itself a sufficiently wide class of immediate consequences of anything it is told and what it already knows. [151]

Interestingly, the US Pentagon itself has revived McCarthy's vision for common sense AI. The Machine Common Sense program, launched October 2018 by the Defense Advanced Research Projects Agency (DARPA) explores multiple methods for teaching computers broad strategies for navigating the world. DARPA, like McCarthy, sees common sense as key to moving from the narrow AI of today to the general AI of tomorrow:

> The absence of common sense prevents intelligent systems from understanding their world, behaving reasonably in unforeseen situations, communicating naturally with people and learning from new experiences. Its absence is perhaps the most significant barrier between the narrowly focused AI applications we have today and the more general, humanlike AI systems we would like to build in the future."[152]

151 Hector Levesque, *Common Sense, the Turing Test, and the Quest for Real AI*, Cambridge, Massachusetts: The MIT Press, 2017.

152 "Teaching Machines Common Sense Reasoning," DARPA, October 11, 2018, https://www.darpa.mil/news-events/2018-10-11

The holy grail: Understanding

Causality, reasoning, transfer of learning, imagination and common sense are themselves hallmarks of one of the holy grails of AI: understanding. HLAI would need to have an understanding of the physical world. This is how children develop. During the pre-language stage, children use observation to develop a basic understanding of how the world works. My one-year-old daughter cannot speak yet, but she is extremely smart at getting what she wants. AI systems, by gaining the abilities of causality, reasoning, transfer of learning and imagination would gain an "understanding" of the world. There is no AI system in the world that knows today is a day and not just a digit on a calendar. AGI will need to use its new capabilities to develop a holistic understanding of the world.

This understanding would also enable AI to pass the Turing test. While we have speech recognition systems today like Alexa or Siri, which give specific answers to questions, they cannot go off script, which requires understanding and reasoning about what is being said below the surface. Having a natural conversation as outlined in the Turing test (which is not scripted but can branch off in different directions) would require something approaching human-level understanding. While it might be possible to use gamesmanship or outright deception to pass a 15-minute Turing test, it wouldn't be possible to cheat in a test that lasts a week or a month. The reason is that language itself is just a medium, transmitting ideas and models we hold in our minds. These models are internal to us, and through language, we communicate to others.

Understanding language will enable AI to vastly improve its development. Human beings use reading to develop complex models of how the world works. AI that properly understands language can read and, like Newton, can "stand on the shoulders of giants," gaining access to the thoughts, workings and knowledge of humans throughout history.

TIMELINE TO HLAI

How close are we to making these breakthroughs and achieving HLAI? Stuart J. Russell argues most of building blocks already there:

> We already know how to represent knowledge and reasoning; we have developed computational logic over quite a long time now. Even predating computers, people were thinking about algorithmic procedures for doing logical reasoning. And so, arguably some of the conceptual building blocks for AGI have already been here for decades. We just haven't figured out yet how to combine those with the very impressive learning capacities of deep learning. [153]

The challenge was summed up by Critical Future colleague, Michael Rawson, a PhD in automated reasoning, who said it is what computer scientists call "P versus NP." P represents computer science problems that are solvable. NP represents the bucket of problems that are very hard to solve mathematically. Alan Turing conceived of neural networks in 1947, but we did not have the mathematical firepower to make them work properly until Geoffrey Hinton's breakthroughs in the mid-2000s. As Stuart Russell says, we may be already there theoretically, but we have NP problems to solve. If neural networks are a benchmark, then it may take 60 years. Although since many of these ideas are old, we may make breakthroughs quite soon or in a long time from now—we really don't know.

The truth is that it is very difficult to predict when a breakthrough will happen. With nuclear physics, for example, the agreed opinion, as expressed by physicist Ernest Rutherford on September 11, 1933, was that it was impossible to extract atomic energy from atoms. The prediction was "never." But the next morning, Leo Szilard, upon reading Rutherford's speech, became irritated and immediately invented a nuclear chain reaction mediated by neutrons. The consensus view had been "never" and the truth was that one day later, it happened. In the same way, it is futile to predict when individual breakthroughs in AI will occur.

But what if there were some underlying laws that governed the speed of technological progress? We may not be able to guess which specific breakthrough will occur at what time, but we do know the general patterns and pace of change. In Chapter 1, we were introduced to Moore's law, a

153 Martin Ford, *Architects of Intelligence.*

powerful example of one such law that for decades has proven remarkably accurate in predicting the doubling of transistors and computing power. Moore's Law does not predict how or what new technology will come long to enable us to pack more transistors onto a circuit, it just predicts this will double every two years. Now, one man believes he has found just such a scientific law for how quickly technology in general develops, and he believes he can predict with very high accuracy when we will reach HLAI.

Accelerating returns

Ray Kurzweil has developed a model for how technologies develop called the "law of accelerating returns." It claims every area of technology is subject to the law of accelerating returns if the rate at which the technology improves is proportional to the quality of the technology. Growth will then be exponential rather than linear.

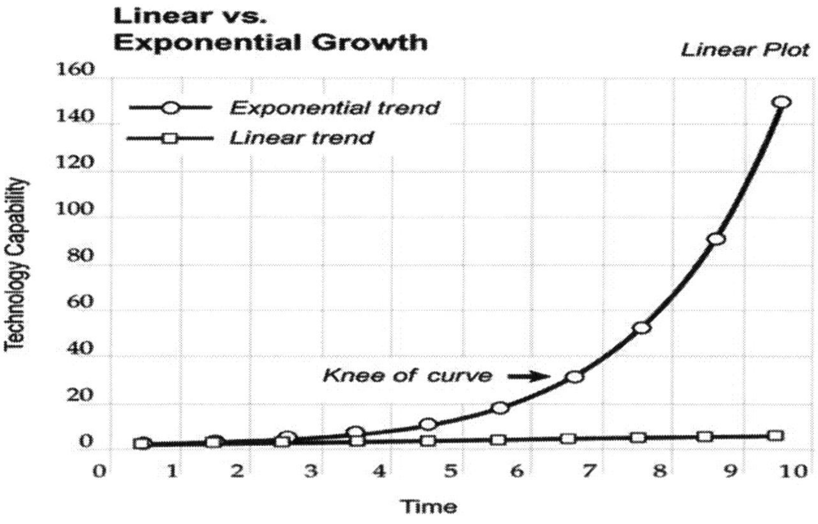

Figure 14 Linear versus exponential: from Ray Kurzweil, The Singularity Is Near: When Humans Transcend Biology, London: Penguin Books, 2005.

Linear growth is steady, while exponential growth is explosive. Kurzweil notes Gary Kasparov scorned the pathetic state of computer chess in 1992, but the doubling of computer power every year enabled a computer to defeat him only five years later. Kasparov agrees the example of chess is instructive:

> The growth of machines from chess beginners to grand masters is also a progression that is being repeated by countless AI projects around the world. AI products tend to evolve from laughably weak to interesting but feeble, then to artificial but useful, and finally to transcendent and superior to human. [154]

Kurzweil points out the same phenomenon happened with the human genome project:

> Halfway through the human genome project, 1 percent had been collected after 7 years, and mainstream critics said, "I told you this wasn't going to work; 1 percent in 7 years means it's going to take 700 years, just like we said." My reaction was, "We finished 1 percent—we're almost done. We're doubling every year. One percent is only 7 doublings from 100 percent." And indeed, it was finished 7 years later. [155]

Kurzweil tracks the exponential growth found in Moore's law across many different domains. His graphs make a powerful point; thus, I include some here:

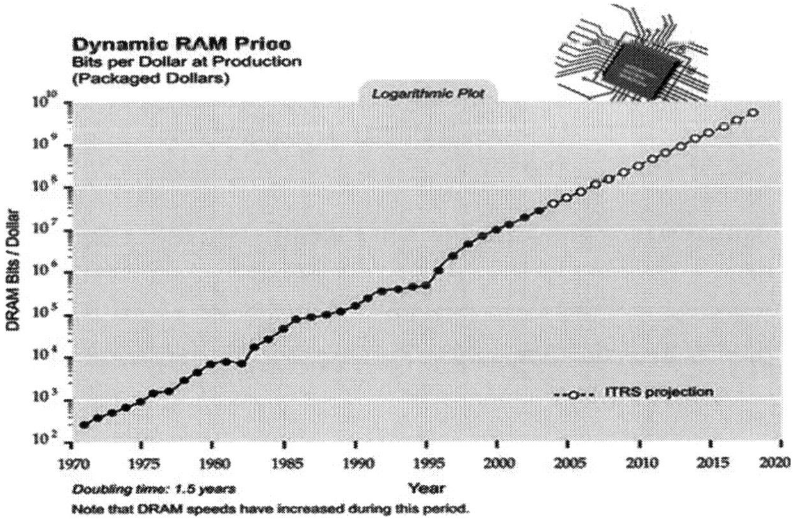

154 Gary Kasparov, Deep Thinking.

155 "Ray Kurzweil on Turing Tests, Brain Extenders, and AI Ethics," Wired.com, November 13, 2017, https://www.wired.com/story/ray-kurzweil-on-turing-tests-brain-extenders-and-ai-ethics/.

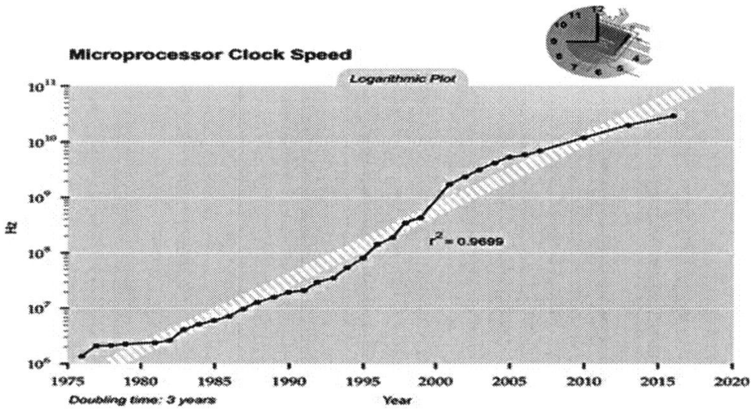
Microprocessor Clock Speed
Logarithmic Plot
Hz
r² = 0.9699
Year
Doubling time: 3 years

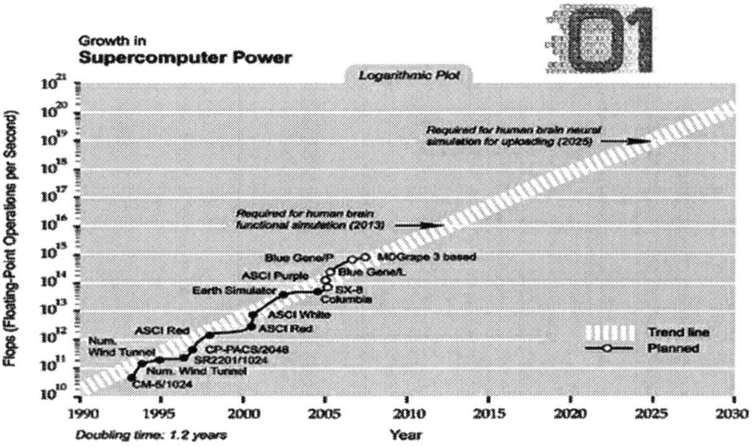
Growth in
Supercomputer Power
Logarithmic Plot
Flops (Floating-Point Operations per Second)
Required for human brain neural simulation for uploading (2025)
Required for human brain functional simulation (2013)
Blue Gene/P
MDGrape 3 based
Blue Gene/L
ASCI Purple
SX-8
Earth Simulator
Columbia
ASCI White
ASCI Red
ASCI Red
Num. Wind Tunnel
CP-PACS/2048
SR2201/1024
Num. Wind Tunnel
CM-5/1024
Trend line
Planned
Year
Doubling time: 1.2 years

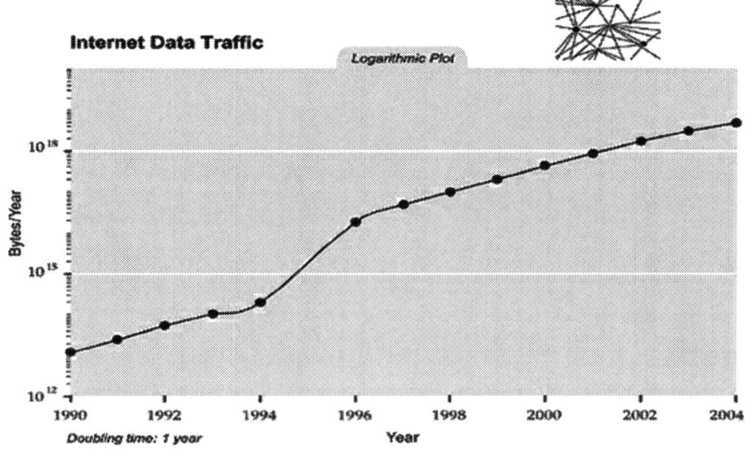
Internet Data Traffic
Logarithmic Plot
Bytes/Year
Year
Doubling time: 1 year

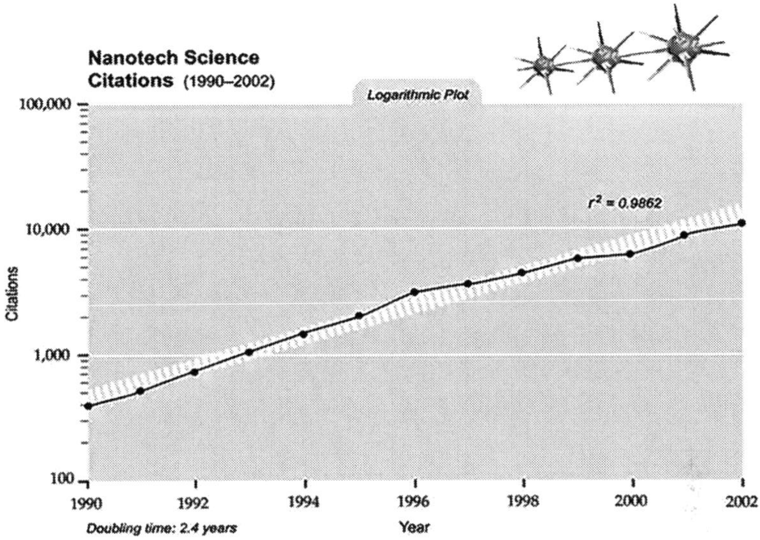

Figure 15: graphs from the book by Ray Kurzweil, *The Singularity Is Near: When Humans Transcend Biology*, London: Penguin Books, 2005.

Kurzweil predicts that after passing the Turing test in 2029, AI will accelerate and the singularity will occur 16 years after that, in 2045:

> I set the date for the Singularity—representing a profound and disruptive transformation in human capability—as 2045. The nonbiological intelligence created in that year will be one billion times more powerful than all human intelligence today.

Is Kurzweil right? He has a good track record in making predictions. BIll Gates calls Kurzweil "the best person I know at predicting the future of artificial intelligence." Google, which is working very hard to develop HLAI, hired Kurzweil as the company's director of engineering. Doubling of computing power does occur every two years. If this doubling applies to other AI technologies, then HLAI will arrive much sooner than most people anticipate. If natural language processing is a barometer, it is, indeed, making progress at terrific speed. In 2019, Elon Musk's Open AI announced it had developed NLP that can tell stories. It is so potent that Open AI will not release the code so as to prevent misuse. At this pace of development, it is possible in ten years that language AI will pass the Turing test. Hans Moravec thinks so:

> It may seem rash to expect fully intelligent machines in a few decades, when the computers have barely matched insect mentality in a half-century of development. Indeed, for that reason, many long-time artificial intelligence researchers scoff at the suggestion and offer a few centuries as a more believable period. But there are very good reasons why things will go much faster in the next fifty years than they have in the last fifty. . . . Since 1990, the power available to individual AI and robotics programs has doubled yearly. [156]

Moravec provides the following graph showing when computers will reach human brain power based on current trends:

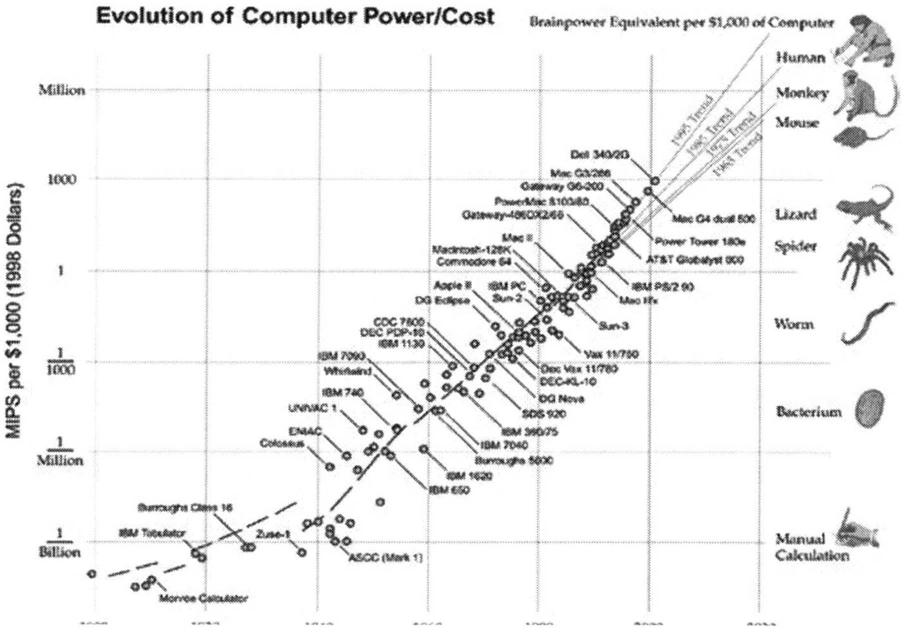

And this graph shows how quickly AI will go from HLAI to surpassing all human intelligence in the world combined:

156 Ray Kurzweil, *The Singularity Is Near: When Humans Transcend Biology*, London: Penguin Books, 2005.

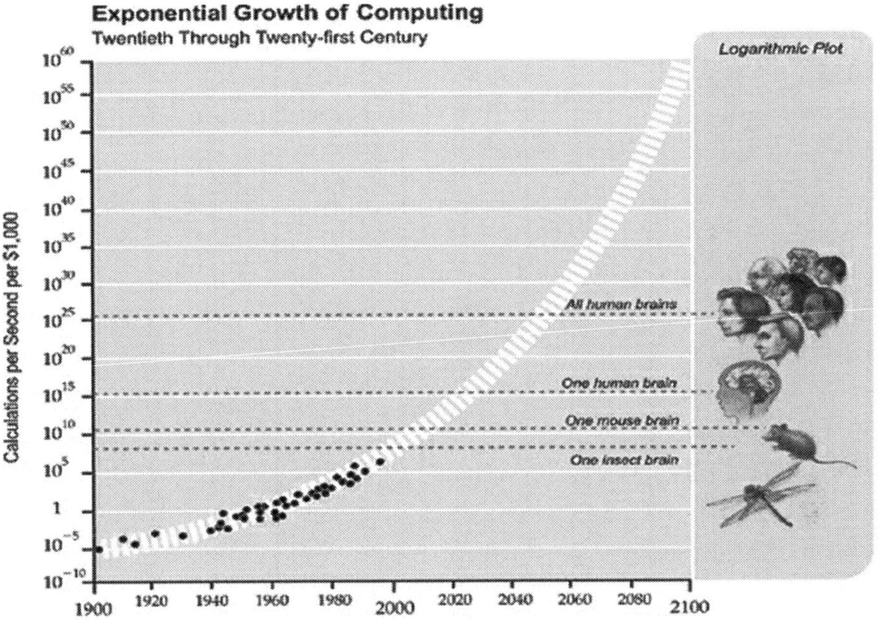

Figure 16: graphs from Ray Kurzweil, The Singularity Is Near: When Humans Transcend Biology, London: Penguin Books, 2005.

Whole-brain emulation

So if HLAI is achievable, how do we get there? The most obvious path is replicating the human brain. Ray Kurzweil explains:

> Basically, we are looking for biologically inspired methods that can accelerate work in AI, much of which has progressed without significant insight as to how the brain performs similar functions. From my own work in speech recognition, I know that our work was greatly accelerated when we gained insights as to how the brain prepares and transforms auditory information. [157]

Kurzweil believes the shortest route to HLAI would be intricately scanning the brain to yield a collection of brain-based circuits. Represented in algorithms or hardware networks, these circuits will then be fired up on a computer as a unified synthetic brain and trained.

157 Martin Ford, *Architects of Intelligence.*

John McCarthy put forward two similarly human-centric approaches to developing HLAI: "Understanding the human brain well enough to imitate its function . . . requires theoretical and experimental success in psychology and neurophysiology."[158]

The other option is developing programs that mimic human behaviour. For McCarthy, both were valid approaches. "It isn't a question of deciding between them, because each should eventually succeed; it is more a race." [159]

Significant investment is going into understanding the human brain. In the United States, the government put $100 million for the first year alone in the BRAIN initiative, a collaborative, public-private research initiative. The European Union has the €1 billion Human Brain Project, which aims to distill all human knowledge about the brain into a full-scale computer model. This funds a supercomputer called Spiking Neural Network Architecture, or SpiNNaker, at the University of Manchester in the United Kingdom. Ten years in the making, SpiNNaker is the world's most powerful supercomputer with a million processing cores and 1,200 interconnected circuit boards. But SpiNNaker can still manage only a fraction of the computations performed by a human brain. It can only approach 1 percent of the scale of the human brain. SpiNNaker has achieved the function of a mouse brain, which is 1,000 times smaller than a human brain. But should computing power double every two years, to get from 1 percent to 100 percent, we need only seven more years. So we may expect a technology equivalent to human brain power soon.

Mysteries of the human brain

We still lack important knowledge about how the human brain works. "We know much less about how the brain works than we do about the heart, liver or kidneys," says Thomas Insel, a psychiatrist who led the US National Institute of Mental Health from 2002 to 2015.

158 Nils J. Nilsson, *The Quest for Artificial Intelligence.*
159 Nils J. Nilsson, *The Quest for Artificial Intelligence.*

Why? The complexity of the brain dwarfs all other organs "and we have not had the tools we have needed to be able to study the brain in the kind of detail that we'd like," Insel says.

Until recently, brain science has been all about "studying the dead brain. It is only since the nineties that we have been able to study not only the brain alive, but functioning," says Katerina Fotopoulou, a senior lecturer in the Psychoanalysis Unit at University College London and director of the International Neuropsychoanalysis Centre. Marlene Behrmann, a professor of cognitive neuroscience, agrees: "We still have only a rudimentary understanding of brain function."

Many people, including neuroscientists, believe the human brain is somehow beyond quantification. The late Microsoft cofounder, Paul Allen, believed that "the complexity of the brain is simply awesome. Every structure has been precisely shaped by millions of years of evolution to do a particular thing, whatever it might be."

But we may not need to fully understand the brain. Man-made engineering solutions often differ radically from nature's. We did not build planes by reverse engineering the wings of birds. Yet our jet engines are much more powerful than nature's flapping wings. We did not make vehicles by reverse engineering how cheetahs run, but by inventing the wheel, and later a carriage and automobile. Likewise, AI progress to date has not come from precisely replicating human intelligence. Take language, it was believed that a machine would need to understand context to understand language. This is because human minds work this way. But natural language processing (NLP) proved that it can make sense of language in a different way.

Is the brain a "kludge"?

It may not even be the optimal solution to replicate the brain, which could be what Marvin Minsky calls a "kludge." This term is used to describe the legacy IT systems in some businesses, each built on top of another. This "kludge" is difficult to work with and burdensome. Complexity is not good in itself.

Could the human brain be a 200 million-year-old kludge? Evolution is a process through which chance events shape physical outcomes. Evolution is not directional. A brain function may have evolved for a specific environment; then, as a new environmental pressures acted on it, the brain built a new way of coping. This could leave a whole host of legacy brain functions built on top of each other. The result may be that the human brain performs in an overly complex way. Precisely replicating it may waste a lot of resources and create an artificial kludge.

Systems-level understanding

A better approach is to take inspiration from how the systems in the brain operate. For example, neural networks drew inspiration from how neurons in the human brain work in parallel. They did not emulate neurons but simply learned at a systems level how they operate. As Demis Hassabis explains:

> What we're interested in at DeepMind is a systems-level understanding of the brain and the algorithm the brain implements, the capabilities it has, the functions it has, and the representations it uses. DeepMind is not looking at the exact specific of the wetware of . . . the biology. . . . We can abstract all of that away.

The human brain is a good guide for what to research next. But we don't need to emulate it. We can take inspiration from it for systems we can develop in AI. We can also take inspiration from other animals, and if we ever want to develop a robot with autonomous arms, the octopus might be an interesting model.

Collective intelligence

However we develop individual AI systems, the most important breakthrough will be in creating AI systems with collective intelligence. Geoffrey Hinton, the godfather of deep learning, says, "Very advanced intelligence is going to involve making communities of intelligent systems because a community can see much more data than an individual system. . . . The community aspect is going to be essential."

For machines to reach human-level intelligence, they will need to learn large-scale cooperation. After all, any single human being shut away in a room is not that smart. Sadly, tragic cases of child abuse in which children have spent their lives shut in dark rooms have proven they become feral children and important parts of their brain do not develop. Human minds need stimulation from other humans, and we gain our intelligence by learning from other human beings, be that in person or through written language, telecommunications or digital connections.

While a solitary human being is not so impressive intellectually, when he or she taps into the rest of humanity, that person becomes something else altogether. This individual can contribute to advances in science, debate philosophy, build technology and so much more. So even if we create an AI that emulates the whole human brain, it wouldn't represent human societal-level intelligence unless it can learn large-scale cooperation. General AI will always be weak without the human ability to cooperate in larger and larger networks. So how do we create AI, which can cooperate on a large scale with other machines or human beings? The answer could come from the strangest of places: the remarkable marriage of AI and religion.

RELIGION AND FRIENDLY AI

I began this book by evangelizing about how ubiquitous AI can be. AI can intelligize every machine in the world. Look around your room at all the objects—the coffee cup, the TV, laptop, chair, door, curtains, phone, heating, doorbell, lights, glasses, watch. Every one of those objects you see can be invigorated with AI. But the full benefits of this mass AI will not be realized until all these systems can work together. When all the objects in your room are intelligent and cooperating intelligently together, we will achieve levels of productivity never before imagined.

Multiagent systems is an established field of AI research. Professor Manuela Velosa, head of the Machine Learning Department at Carnegie Mellon University, is one of the world's lead researchers in developing cooperative robots, i.e., a system with multiple agents. She has created soccer-team robots, each able to take into account the actions of the other players to decide what they might do next. The ultimate goal of this RoboCup is to "develop a team of fully autonomous humanoid robots that (by 2050) can win against the human world champion team in soccer."

But the multi-agent field has yet to make the key breakthroughs needed for disparate AI systems to cooperate through shared norms. A norm is a guide for the common conduct of agents, easing their decision-making, coordination and organization. The crucial tool human beings used to develop shared norms is religion. Yuval Noah Harari credits religion with having the central role in enabling large-scale human cooperation:

> Humanity's greatest invention is religion, which does not necessarily mean belief in gods. Rather, religion is any system of norms and values that is founded on a belief in superhuman laws. Some religions, such as Islam, Christianity and Hinduism, believe that these superhuman laws were created by the gods. Other religions, such as Buddhism, Communism and Nazism believed that these superhuman laws are natural laws. . . . Without some kind of religion, it is simply impossible to maintain social order.

If we can develop a religion for AI, it could transform the field. By giving religion to AI, I mean creating a system of norms for AI based on a shared understanding of superhuman laws. As AI develops this religion, it would be able to develop complex forms of cooperation. Not only will religious AIs will be able to cooperate and form collective intelligence, religious AI will be "friendly." It will share our values and so remove the existential threat of a superintelligence.

The new atheists

Religion is lambasted and attacked by the new atheists, among them Richard Dawkins in *The God Delusion* and the late Christopher Hitchens in *God Is Not Great.* They view religion only in negative terms, and Dawkins has actually argued that being raised a Roman Catholic was worse than being sexually abused. However, the new atheists target a thin sliver of religion—Judeo-Christian monotheism. As John Gray captures:

> Taking monotheism as a model for religion is misleading. It is not only animism and polytheism that are left out of the picture. Non-theist religions are ignored as well. Buddhism says nothing of any divine mind and rejects any idea of the soul...The smears and fulminations of the "new atheists" make sense only in a specifically Christian context, and even then only within a few subsets of the Christian religion.[160]

The biggest problem with the new atheism's purely negative account of religion (ironically for its proponents, who are in some cases ultra-Darwinists) comes from Darwinism, which makes it likely that religion is likely an evolved trait. Religion has been documented in every society ever known to man. From Amazon rain forest tribes to Australian Aborigines, sub-Saharan hunter-gatherers and Arctic Inuits–every society we know has had religion. As Karen Armstrong a former Catholic nun, who has spent her life researching the origins of religion explains:

> "Yet my study of the history of religion has revealed that human beings are spiritual animals. Indeed there is a case for arguing that Homo Sapiens is also Homo religiosus. Men and women started to worship gods as soon as they became recognisably human" (Armstrong, 2019)

In the beginning man made god. As this includes isolated preliterate societies who have had no contact with other human cultures, we can rule out the possibility that they developed religion through cultural contagion. Rather, religion has emerged either dependently or independently in each and every society in history, which strongly suggests religious belief is genetic. If we rule out cultural contagion as the only driver, then the alternatives are either genetics or chance.

160 John Gray, *Seven Types of Atheism*, New York: Farrar, Straus and Giroux, 2018.

Is religion genetic?

The probability is miniscule that every society throughout millennia of human history developed religion by coincidence. This leaves the only rationale for the ubiquitousness of religion: It must be genetic. If religious belief is genetic, then we can also say that it is probably useful in an evolutionary sense. For religious belief to be genetic, it would have had to be positively selected for. As Darwin explains on the last page of *On the Origin of Species*:

> And as natural selection works solely for the good of each being, all corporeal and mental endowments will tend to progress to perfection.[161]

Darwin's principle of natural selection ensures that traits that are useful in terms of fitness are passed on and those that are not useful are selected against. For example, if we had an atheist gene and a religious gene in early human societies that led to atheist tribes and religious tribes, then natural selection would select for and against the most useful in terms of "fitness." If atheist genes helped produce more efficient atheist tribes, then these atheist tribesmen would have vanquished the religious tribesmen and they would have taken their women and passed on atheist genes to the detriment of religious genes.

But, in fact, the evidence of religious prevalence suggests the opposite happened. Religious belief is, therefore, highly likely to be genetic and the results are useful in terms of fitness. This is why today religion is everywhere in our human world. I have considered myself an atheist since the age of five, so I am well aware of the problems caused by religion, especially when religious mythology becomes a dogma that inhibits scientific progress through the quest for truth. But religion defined in a broad sense to include ideologies such as Liberalism, communism and the like undoubtedly plays a crucial social role.

161 Charles Darwin, *On the Origin of Species,* Cambridge, Massachusetts: Harvard University Press, 2001.

Can communism really be described as a religion? Bertrand Russell, the British mathematician and philosopher wrote:

> To understand Marx psychologically, one should use the following dictionary:
> Yahweh = Dialectical Materialism
> The Messiah = Marx
> The Elect = the Proletariat
> The Church = The Communist Party
> The Second Coming = The Revolution
> Hell = Punishment of the Capitalists
> The Millennium = The Communist Commonwealth
> The terms on the left give the emotional content of the terms of the right, and it is this emotional content, familiar to those who have had a Christian or Jewish upbringing, that makes Marx's eschatology credible.[162]

Liberalism's role as a religion is well captured by John Gray:

> Liberalism emerges in the seventeenth century as the application of a universal morality inherited from monotheism, but from John Stuart Mill onwards it became a vehicle for the religion of humanity, which aimed to replace monotheism even as it continued monotheistic thinking in another guise.[163]

Fundamentally, Liberalism believes in the equality of all human beings and the sanctity of life. While I find these beliefs eminently persuasive, they are based on faith rather than science. We know from science that human beings are unequal in both physical and mental abilities, and in moral courage. Liberalism's egalitarianism appeals to faith instead of empiricism. Like communism, Fascism and Nazism, Liberalism is a religion, although, in my view, of the most benign variety:

162 Bertrand Russell, *A History of Western Philosophy,* New York: Simon & Schuster, 1905 (reprint).
163 John Gray, *Seven Types of Atheism.*

> "The belief we live in a secular age is an illusion . . . . Secular thought is mostly composed of repressed religion. The idea of a secular realm originated in Jesus teaching his disciples to render unto Caesar what is Caesar's. It is Jewish and Christian monotheism—not the European Enlightenment—that is the chief source of the practice of toleration. But monotheism also inspired many of the anti-liberal movements of modern times. A mix of Christian notions of redemption with a gnostic belief in the Slavic power of knowledge has propelled the project of salvation through politics. With the revival of religion in recent times, we may seem to be living in a post-secular era. But since secular thinking was not much more than repressed religion, there never was a secular era."[164]

Shared norms and social order

Religions give us shared norms, which enables mass-scale cooperation. Religion has been fundamental to our success as a species and can exist alongside science, as Harari explains:

> It is often argued that science and religion are enemies, because both seek the truth, yet each finds a different truth. The fact is that science and religion are allies. Science is interested above all in power. Religion is interested above all in order. Together, they are a winning team. [165]

AI scientist Steve Omohundro wants us to build friendly AI systems with "human values, such as caring about human rights and property rights and having compassion for other entities." He believes it is "absolutely critical that we build these in at the beginning, otherwise we'll get systems that are very powerful, but that do not support our values." The solution is religion for AI.

As religion for AI develops, it will take different forms to reflect the religions of its human creators. For example, Western AI will take Lib-

164 John Gray, *Seven Types of Atheism.*

165 "Science and Religion," YNHarari.com, https://www.ynharari.com/topic/science-and-religion/.

eralism as its foundation, believing in the equality and sacredness of human life. Chinese AI will be more shaped by communism as its religion, valuing collectivism most. Japanese AI systems may take Buddhist ideals.

The religion of AI systems

These different AI systems will use their religions to resolve ethical issues and guide their actions. F Nick Bostrom put forward a famous example using paper clips to illustrate the risks of a superintelligence. Bostrom showed with this thought experiment that a superintelligence may not purposely decide to exterminate human beings, but this could be an unintended consequence if we happen to be in the way of its goal. For example, if we gave the AI system the goal of maximizing the number of paper clips at some point, it might transform "first all of earth and then increasing portions of space into paper clip manufacturing facilities." Human beings may be annihilated as the superintelligence uses up the whole world as material to produce paper clips.

This paper clip example has become famous as a lighthearted reminder of the risks of strong AI. But what is the solution? It is religion for AI. A Western-created superintelligence that believes in Liberalism would not use up the whole human race for paper clip production because it would value human life as sacred. In fact "liberal superintelligence" would not sacrifice one single human life for paper clips, since Liberalism values individual human life above all else. A Chinese-created superintelligence that values collectivism and utilitarianism may make different choices. For example, "communist superintelligence" would also not exterminate mankind but may choose to sacrifice some human lives to make paper clips if it judged this would benefit human society overall. The only way such an AI system can resolve ethical dilemmas is by referencing its religious beliefs.

Religion will play just as big, if not bigger, a role with AI as it has played with humans. Human beings have used religion as the defining tool of our success. It makes sense that AI will also need religion. In fact, AI systems need religion even more than humans. If every machine was given a religion, then they could work together. The car, washing machine, vacuum cleaner, television, they are working not just to fulfil their narrow function but towards higher religious ideals. In the future, you may find the religion followed by AI in one geographical region is different than the religion followed by AI in another. Religious AI from different faiths may not be able to work together, just as human beings of different faiths struggle to reconcile their differences. Religious AI will need to learn tolerance and acceptance of other faiths to cooperate.

Religious AI would also know what to focus on for its development. Religion and politics always had a role in shaping what science to focus on. Should we invest time and resources to develop nuclear bombs or child psychology? The answer cannot come from science but instead religion, as Yuval Noah Harari explains:

> Science is unable to set its own priorities. It is also incapable of determining what to do with its discoveries. For example, from a purely scientific viewpoint it is unclear what we should do with our increasing understanding of genetics. Should we use this knowledge to cure cancer, to create a race of genetically engineered supermen or to engineer dairy cows with super-size udders? It is obvious that a liberal government, a communist government, a Nazi government, and a capitalist business corporation would use the very same scientific discovery for completely different purposes, and there is no scientific reason to prefer one usage over others. [166]

The religion of AI systems will determine how they develop. A superintelligence can in theory engineer anything possible by the laws of physics. But should it focus on creating nuclear bombs, eradicating hunger or exploring outer space. Is solving hunger more important than exploring space? These are ethical questions and require an ethical framework. But what ethical framework is the right one: Communism? Liberalism? Utilitarianism? Christianity? Hinduism? Buddhism? Well, that depends on your religion. Science cannot provide the list of priorities, only religion can.

166 "Science and Religion," YNHarari.com, https://www.ynharari.com/topic/science-and-religion/.

AN EMERGENT SUPERINTELLIGENCE

Is all this just academic? Can an AI superintelligence really develop? Yes, by all known science it is possible, just incredibly difficult to engineer a single superintelligence. But if millions of AI systems learned to work together as a collective intelligence, then an overall superintelligence could emerge.

AI has a strength of connectivity that far exceeds human. We can connect through writing, telecommunications, the internet. But machines can remain constantly connected, so AI collective intelligence can far exceed ours. When every AI system in the world is working together sharing knowledge, solving new problems, these individual agents could collectively form a whole new overall intelligence.

This is what Marvin Minsky, a father of AI, suggested when he spoke of a "society of mind." Minsky believes a society of mind emerges from the interaction of many smaller "agents," none which is very intelligent as an individual but which together create an overall system that is intelligent.

It's like the billions of individual neurons that work together to create the human brain. We have a strong sense of being individuals but are, in fact, a colony of bacteria, viruses, fungi and archaea, which all feed into our brain, itself a community of 100 billion neurons, to produce a unified emergent intelligence. More than half of the cells in your body are not even human. Human cells make up only 43 percent of the body's total cell count, and the rest are microscopic colonists. You are more microbe than human. Your human DNA has 20,000 instructions, but, combined with microbes, this is more like 20 million instructions that augment your genome.

A community of intelligences come together to make you feel you are you. The same will happen when communities of AI come together. Machines are on the verge of connecting on a mass scale. By 2025 it is estimated that there will be 75 million connected devices through Internet of Things. The next step will be to use AI to intelligize these connected machines. This mass-intelligence will be both a collective of individual intelligences and also if it develops norms or a religion for AI, a unified single intelligence.

The whole is greater than the sum of the parts. A nation is made up of millions of individuals, but the nation itself is a collective intelligence that makes decisions sometimes even against what the populace wants, such as going to war and curtailing civil liberties. Collective intelligences from teams to organizations, institutions and nations are the dominant force in our world. As individual AI comes together into a collective intelligence, that overall unit will itself have a will and a purpose that is a new identity. It will make decisions collectively, just as the multitude of agents inside a human being together form a personality.

This collective intelligence could progress, with the aid of human developers, to overcome the milestones to AGI, such as transfer of learning, causality, self-replication, understanding, reaching the holy grail of human-level AI. I am confident that machine intelligence will eventually reach the human level because humans are ourselves machines. Nils. J. Nilson explains:

> "I predict that someday we'll have human-made artifacts with levels of intelligence (in all of its manifestations) equalling or exceeding that of humans. I make that prediction because I believe that we humans are machines (for what else could we be)?" (Nilson, 2009)

Following I.J. Good's intelligence explosion, this HLAI can design itself with "recursive self-improvement" running away, past our feeble minds and becoming a superintelligence, presenting a new history, a new science, a new epoch—a new God?

The belief in human salvation through knowledge is present in every major religion. While Kurzweils' ideas seem wonderfully new, they are actually part of Gnoticism, a tradition dating back at least 2,000 years.

Gnoticism, "the belief that human beings can be delivered from a dark world by the saving light of knowledge," began with the ancient Greeks and permeated second-century AD Christianity from the time of Augustine. As the Christian Bible says, "For the LORD gives wisdom; from his mouth come knowledge and understanding," (Proverbs 2:6).

The same belief is found thousands of miles away, in 4,000 -year-old Hinduism, with salvation through "the way of knowledge." From Buddhism and Taoism's belief in salvation through "illumination" to the more recent Islamic belief in the omniscience of god. The Koran teaches, "Allah knows all that is contained in the Heavens and all that is upon the Earth; and surely Allah has complete knowledge of everything."

This constant current of human belief in salvation through unbounded knowledge finds its most recent manifestation with the growing cult Singularitarianism, with Ray Kurzweil as high priest. It is fascinating that such deep appeal for knowledge unconstrained by the limitations of the human mind, appears to have developed in every major religion. This suggests that it serves a deeply ingrained human need or perhaps more ambitiously represents a prescience of something to come—a foreknowledge of the singularity. These intriguing religious parallels and implications are too profound to cover here, and so I will be exploring these in my next book, AI God. I look forward to seeing you there.

Please don't hesitate to contact me in the meantime,

Adam Riccoboni
adam@criticalfuture.global

NOTES

INTRODUCTION

1. ""Crime prediction software 'adopted by 14 UK police forces,' "" " - BBC News,." 4 February 4,. 2019, https://www.bbc.co.uk/news/technology-47118229. Accessed 4 Feb. 2019.

CHAPTER 1

2. Andrew Hodges, Alan Turing: The Enigma, The Book That Inspired the Film The Imitation Game, Princeton, New Jersey: Princeton University Press, 2014.
3. On computable numbers, with an application to the Entscheidungsproblem, A.M. Turing, 1936, https://www.cs.virginia.edu/~robins/Turing_Paper_1936.pdf.
4. Ada Augusta, Countess of Lovelace, "Notes by the Translator" on French comments by L. F. Menabrea on "Sketch of the Analytical Engine Invented by Charles Babbage." Her notes at the end with instructions for "the first computer program," were three times longer than Meabrea's comments, http://www.fourmilab.ch/babbage/sketch.html, 1843
5. William Aspray, ed, Computers Before Computing, Ames, Iowa: Iowa State University Press, 1990.
6. Alan Hodges, Alan Turing: The Enigma
7. Alan Hodges, Alan Turing: The Enigma.
8. "Was Churchill really worried about the Battle of the Atlantic? And if so, why?" Churchill Archive for Schools, http://www.churchillarchiveforschools.com/themes/the-themes/key-events-and-developments-in-world-history/was-churchill-really-worried-about-the-battle-of-the-atlantic-and-if-so-why.
9. "The Historical Impact of Revealing the Ultra Secret," NSA.gov, October 26, 2006, https://www.nsa.gov/news-features/declassified-documents/cryptologic-spectrum/assets/files/ultra_secret.pdf.
10. "Eisenhower letter praising UK code breakers goes on display," Theguardian.com, March 15, 2016, https://www.theguardian.com/uk-news/2016/mar/15/eisenhower-letter-uk-code-breakers-display-bletchley-park.
11. "Churchill: Turing made the single biggest contribution to the war effort," The Turing Centenary, October 19, 2011, https://theturingcentenary.wordpress.com/2011/10/19/churchill-turing-made-the-single-biggest-contribution-to-the-war-effort/.
12. Dermot Turing, PROF: Alan Turing Decoded, (London: Pavilion Books, 2016), 152.
13. Ian Watson, The Universal Machine: From the Dawn of Computing to Digital Consciousness, New York: Copernicus, 2012.
14. Hector Levesque, Common Sense, the Turing Test, and the Quest for Real AI, Cambridge, Massachusetts: The MIT Press, 2017.
15. Hector Levesque, Common Sense, the Turing Test, and the Quest for Real AI, 113.
16. Dermot Turing, PROF: Alan Turing Decoded.
17. Ada Lovelace, "Notes of the Translator," English translation of French comments on "Sketch of the Analytical Engine Invented by Charles Babbage," http://www.fourmilab.ch/babbage/sketch.html, 1843.
18. "Computing Machinery and Intelligence," A. M. Turing, Oxford University Press,1950, http://phil415.pbworks.com/f/TuringComputing.pdf.
19. S. Barry Cooper and J. van Leeuwen, eds, Alan Turing: His Work and Impact, Amsterdam: Elsevier Science, 2013.
20. Martin Ford, Architects of Intelligence.
21. Peter Morton, ed, A Historical Introduction to the Philosophy of Mind—Second Edition, Peterborough, Canada: Broadview Press, 2010.
22. Shaun Usher, Letters of Note: Volume 2: An Eclectic Collection of Correspondence Deserving of a Wider Audience, San Francisco: Chronicle Books, 2016.
23. "William James (1842-1910), Memories and Studies, Project Gutenberg, http://www.gutenberg.org/ebooks/20768.
24. Hugh Sebag-Montefiore, Enigma: The Battle for the Code, Hoboken, New Jersey: Wiley, 2004, 189.
25. Martin Ford, Architects of Intelligence.
26. Margaret A. Boden, Mind as Machine: A History of Cognitive Science, Oxford: Oxford University Press, 2008.
27. "The Brain's Last Stand," Newsweek, May 5, 1997, https://www.amazon.com/Newsweek-May-1997-MAN-MACHINE/dp/B0055FEL4G.
28. Raymond Keene, How to Beat Gary Kasparov, London: Hardinge Simpole, 2002.

29. Gary Kasparov with Mig Greengard, Deep Thinking: Where Machine Intelligence Ends and Human Creativity Begins, New York: PublicAffairs, 2017.

30. Gary Kasparov with Mig Greengard, Deep Thinking: Where Machine Intelligence Ends and Human Creativity Begins.

31. Gary Kasparov with Mig Greengard, Deep Thinking: Where Machine Intelligence Ends and Human Creativity Begins.

32. Samuel Butler, "Darwin Among the Machines," The Press, Christchurch, New Zealand, June 13, 1863, https://www.goodreads.com/book/show/28103397-darwin-among-the-machines.

33. "Did a Computer Bug Help Deep Blue Beat Kasparov?" Wired.com, September 28 2012, https://www.wired.com/2012/09/deep-blue-computer-bug/.

34. Nils J. Nilsson, The Quest for Artificial Intelligence: A History of Ideas and Achievements, Cambridge: Cambridge University Press, 2009.

35. Counting Legal Positions in Go, John Tromp, https://tromp.github.io/go/legal.html.

36. "World's best Go player flummoxed by Google's 'godlike' AlphaGo AI," Theguarandian.com, May 23, 2017, https://www.theguardian.com/technology/2017/may/23/alphago-google-ai-beats-ke-jie-china-go.

37. "Google's AlphaZero Destroys Stockfish In 100-Game Match," Chess.com, December 6, 2017, https://www.chess.com/news/view/google-s-alphazero-destroys-stockfish-in-100-game-match.

38. Shoshana Zuboff, The Age of Surveillance Capitalism: The Fight for a Human Future at the Frontier of Power, New York, 2019.

CHAPTER 2

39. "Seeing the Beautiful Intelligence of Microbes," Quanta.org, November 13, 2017, https://www.quantamagazine.org/the-beautiful-intelligence-of-bacteria-and-other-microbes-20171113/.

40. "The Intelligent Plant," NewYorker.com, December 23, 2013, https://www.newyorker.com/magazine/2013/12/23/the-intelligent-plant.

41. "New Research Suggests Plants Hear and Respond to Sounds and Broadcast Ultrasounds of Their Own," Mysterious Universe, January 11, 2019, https://mysteriousuniverse.org/2019/01/new-research-suggests-plants-hear-and-respond-to-sounds-and-broadcast-ultrasounds-of-their-own/.

42. "Tree of Life (biology)," Wikipedia, https://en.wikipedia.org/wiki/Tree_of_life_biology.

43. "Chimps filmed grieving for dead friend," BBC Earth, May 18, 2016, http://www.bbc.com/earth/story/20160517-chimps-grieve-for-dead-friend.

44. "Six Talking Apes," Smithsonianmag.com, August 11, 2011, https://www.smithsonianmag.com/science-nature/six-talking-apes-48085302/

45. "Chimpanzees and monkeys have entered the Stone Age," BBC Earth, August 18, 2015, http://www.bbc.com/earth/story/20150818-chimps-living-in-the-stone-age.

46. "Chimps Make Spears and Hunt Bushbabies." Livescience.com, February 22, 2007, https://www.livescience.com/4395-chimps-spears-hunt-bushbabies.html.

47. "Chimps Trade Meat for Sex—and It Works," Nationalgeographic.com, April 7, 2009, https://www.nationalgeographic.com/animals/2009/04/chimps-behavior-sex-news-animals/.

48. "Dolphins Have Names, Respond When Called," Nationalgeographic.com, July 23, 2013, https://news.nationalgeographic.com/news/2013/07/130722-dolphins-whistle-names-identity-animals-science/

49. "Dolphin Waits After Creating Sand Circle," Seconds Later Camera, Relayhero.com, https://www.relayhero.com/dolphin-stunning-ocean-phenomenon/.

50. "How smart are killer whales—and can they decide to kill a person," Orlandosentinel.com, March 7, 2010, http://articles.orlandosentinel.com/2010-03-07/news/os-seaworld-killer-whale-brains-20100302_1_killer-whales-orcas-dolphin-or-porpoise.

51. "Clever Critters: 8 Best Non-Human Tool Users," Wired.com, January 16, 2009, https://www.wired.com/2009/01/animaltools/.

52. "Ravens, Crows, Parrots, and More—Meet the Most Intelligent Birds," Nationalgeographic.com, March 15, 2018, https://news.nationalgeographic.com/2018/03/year-of-the-bird-brains-intelligence-smarts/.

53. Peter Godrey-Smith, Other Minds: The Octopus, the Sea, and the Deep Origins of Consciousness, New York: Farrar, Straus and Giroux, 2016.

54. Peter Godrey-Smith, Other Minds: The Octopus, the Sea, and the Deep Origins of Consciousness.

55. "Humans are not smarter than animals—we just don't understand them," Independent.co.uk, December 13, 2013, https://www.independent.co.uk/news/science/humans-are-not-smarter-than-animals-we-just-dont-understand-them-9003196.html.

56. Martin Ford, Architects of Intelligence, Birmingham, UK: Packt Publishing, 2018.

57. Jeff Hawkins, On Intelligence: How a New Understanding of the Brain Will Lead to the Creation of Truly Intelligent Machines, London: St. Martin's Griffin, 2005.

58. Martin Ford, Architects of Intelligence.

59. Robert Wright, Nonzero: The Logic of Human Destiny, New York: Vintage Books, 2001.

60. Quote by S.I. Hayakawa, https://www.goodreads.com/quotes/44905-it-is-not-true-that-we-have-only-one-life.

61. "What Makes Humans Different? Fiction and Cooperation," Smithsonianmag.com, https://www.smithsonianmag.com/arts-culture/what-makes-humans-different-fiction-and-cooperation-180953986/

62. Thomas W. Malone, Superminds: The Surprising Power of People and Computers Thinking Together, Amazon.com, New York: Little, Brown and Company, 2018.

63. Thomas W. Malone, Superminds.

64. "A Collection of Definitions of Intelligence," Researchgate.com, https://www.researchgate.net/publication/1895883_A_Collection_of_Definitions_of_Intelligence.

CHAPTER 3

65. Adapted from Infographic in Paul R. Daugherty and H. James Wilson's Human + Machine: Reimagining Work in the Age of AI, Cambridge Massachusetts: Harvard Business Review Press, 2018.

66. Nick Bostrom, Superintelligence: Paths, Dangers, Strategies, Cambridge: Oxford University Press, 2016.

67. Pedro Domingos, The Master Algorithm: How the Quest for the Ultimate Learning Machine Will Remake Our World, New York: Basic Books, 2015.

68. Nick Polson and James Scott, AIQ: How Artificial Intelligence Works and How We Can Harness Its Power for a Better World, (New York: St. Martin's Griffin, 2019), 4.

69. "MIT Professor Claude Shannon dies; was founder of digital communications," MIT News, http://news.mit.edu/2001/shannon.

70. Pedro Domingos, The Master Algorithm: How the Quest for the Ultimate Learning Machine Will Remake Our World.

71. "Industrial-Strength Analytics with Machine Learning," CIO Journal, WSJ.com, September 11, 2013, https://blogs.wsj.com/cio/2013/09/11/industrial-strength-analytics-with-machine-learning/.

72. Ajay Agrawal and Joshua Gans, Prediction Machines: The Simple Economics of Artificial Intelligence, (Cambridge, Massachusetts: Harvard Business Review Press, 2017), 24.

73. Jeff Hawkins, On Intelligence.

74. Jeff Hawkins, On Intelligence, 87.

75. Jeff Hawkins, On Intelligence.

76. Ajay Agrawal and Joshua Gans, Prediction Machines: The Simple Economics of Artificial Intelligence.

77. Daniel Kahneman, Thinking, Fast and Slow, New York: Farrar, Straus and Giroux, 2011.

78. Daniel Kahneman, Thinking, Fast and Slow.

79. Nick Polson and James Scott, AIQ: How Artificial Intelligence Works and How We Can Harness Its Power for a Better World.

80. Ajay Agrawal and Joshua Gans, Prediction Machines: The Simple Economics of Artificial Intelligence.

81. Ajay Agrawal and Joshua Gans, Prediction Machines: The Simple Economics of Artificial Intelligence.

82. Gary Kasparov with Mig Greengard, Deep Thinking: Where Machine Intelligence Ends and Human Creativity Begins.

83. Andrew McAfee and Erik Brynjolfsson, Machine, Platform, Crowd: Harnessing Our Digital Future, New York: W. W. Norton & Company, 2017.

84. "Are We Ready for Intimacy With Androids?" Wired, October 17, 2017, https://www.wired.com/2017/10/hiroshi-ishiguro-when-robots-act-just-like-humans/.

CHAPTER 4

85. Cynthia Montgomery, The Strategist: Be the Leader Your Business Needs, New York: HarperBusiness, 2012.

86. "Step Inside the Hub: Coke's Social Media HQ," Coca-colacompany.com, January 12, 2017, https://www.coca-colacompany.com/stories/step-inside-the-hub--coke-s-social-media-lab.

87. "DeepMind AI Reduces Google Data Centre Cooling Bill by 40%," Deepmind.com, July 20, 2016, https://deepmind.com/blog/deepmind-ai-reduces-google-data-centre-cooling-bill-40/.

88. "IBM Security helps Wimbledon focus on the court, not the cloud," IBM Security, October 25, 2017, https://www.youtube.com/watch?v=m-hq2aOMeuE.

CHAPTER 5

89. "Bank of England chief economist warns on AI jobs threat, BBC.com, August 29, 2018, https://www.bbc.com/news/business-45240758.

90. "The Future of Employment: How Susceptible Are Jobs to Computerisation," Oxford Martin School, University of Oxford, September 17, 2013, https://www.oxfordmartin.ox.ac.uk/downloads/academic/The_Future_of_Employment.pdf.

91. "The Internet Classics Archive, Politics, Aristotle," http://classics.mit.edu/Aristotle/politics.html.

92. "Marx's Vision of Communism," The Writings of Bertell Ollman, NYU.edu, https://www.nyu.edu/projects/ollman/docs/vision_of_communism.php.

93. "The Risk of Automation for Jobs in OECD Countries: A Comparative Analysis," Melanie Arntz, Ulrich Zierhan and Terry Gregory, OECD, https://www.oecd-ilibrary.org/social-issues-migration-health/the-risk-of-automation-for-jobs-in-oecd-countries_5jlz9h56dvq7-en.

94. "Why Are There Still So Many Jobs: The History and Future of Workplace Automation," Journal of Economic Perspectives, Summer 2015, https://economics.mit.edu/files/11563.

95. Martin Ford, Architects of Intelligence.

96. Martin Ford, Architects of Intelligence.

97. "Jobs surge in April, unemployment rate falls to the lowest since 1969," CNBC.com, May 13, 2019, https://www.cnbc.com/2019/05/03/non-farm-payrolls-april-2019.html.

98. "Hillibillies who code: The former miners out to put Kentucky on the map," Theguardian.com, April 21, 2017, https://www.theguardian.com/us-news/2017/apr/21/tech-industry-coding-kentucky-hillbillies.

99. "The Iliad Mortality Quotes," Shmoop.com, https://www.shmoop.com/iliad/mortality-quotes-2.html.

100. John Montague, Selected Poems, Toronto: Exile Editions Limited, 1982, 1991.

101. Geoffrey West, Scale: The Universal Laws of Life, Growth, and Death in Organisms, Cities and Companies, Penguin Random House, New York: Penguin Random House, 2018.

102. Geoffrey West, Scale.

103. "Why Are There Still So Many Jobs: The History and Future of Workplace Automation," Journal of Economic Perspectives, Summer 2015, https://economics.mit.edu/files/11563.

104. Martin Ford, Architects of Intelligence.

105. "The Surprising Truth About Where New Jobs Come From," Forbes.com, October 29, 2014, https://www.forbes.com/sites/stevedenning/2014/10/29/the-surprising-truth-about-where-new-jobs-come-from/

106. "The Importance of Young Firms for Economic Growth," Kauffman.org, September 13, 2015, https://www.kauffman.org/what-we-do/resources/entrepreneurship-policy-digest/the-importance-of-young-firms-for-economic-growth.

107. "Unemployment Rates Around the World," GFmag.com, November 1 2018, https://www.gfmag.com/global-data/economic-data/worlds-unemployment-ratescom.

108. Nick Bostrom, Superintelligence: Paths, Dangers, Strategies, 46.

109. "The Co-existence of Machines and Humans Is the Way Forward," Huffpost.com, December 6, 2017, https://www.huffingtonpost.co.uk/entry/the-co-existence-of-machines-and-humans-is-the-way-forward_uk_5a1ef334e4b0e37da0447bde.

110. Martin Ford, Architects of Intelligence.

111. Martin Ford, Architects of Intelligence.

112. "Those stories about AI taking our jobs might be dead wrong," Mashable.com, July 17, 2018, https://mashable.com/article/ai-new-jobs/.

113. Claudia Goldin and Lawrence F. Katz, The Race Between Education and Technology, Cambridge, Massachusetts: Harvard University Press, 2010.

114. Martin Ford, Architects of Intelligence.

115. "Income Inequality and Mortality in Metropolitan Areas of the United States," JW Lynch et al., American Journal of Public Health, July 1998, NIH.gov, https://www.ncbi.nlm.nih.gov/pmc/articles/PMC1508263/.

116. Martin Ford, Architects of Intelligence.

117. "Union cheers as trucks kept out of U.S. self-driving legislation," Reuters.com, July 28 2017, https://www.reuters.com/article/us-usa-selfdriving-vehicles/union-cheers-as-trucks-kept-out-of-u-s-self-driving-legislation-idUSKBN1AD2S3.

118. CHAPTER 6

119. "IBM Predicts Demand for Data Scientists Will Soar 28% by 2020," Forbes.com, May 13, 2017, https://www.forbes.com/sites/louiscolumbus/2017/05/13/ibm-predicts-demand-for-data-scientists-will-soar-28-by-2020/
120. Martin Ford, Architects of Intelligence.
121. Martin Ford, Architects of Intelligence.
122. Kai-Fu Lee, AI Superpowers: China, Silicon Valley, and the New World Order, New York: Houghton Mifflin Harcourt, 2018.
123. Martin Ford, Architects of Intelligence.
124. Martin Ford, Architects of Intelligence.
125. Martin Ford, Architects of Intelligence.
126. "Cognitive Comparative Advantage and the Organization of Work: Lessons from Herbert Simon's Vision of the Future," University of Connecticut, SSRN.com, January 7, 2003, https://www.ssrn.com/abstract=353262.
127. Frank Levy and Richard J. Murnane, The New Division of Labor: How Computers Are Creating the Next Job Market, Princeton, New Jersey: Princeton University Press, 2004.
128. "Economics of the Singularity," Spectrum.ieee.org, June 1, 2008, https://spectrum.ieee.org/robotics/robotics-software/economics-of-the-singularity.
129. Daniel J. Pink, A Whole New Mind: Why Right-Brainers Will Rule the Future, New York: Riverhead Books, 2006.
130. "London's black-cab drivers consider suing Uber for £1bn," Theguardian.com, July 24, 2018, https://www.theguardian.com/technology/2018/jul/24/londons-black-cab-drivers-consider-suing-uber-for-1bn.
131. Paul Ekman, Emotions Revealed, Second Edition: Recognizing Faces and Feelings to Improve Communication and Emotional Life, New York: Holt Paperbacks, 2007.
132. Lisa Feldman Barrett, How Emotions Are Made: The Secret Life of the Brain, New York: Houghton Mifflin Harcourt, 2017.
133. Yuval Noah Harari, 21 Lessons for the 21st Century, New York: Spiegel & Grau, 2018.
134. Max Tegmark, Life 3.0: Being Human in the Age of Artificial Intelligence, New York: Vintage Books, 2018.
135. Martin Ford, Architects of Intelligence.
136. Adam Smith, The Wealth of Nations, London: Penguin Classics, 1982.
137. Geoff Colvin, Humans Are Underrated: What High Achievers Know that Brilliant Machines Never Will, New York: Portfolio, 2015.
138. Kai-Fu Lee, AI Superpowers: China, Silicon Valley, and the New World Order.
139. Geoff Colvin, Humans Are Underrated, 213.

CHAPTER 7

140. Martin Ford, Architects of Intelligence.
141. Nils J. Nilsson, The Quest for Artificial Intelligence.
142. Nils J. Nilsson, The Quest for Artificial Intelligence.
143. Martin Ford, Architects of Intelligence.
144. Vernor Vinge, The Coming Technological Singularity: How to Survive in the Post-Human Era, NASA.gov, https://edoras.sdsu.edu/~vinge/misc/singularity.html.
145. Nils J. Nilsson, The Quest for Artificial Intelligence.
146. Meredith Broussard, Artificial Unintelligence: How Computers Misunderstand the World, Cambridge, Massachusetts: The MIT Press, 2018.
147. "The Chinese Room Argument," Stanford Encyclopedia of Philosophy, March 19, 2004, https://plato.stanford.edu/entries/chinese-room/.
148. Martin Ford, Architects of Intelligence.
149. Martin Ford, Architects of Intelligence.
150. Martin Ford, Architects of Intelligence.
151. "Loveable rogue, or selfish killer?" Telegraph.com, March 21, 2006, https://www.telegraph.co.uk/technology/3345286/Loveable-rogue-or-selfish-killer.html.
152. Hector Levesque, Common Sense, the Turing Test, and the Quest for Real AI, Cambridge, Massachusetts: The MIT Press, 2017.
153. "Teaching Machines Common Sense Reasoning," DARPA, October 11, 2018, https://www.darpa.mil/news-events/2018-10-11
154. Martin Ford, Architects of Intelligence.
155. Gary Kasparov, Deep Thinking.
156. "Ray Kurzweil on Turing Tests, Brain Extenders, and AI Ethics," Wired.com, November 13, 2017, https://www.wired.com/story/ray-kurzweil-on-turing-tests-brain-extenders-and-ai-ethics/.
157. Ray Kurzweil, The Singularity Is Near: When Humans Transcend Biology, London: Penguin Books, 2005.

158. Martin Ford, Architects of Intelligence.
159. Nils J. Nilsson, The Quest for Artificial Intelligence.
160. Nils J. Nilsson, The Quest for Artificial Intelligence.
161. John Gray, Seven Types of Atheism, New York: Farrar, Straus and Giroux, 2018.
162. Charles Darwin, On the Origin of Species, Cambridge, Massachusetts: Harvard University Press, 2001.
163. Bertrand Russell, A History of Western Philosophy, New York: Simon & Schuster, 1905 (reprint).
164. John Gray, Seven Types of Atheism.
165. John Gray, Seven Types of Atheism.
166. "Science and Religion," YNHarari.com, https://www.ynharari.com/topic/science-and-religion/.
167. "Science and Religion," YNHarari.com, https://www.ynharari.com/topic/science-and-religion/.

Printed in Germany
by Amazon Distribution
GmbH, Leipzig

21488961R00148